Making Punches Count

Making Punches Count

The Individual Logic of Legislative Brawls

NATHAN F. BATTO
and
EMILY BEAULIEU

OXFORD
UNIVERSITY PRESS

OXFORD
UNIVERSITY PRESS

Oxford University Press is a department of the University of Oxford. It furthers
the University's objective of excellence in research, scholarship, and education
by publishing worldwide. Oxford is a registered trade mark of Oxford University
Press in the UK and certain other countries.

Published in the United States of America by Oxford University Press
198 Madison Avenue, New York, NY 10016, United States of America.

© Oxford University Press 2024

All rights reserved. No part of this publication may be reproduced, stored in
a retrieval system, or transmitted, in any form or by any means, without the
prior permission in writing of Oxford University Press, or as expressly permitted
by law, by license, or under terms agreed with the appropriate reproduction
rights organization. Inquiries concerning reproduction outside the scope of the
above should be sent to the Rights Department, Oxford University Press, at the
address above.

You must not circulate this work in any other form
and you must impose this same condition on any acquirer.

Library of Congress Cataloging-in-Publication Data
Names: Batto, Nathan F., author | Beaulieu, Emily, author.
Title: Making punches count : the individual logic of legislative brawls /
Nathan F. Batto and Emily Beaulieu.
Description: New York, NY : Oxford University Press, [2024] |
Includes bibliographical references and index.
Identifiers: LCCN 2023054948 (print) | LCCN 2023054949 (ebook) |
ISBN 9780197744420 (hardback) | ISBN 9780197744437 (paperback) |
ISBN 9780197744468 | ISBN 9780197744444 (epub)
Subjects: LCSH: Political violence. | Legislators—Violence against. |
Legislators—Violence against—Taiwan. | Legislators—Violence
against—Ukraine. | Political violence—Taiwan. | Political
violence—Ukraine. | Political atrocities—Social aspects.
Classification: LCC JC328.6 .B42 2024 (print) | LCC JC328.6 (ebook) |
DDC 303.609477—dc23/eng/20240129
LC record available at https://lccn.loc.gov/2023054948
LC ebook record available at https://lccn.loc.gov/2023054949

DOI: 10.1093/oso/9780197744420.001.0001

Paperback printed by Marquis Book Printing, Canada
Hardback printed by Bridgeport National Bindery, Inc., United States of America

Contents

Acknowledgments vii

1. Introduction 1
2. Brawls in Taiwan, in Ukraine, and around the World 20
3. An Individual Theory of Parliamentary Brawls 52
4. Who Brawls 81
   Appendix 4.1 Legislative Behavior Coding for Video Coverage of Taiwan's Legislative Yuan 101
5. Media and Signal Transmission 103
   Appendix 5.1 Media Coverage of Brawling in Taiwan—Data Collection and Analysis 114
   Appendix 5.2 Media Coverage of Brawling in Ukraine—Data Collection and Analysis 120
6. The Audience for Brawls 122
7. Brawling and Re-election 146
8. Conclusions 170

Notes 189
References 193
Index 203

Acknowledgments

It is safe to say that when we entered the same PhD program at University of California, San Diego, in 2000, we never imagined writing this book. Even when we ended up working with the same dissertation advisor, there was no hint of what was to come. Nathan wrote a dissertation on party strategies in the Taiwan legislature and, after three years at the University of the Pacific, took a job in Taiwan. Emily wrote a dissertation on election boycotts and moved to Kentucky.

In 2014, Nathan attended a panel at the Midwest Political Science Association annual meeting, where Emily was presenting a paper on parliamentary brawling—having been inspired to pursue the topic after a conversation with her Midwest Political Science Association (MPSA) women's caucus mentor, Candice Ortbals-Wiser, the year before. The paper was coauthored with Christopher Gandrud, whom Emily had found thanks to a paper he posted to the SSRN, which later became his article in the *Journal of Peace Research* on parliamentary brawls. Emily remembers two things happening at that panel. First, Jose Cheibub, discussant for the panel, cautioned her and Christopher that they needed to move beyond the "sexy" nature of the topic and engage in some serious scholarship. Second, after the panel Nathan told her: "Brawling is a major problem in Taiwan; I want to work on this with you!"

Two years later, thanks to a grant from Taiwan's Ministry of Science and Technology, Emily found herself in Taiwan with Nathan and Christopher, working for three weeks on a National Science Foundation proposal to study parliamentary brawls. The proposal was not funded and Christopher subsequently left academia, but we continued to work on what would ultimately become the monograph you hold today.

The project received three grants from the Republic of China Ministry of Science and Technology (now the National Science and Technology Council), projects MOST 104-2410-H-001-057-MY2, MOST 106-2410-H-001-033-MY2, and MOST 108-2410-H-001-073-MY2. We also received support from the Election Study Center (ESC), National Chengchi University, which funded the June 2016 telephone survey cited in Chapter 6.

Our project benefited from so many people's efforts and input along the way. Early stages of the research were presented at University of Colorado Boulder, Rice University, Louisiana State University, Soochow University, and the School of Oriental and African Studies, University of London. Other parts of what would become this book were presented at conferences organized by the American Political Science Association, the MPSA, the World Congress for Taiwan Studies, Asian Election Studies, and the Center of Legislative Study, Soochow University.

Data collection and analysis in Taiwan were aided by several people and institutions. We owe our biggest debt to Tsai Yun-chu, who was co–principal investigator (PI) on all three of the grants. She was intimately involved in every aspect of the Taiwan project, including building various databases, survey design, in-depth interviews, video analysis, and several topics that did not make it into this book. Yun-chu's fingerprints are all over this manuscript. Weng Ting-wei was our research assistant for the first grant, and he did most of the early work combing through the *United Daily News* (UDN) archives. Lin Yi-ting was the research assistant for the second grant, and she coded all the video behavior. Institutionally, both Ting-wei and Yi-ting were based at the Election Study Center (where Nathan holds a joint appointment), which also executed all the surveys produced in this project. Eric Yu Chen-hua was co-PI for the first two grants, and we owe a great deal to the entire ESC family. Nathan's primary appointment is at the Institute of Political Science, Academia Sinica (IPSAS), and IPSAS has consistently provided support for our project, including, as mentioned above, hosting Emily and Christopher's 2016 visit. Sophie Yates translated the newspaper story about the 1954 Japanese brawl, and she also dug up Jennings's 1881 book on UK parliamentary history.

Data collection, translation, and analysis in Ukraine never would have happened without Dina Klimkina and Olexander Tyron.

We are incredibly grateful for the input of Nicholas Kerr, Simanti Lahairi, Andy Baker, Bob Stein, Randy Stevenson, Justin Esarey, SongYing Fang, Rick Wilson, Tom Flores, Daniel Corstange, Irfan Nooruddin, Sarah Croco, Jennifer Fitzgerald, Carew Boulding, Claudio Holzner, Susan Hyde, Tiffany Barnes, Khemverg Puente, Kathleen Searles, and the late Martin Johnson. We would also like to thank Hawang Shiow-duan, Sheng Shing-yuan, Liao Da-chi, Jeon Jin Young, Sohn Byoung Kwon, Lee Jaemook, Jacob Reidhead, Wu Chung-li, Chiou Fang-yi, Wu Chin-en, Wu Wen-chin, Tsai Chia-hung,

Yu Ching-hsin, Chen Lu-huei, Huang Chi, Cheng Su-feng, Ben Nyblade, Shelley Rigger, Dafydd Fell, and Albert Chiu.

We owe a deep debt of gratitude to our dissertation advisor, Gary Cox. The title for this book was, of course, inspired by his seminal (1997) work *Making Votes Count*. And although we did not use his suggestion for the subtitle (*Strategic Pugilism in the World's Legislative Arenas*), we agreed that he always has the best words. More importantly, it is thanks to his mentorship, guidance, and example of intellectual curiosity and rigor that we are in any position to offer this modest contribution to our collective understanding of how representative democracy works.

Much has changed in both of our lives in the intervening seven years since we first began working together in Taiwan. Some of that change has been for the better and some for the worse. Throughout it all, though, we have been fortunate to rely on each other as well as friends and family. Emily is thankful for the love of her three sons, Ewan, Layne, and Percy; for the unfailing love and support of her mother, Ann; and for the genuine enthusiasm and steady encouragement of her husband, George Steele. Nathan is thankful for the constant stream of love, support, inspiration, and intellectual challenges from his wife, Lavai Fu-yi Yang.

And though much has changed, one constant that has remained as we have researched and written this book is the fact that it is the most fun we've ever had engaging in scholarship. Even though we took Jose Cheibub's charge to heart and did our best to make this a serious scholarly work, we feel the project cannot help but exude a certain sexiness. We hope you will be as thrilled reading this work as we are to share it with you.

1
Introduction

May 30, 2006, was the last day of Taiwan's legislative session, and the Kuomintang (Chinese Nationalist Party, KMT) had one item that it wanted to pass. The KMT, favoring closer economic ties with China, hoped to pass a law allowing regular direct charter flights between Taiwan and China, something that had been forbidden for decades. The KMT was Taiwan's longtime ruling party, and although it had lost the presidency, it still ran the legislature (along with a junior partner in the blue coalition) and, as such, was in a position to see this legislation pass.[1] The Democratic Progressive Party (DPP), which held the presidency, was wary of closer ties with China. Presently, it could use its control of the executive branch to turn down most applications for special charter flights, but if the bill passed it would be required by law to allow most flights. Unfortunately for the DPP, its green coalition only had a minority of seats in the legislature. If it came to a vote, the blue coalition would prevail.

The Speaker announced that discussion on the bill was to begin, and a KMT legislator tried to move to the podium near the front of the chamber, from which backbenchers make all their speeches. However, the podium was surrounded by DPP legislators who physically blocked his path. The legislator yelled out that he wanted to propose a motion to stop discussion and move directly to a vote, but he was unable to formally do so since he was physically blocked from reaching the podium. As the session was in chaos and it was impossible to proceed, the Speaker announced a 10-minute recess. This scenario was replayed four different times that day. Each time a KMT party member tried to approach the podium to call for a vote, DPP legislators physically blocked the regular legislative proceedings, and the Speaker capitulated by calling a recess. The later episodes became more violent than the first, escalating from mild jostling and pushing to more aggressive pushing, a few punches, some hair pulling, throwing water, spitting, and choking. Several brawling legislators were mentioned by name in the subsequent media reports. The legislator who grabbed the most attention was a heretofore anonymous DPP member, Wang Shu-hui. When the KMT attempted to submit a formal, written motion to the legislative staff to stop discussion and move to a vote, Wang snatched the paper away from the bureaucrat. She was immediately surrounded by KMT legislators, who tried to recapture the document. Wang surprised everyone by crumpling up the sheet of paper and stuffing it into her mouth. A few KMT legislators continued to grab at her hair, but most stood stupefied as Wang simply walked away from the scrum with her prize safely stowed away (C. Chen 2006; J. Huang 2006; Yang 2006).

At the end of the day, the KMT and its blue coalition admitted defeat. The bill did not pass that day or in the remaining year and a half of the legislative term. Some KMT members complained that their party had not shown enough backbone. Hung Hsiu-chu, a KMT hardliner, criticized her party's floor leaders, asking, "When you are dealing with thugs, what is the point of acting politely?" (C. Wang 2006, paragraph 5). She and other KMT hawks demanded that the Speaker use his police powers to clear out the disruption. Speaker Wang Jin-pyng wearily replied, as he had for nearly two decades, that police were not allowed to physically clash with or arrest legislators, so bringing in the police would only make things worse (M. Huang 2006). KMT chair and future president Ma Ying-jeou groused that the legislature should act rationally and that the DPP's actions were causing Taiwan to lose face in front of the world (J. Huang 2006).

On the green side, the mood was quite different. At that moment, the DPP was besieged. The president was accused of corruption, and there were massive demonstrations calling for his removal. Only a few days later, he would try to alleviate this pressure by announcing he would devolve most power to the premier and retreat to the second line of politics. In this context, the DPP's legislative victory provided a much-needed morale boost. The pro-DPP *Taiwan Daily* ran an analysis piece with the title, "Fighting for Taiwan, Wang Shu-hui Wakes Up the DPP," which lamented the DPP's recent travails and climaxed, "Wang Shu-hui is not a person who loves grandstanding, but for the sake of Taiwan, she will fight with her life. And it is not just her; the DPP has a large group just like her. With this willingness to fight for Taiwan, Taiwanese need not despair. As long as we still have breath, we still have hope and need never bow our heads to accept defeat!" (F. Cheng 2006, paragraph 7).

This is a book about legislative brawling—instances in which legislators engage in physical conflict in the course of their duties. Traditionally, both legislative scholars and the popular media have treated brawling as an aberration rather than a rational part of the political process. It is often seen as little more than comic relief from the otherwise sober stuff of real politics, which involves policy platforms, political debate, issue spectrums, roll-call votes, and so on. Brawls seem to be episodes in which everything temporarily goes off the rails, in which civilized grown men and women suddenly turn into immature children who cannot control their passionate impulses. Fortunately, after the brawl, everything goes back to normal, so legislative scholars and reporters can return to looking at pork-barrel proposals, voting alliances, and legislative agendas. Moreover, our previous story notwithstanding, brawls usually do not change outcomes. The brawl slows things down for a while, but the majority usually gets what it wants. That is, the eventual outcome appears to be the one that would have happened in the absence of a brawl. If brawls are just an irrelevant, irrational blip in politics-as-usual, there is no point in spending time, energy, and money to figure out what is happening. It is better to watch a video clip on YouTube, laugh a bit, and move on to more weighty matters.

We want to challenge this premise and take legislative brawls seriously. For one thing, brawls are not nearly as rare as one might think. The most comprehensive search to date, based on internet searches of several media databases in seven different languages, uncovered 375 instances of brawls in 73 countries from 1980 to 2018, with 348 after 1990 (Schmoll and Ting 2023). That is not a small number, and it is probably a significant undercount. Using local media sources, we count 202 brawls from 1987 to 2019 in Taiwan alone, and it is possible that the number of brawls has been underestimated in other countries as well, particularly those in which the media do not use one of the common international languages, such as Turkey, South Korea, and Thailand. Finally, if one expands the time horizon, several countries that currently have well-behaved legislatures have a rich history of legislative brawling, including the US and UK.

Beyond their frequency, there are other reasons brawls may be important to consider. Although they often do not change the legislative outcome at issue, they can. In fact, in our opening anecdote, the brawl prevented a bill from passing. More subtly, the very threat of a brawl may induce the majority party or coalition to make concessions to ensure smooth passage of the item at hand. Joanne Freeman argued, in her book on violence in the antebellum US Congress, that the threat of violence had "an enormous impact on congressional debate" (Freeman 2018, 6). Thus, brawling may be an important yet overlooked piece of the legislative bargaining game. Furthermore, the process matters. Democratic legislatures derive their legitimacy from acting according to prescribed procedures. In contrast to other forms of legislative disruption—such as coordinated walkouts, sit-ins, singing, or chanting—a resort to physical violence signals a temporary abandonment of, and potential threat to, democratic norms of nonviolence and civility. As such, brawls may cause concerns about the health and longevity of democracy and the potential for broader civil conflict. For example, Freeman (2018) has argued that violence in the antebellum US Congress portended the coming Civil War.

The most perplexing feature of brawls is that citizens do not like them. In surveys, large majorities have negative reactions to brawls. Furthermore, their evaluations of legislative performance and democratic quality decline in the aftermath of brawling. Not only does the negative impact of brawls on citizens' attitudes toward individual legislators and the entire democratic regime suggest a reason to study them systematically, but it also highlights an important puzzle. Why would legislators brawl if citizens don't like it? This paradox may well explain the casual popularity of explanations of brawls focusing on passions and inflamed tempers—maybe citizens don't want them to brawl but sometimes legislators just can't help themselves. Instead, we argue that legislators are making strategic calculations, balancing the potential risks of brawling against possible payoffs.

As such, political communication and the interests of individual legislators are at the theoretical heart of this book. Because they are highly visible episodes of visceral conflict, brawls offer opportunities for legislators to present both themselves and their opponents to the general public and to communicate with target audiences. In the course of unpacking that statement and exploring its repercussions, we will argue that, while each brawl is of course unique, there are many recurring patterns that point to a systematic, individualistic logic of brawling.

Indeed, we offered the opening story of the Taiwanese brawl over direct flights precisely because it is so utterly normal. The brawl was over a partisan dispute between a majority that wanted to pass something and a minority that lacked the votes to block it. The minority disrupted the normal process, temporarily preventing the majority from exploiting its numerical advantage to process the item, by physically blocking a strategic location. The majority responded by trying to dislodge minority members from that location, an act that required some physical interaction. Within this physical conflict, some individual legislators escalated the level of violence, doing things such as punching, spitting, and destroying documents, thereby drawing attention to themselves. The fact that minority legislators were more enthusiastic participants than their majority counterparts is not an accident—in these disruptive situations, majority legislators are often more ambivalent.

The responses to the brawl were also telling. No one apologized. One of our core arguments is that brawlers are trying to communicate messages about themselves to specific audiences, and one of the most common messages in political systems where parties are strong is that the legislator is a loyal party soldier. Such a message is particularly resonant with a party's strongest supporters, for whom there is not much difference between a fighter for the country and a fighter for party goals. Because the brawl occurred in the context of a bitter partisan fight and also because the level of violence never got completely out of hand, the loudest public reactions were driven by opinions about the substantive conflict rather than by disgust toward the brawling behavior itself. The response from KMT party chair and presidential candidate-in-waiting Ma Ying-jeou is also instructive. Although specific audiences react positively to brawling, most voters dislike it. By expressing disapproval of brawling and trying to paint the DPP as a violent party, Ma was trying to ensure the DPP paid a heavy price with ordinary voters for its actions. All in all, this was a classic example of a brawl occurring in the context of opposition disruption—one of the most common categories of brawls we will introduce in this book. First, however, let us offer clarification of some of our core concepts and questions.

What Is a Brawl?

Brawls involve physical violence that disrupts legislative proceedings. We can think of brawls as an extreme end of a continuum of legislative disruption. In a broad sense, disruption is any activity that intentionally interrupts normal legislative proceedings. This includes many of the various institutionally permitted dilatory tactics that minority parties rely on to resist majorities, such as quorum calls, filibusters, demands for votes and revotes on every item, proposing scores of nongermane amendments, and so on (Binder 1997; Dion 2001). We, however, are not concerned with tactics such as these that are formally permitted by the rules. Neither are we concerned with disruptions that are not explicitly forbidden but which also do not necessarily interrupt the legislative process. Actions such as coordinated walkouts, an individual shouting "you lie" at the president of the US during a State of the Union address, or two legislators pounding their fists on their desks while screaming at each other may violate norms of civil behavior, but the legislative process can continue.

In this book, we reserve the term "disruption" for physical actions that are not formally sanctioned by the rules *and* that prevent the normal legislative process from continuing. Some examples of disruption include barricading the doors; occupying the Speaker's podium; overturning tables and chairs; removing or destroying necessary items such as documents, microphones, or ceremonial scepters; and physically assaulting members of the legislature.

By our definition, disruptions are inherently physical, but they do not always involve direct contact or violence. For example, if the minority occupies the podium or bars the doors and the majority decides to acquiesce to minority demands rather than to respond to this challenge, the disruption can be entirely peaceful. More importantly, we do not consider all physical contact to be violence. Incidental contact is clearly not violent—recall the May 2016 "scuffle" between Canadian Prime Minister Trudeau and members of parliament (MP) where Trudeau put his hand on the party whip to move him toward his seat and elbowed another MP in the process (Tasker 2016). While some clutched pearls at this incident, the contact was so incidental that it could only be discerned in slow motion. More generally, we do not consider mild physical contact or conflict as violence. For example, podium occupations can involve some physical contact such as mild jostling or low-level pushing, as legislators try to occupy prime places near the podium. Indeed, on some occasions physical contact, such as holding an individual's arms back, is meant to prevent violence. To reiterate, nonviolent disruptions can involve some degree of physical contact so long as that contact is either incidental, mild, or intended to minimize the potential for actual violence to erupt.

Brawls involve physical conflict that is unambiguously violent. Violence requires intense or excessive physical contact that appears intended to physically assault another person or damage an object. Assessing physical actions can be a challenge. In practice, we look for several behavioral markers. If individuals who are directly confronting each other extend their hands with force—to shove, choke, slap, or punch—this is a strong indication of violence. Further, when such actions result in their targets losing their footing or showing the marks of that physical contact such as blood or a black eye, the disruptive action can be characterized as violent. Not all violence is hand to hand. Throwing objects such as books, shoes, chairs, or even projectiles that only incur symbolic damage such as spit or a beverage is also considered violent. Other violence is aimed at objects rather than people. Legislators may rip out microphones, overturn tables, or destroy documents. In all of these cases, the violent nature of the confrontation has escalated the disruption into the category of a brawl.

Most brawls occur in the context of opposition disruption. Opposition disruption involves a large number of opposition members making a coordinated attempt at disruption, such as podium occupation, typically aimed at protesting the passage of a specific piece of legislation, though it can also be staged to protest government policies or actions more broadly. At some point in the coordinated disruption, a legislator may choose to employ a higher level of violence. Thus, while political parties and opposition coalitions are key actors in producing nonviolent disruptions or even mild physical conflicts, it is most often individuals who introduce or escalate the violence to more extreme levels. To wit, the more extreme violence is often confined to a few scattered individuals wrestling or throwing punches, while the bulk of participants engage in less violent or even nonviolent disruption where physical contact is minimal. Those few individuals engaged in violence, however, are taking advantage of the context of opposition disruption to send signals to particular audiences.

Not all brawls involve opposition disruption or an attempt to derail the legislative agenda. Most of the remaining brawls involve questions of honor. These brawls generally break out because of personal insults, often involving accusations of corruption, or other ethical concerns. These honor brawls, which typically feature only two participants, can be quite violent. In Schmoll and Ting's data set of brawls worldwide, just over one-fifth of their cases were coded as involving personal insults or accusations of unethical behavior (Schmoll and Ting 2023). While we will address honor brawls throughout this book, the main focus will be on the far more numerous, theoretically more tractable, and substantively more consequential opposition disruption brawls.

The Question

This book helps us to understand legislative violence by investigating its microfoundations. Why would an individual legislator choose to engage in a brawl during the course of their work? Legislative brawling is clearly outside the scope of normal legislative activities, and causing violence in the legislature does not come without penalties. In some legislatures, those who engage in violence may be subject to internal discipline, fines, or even arrest. Further, there are potential reputational costs to brawling, as we have indicated that the general public does not approve of this activity. Finally, there is the obvious risk of physical harm—no one enjoys getting punched in the nose. As such, we want to understand the individual legislator's motivations behind brawling and how these choices affect their careers.

This book is *not* trying to explain why brawls happen in some places and not others, nor why brawling happens repeatedly in some legislative contexts. Others have made some progress in that regard, finding brawls more likely in young democracies and majoritarian electoral systems (Gandrud 2016), and there are some general descriptive patterns that we can add to existing research. For instance, countries where brawling occurs repeatedly (what we might term "serial brawling"), such as Taiwan, Ukraine, South Korea, and Turkey, are often places experiencing a major security threat and/or a single, dominant political cleavage.

In this book, however, we focus on the motivations of individual legislators, which allows us to explain several key features of legislative violence and to consider the implications of those choices to engage in violence for the stability of democratic institutions and democratic representation more broadly. To this end, our empirical analysis centers around two countries: Taiwan and Ukraine. Both of these legislatures can be characterized as having a serial brawling problem (discussed at length in Chapter 2), and both countries have features that make brawling more likely: they are both younger democracies with some majoritarian elements to their political systems. Further, both countries face an existential security threat. Ukraine has been in a state of rivalry or active conflict with Russia for close to a decade. Taiwan exists in a kind of diplomatic limbo, under constant threat that China will take action based on its claims that Taiwan belongs to the People's Republic of China.

While focusing on these two countries provides numerous empirical advantages, which we discuss below, choosing two countries with similar institutional and geopolitical circumstances in which brawls occur frequently does not provide sufficient variation to explain why brawling happens at certain times in certain countries but not others. However, those similarities, along with the ample data generated by serial brawling, do allow us to leverage some of the important differences in the two political systems, particularly those concerning the role of political parties, to draw meaningful conclusions about individuals' choices. In the end, this focus on individual legislators' choices to brawl helps us to generate insights about the legislative process that offer clear implications for the well-being of democracy and the potential to curb violence in legislatures more broadly.

Challenges to Existing Literature

In asking and answering the question of legislative brawling the way we do, this book challenges two conventional explanations for political violence that have been applied to both popular and scholarly understandings of legislative brawls. One such explanation for political violence may be thought of as psychological, in the tradition of Ted Gurr (1970), where individuals' frustrations lead them to aggressive behavior. Another might be characterized as anthropological, that cultural norms encourage such behavior or at least provide a context in which it is acceptable and meaningful. Our explanation, in contrast to these two, is purely political. We focus on the strategic calculations of legislators as they navigate their political careers within existing political institutions and contexts.

Psychological explanations for political violence shape conventional understandings of the behavior, even if their scholarly treatment has been largely implicit. Conventional portrayals of brawls often emphasize tensions or passions running high and spilling over into physical violence. When we first began studying this phenomenon, for example, an esteemed colleague asked: You think legislative brawls are strategic? Have you ever been in a bar fight?[2] A few brawling participants that we have interviewed have also explained their own or their colleagues' behavior as a simple loss of control over their tempers. One of the brawlers we interviewed in Ukraine, for example, characterized his actions in this way, saying: "This is a matter of emotional strain. There are things, there are values that simply cannot be ignored."[3] There is a certain plausibility to psychological explanations that link aggression to frustration, given how brawls occur. Under circumstances of partisan brawling, an opposition that is powerless to stop legislation could become frustrated enough to turn to violence absent all other options. Freeman, for example, notes that late-night sessions of antebellum Congress were "sure to enflame tempers and push people to extremes" (Freeman 2018, 238). The behaviors of legislators before and after many brawls, however, suggests it is rarely as passionate and uncontrolled as it may appear in the moment.

Another possible explanation that focuses on individual psychology comes from the contentious politics literature. This line of argument suggests that certain types of individuals are more prone to violence. If certain contentious circumstances are not dominated by more moderate individuals, committed to nonviolent disruption, then violence will occur at the hands of more "militant" individuals (Tarrow 1998, 98). In the case of legislative brawling, it could be that certain legislators are just more violence prone and thus produce legislative brawls.[4] Shukan (2013) argues along these lines that one of the main reasons for parliamentary violence in Ukraine was that several violence-prone individuals were elected to Ukraine's legislature, having previously held careers in sports, police work, or the world of business.

However, we cannot find many individuals in either of our main countries of interest (Ukraine and Taiwan) who fit this description. In Ukraine in the mid-1990s, certain MPs who were loyal to then-president Yanukovych had reputations as being thugs, with a common understanding that when legislative proceedings did not go the president's way, it was their job to intervene violently. Shukan's (2013) study identifies 10 such individuals. Taiwan's most famous brawler in the late 1980s and early 1990s was dubbed "Rambo" because of a perceived penchant for physical altercations. Taiwan has also had a few legislators with ties to organized crime who brawled frequently. And while some might see individuals labeled "criminals" as a type with a penchant for violence, we follow in the tradition of Diego Gambetta's *Codes of the Underworld: How Criminals Communicate* (2011) and argue that violence serves strategic purposes for legislators much as it does for those in organized crime. Even if we concede that some individuals appear to brawl out of a sincere desire to commit violence, such individuals represent a tiny fraction of those who actually participate in brawls, most of whom have no such reputations as being prone to violence.

Further, Ukraine and Taiwan provide a pair of examples that refute this logic of brawls being driven by specialists in violence. The 2010s in Ukraine saw the political ascendancy of Vitali Klitschko—a boxer who held the world heavyweight title from 1999 to 2013. He served as an MP from 2012 to 2014, was active in the 2014 Euromaidan protests, and then became mayor of Kyiv—his true political ambition even before entering the legislature. As a testament to his political influence, other progovernment parliamentarians have continued to identify as part of a Klitschko bloc, even since his 2014 departure from the legislature. And despite his obvious aptitude for physical violence, Klitschko was never reported to be involved in a legislative brawl. In fact, when brawls erupted during his time in the legislature, he was conspicuous in placing himself on the sidelines. Similarly, Huang Chih-hsiung, who served three terms in Taiwan's legislature (2005–2016), won bronze and silver medals in Taekwondo at the 2000 and 2004 Olympics, respectively. There were numerous brawls during his 11 years in office, but he was never involved in anything more violent than jostling. That is, in the few times he got involved in brawls, he always played a supporting role rather than taking the lead. If brawls occur because some individuals are good at and comfortable with physical violence, these two should have been at the fore of such incidents. They never were.

The second explanation we are challenging is more anthropological: that cultural norms encourage and shape brawling behavior. This line of argument has enjoyed the most scholarly attention in the study of legislative disruption and brawls to date. Carole Spary's work on legislative disruptions, for example, emphasizes the ritualistic nature of legislative proceedings and the need to understand disruptions to those proceedings as a way to "perform" representation (Spary 2010, 22; 2013). Such performances, she argues, should not be understood in terms of narrow self-interest, but rather as embedded within "cultural scripts" (Spary 2013, 392). Joanne Freeman's historical account of violence in the antebellum US Congress offers one such example, where congressional violence reflected and reinforced a "violent age of aggressive manhood" (Freeman 2018, 68) and was employed to provoke representatives on opposing sides of the debate over slavery. Brawls and fighting in the antebellum Congress were consistent with one view of American political culture in this period—as casually embracing violence (Freeman 2018, 247). However, Freeman also argues that regional cultural differences mattered, as "different men from different regions had different ideas about manhood, violence, lawfulness, and their larger implications" (Freeman 2018, 72). Because violence was more culturally acceptable in the US South and West than in the North, southern congressmen could exploit these differences and use the threat of violence to shame and emasculate their northern colleagues, a powerful political weapon in a cultural context in which questions of a man's honor were paramount.

Our political explanation presents a challenge to both psychological and anthropological explanations. First, implicit in psychological explanations is an idea that brawlers are behaving sincerely—acting violently either out of anger because they are upset or because they genuinely like to employ violence. By contrast, we replace the image of a hot-headed fighter with that of a cool, calculating politician and characterize brawling behavior as strategic. Legislators are attentive to the actors whose support they will need to further their careers and use brawling as a way to signal that they are deserving of such support. With respect to anthropological explanations, while our explanation acknowledges the importance of the context in which brawlers are fighting, our argument still presents challenges to cultural explanations of the phenomenon. First, different individuals make different choices about brawling, variation that is difficult to explain merely with reference to an overarching political culture to which all individuals are subject. Even within the warrior culture of the antebellum US South, for example, some southern congressmen were more prone to violence than others. Further, by offering an empirical investigation of brawling in different countries in very different cultural settings, we once again call into question the ability of culture to provide a satisfactory explanation for individuals' participation in legislative brawls across those settings.[5] In this book, we argue that political and institutional factors, such as the strength of political parties and the electoral rules, offer a better explanation than political culture for why individuals participate in legislative brawls.

The Theory

Our explanation of individuals' participation in legislative brawls draws on theories from across political science, both institutional theories and theories that explain settings where institutions do not shape behavior as expected. In the case of brawling, it is clear that the legislative institutions have failed to shape behavior as expected.

We begin with the basic premise that legislators want to continue their political careers. In most settings, this means they hope to be re-elected, but this may not always be the case. In systems where re-election may not be possible (either because of the irregularity of elections or because of institutional rules barring re-election), legislators may be looking to move on to other elected or appointed political positions. From this basic premise of a desire to further one's career, we argue that legislators use brawls to send signals to those audiences who are particularly influential for the future of their careers.

Signaling theory has been employed in scholarly work that seeks to explain behaviors in the absence of institutional oversight, such as how states communicate with each other in the international system (Hyde 2011) or how criminals coordinate their enterprises without the benefit of legal contracts (Gambetta 2011). Signaling theory assumes that individuals have a certain underlying type that other actors would like to discern in order to make their decisions but cannot actually know. Country A would like to know whether Country B is actually willing to go to war before deciding how to proceed, but of course Country B has every incentive to put on a good show even if it is ultimately going to back down. The mob boss would like to know if this foot soldier is truly committed to the family before promoting him, and every foot soldier wants to appear worthy of promotion. Individuals with political support to offer would like to know if a particular politician is truly worthy of that support, something that every politician will claim is true.

From this basic premise, signaling theory introduces the idea of a costly signal. Costly signals are ones that allow individuals to signal their true underlying type, as such signals would not be sent by individuals engaging in cheap talk and claiming to be a type that they actually were not. Hyde (2011), for example, argued that toward the end of the 20th century, democratizing leaders invited international election monitors to observe elections to send a costly signal of a commitment to democracy to international democracy promoters, as observers would make election rigging more difficult and could only be tolerated by leaders who were not trying to rig elections. Based on this logic, we argue that physical violence in the legislature can function as a costly signal. By risking the reputational, disciplinary, and physical costs associated with legislative violence, throwing punches on the floor of the legislature allows an individual MP to differentiate themselves from those members who might merely claim to be committed to a particular party or cause. And the reputational costs may be substantial. Most citizens strongly dislike brawling, so legislators risk alienating large numbers of ordinary voters when they choose to brawl.

Signaling theory addresses not only the sender of signals but also the recipient: Country A, the mob boss, the political patron, etc. To whom are legislators hoping to send signals when they engage in brawling? If legislators want to be re-elected as we assume, it is tempting to suppose that brawlers' intended target audience is the electorate at large. In general, however, we know that citizens don't approve of conflict and incivility in politics (Mutz and Reeves 2005; Harbridge and Malhotra 2011) and our own research shows that the general public disapproves of brawling (Batto and Beaulieu 2020).

More importantly, perhaps, electoral rules rarely leave legislators dependent on the electorate as a whole for re-election. There are usually small slices of the electorate that have a disproportionate or even decisive influence on a given legislator's electoral fortunes. In cases of opposition disruption, the strength of political parties will affect the intended audience of a brawl. Strong parties have two characteristics. First, they can be thought of as institutionalized. That is, they exist for a long period of time throughout multiple elections; they have citizens who identify as supporters; and they are seen as essential institutions for legislators looking to further their careers (in other words, a political career as an "independent" is seen as limiting to political ambition).[6] Second, parties exert control over how members of the legislature are elected to their seats. That is, parties must have some degree of control, formal or informal, over ballot access, or they must be able to affect voters' behavior. In systems where political parties are strong, specific party actors will be the intended audience of brawls. Depending on who has influence over ballot access and who needs additional information about legislators' types, the target audience may be either party leaders or loyal partisans in the electorate.

Where political parties are weaker, brawlers signal to two potential audiences: nonpartisan elites with the resources to fund future campaigns and small segments of the electorate that legislators hope to capture as voting blocs. In political systems where parties are strong, parties provide a number of resources that legislators need to campaign and stay in office: the information shortcut of the party label, media access, etc. Even where parties are weak and political party support is not important, resources to run campaigns and stay in office still matter. Under such circumstances, legislators hoping to further their careers must either possess those resources themselves or appeal to elites in society who do. Alternatively, legislators might appeal to a small segment of the electorate whose support they can claim and leverage to acquire the necessary resources for political support.

Honor brawls are theoretically more complicated than disruption brawls, but they ultimately also involve sending signals. We must consider the person whose honor has been questioned and the person making the accusation separately. The brawler whose honor has been questioned may be trying to communicate with one of the target audiences we have already mentioned. Alternatively, the brawler might be trying to avoid looking weak and vulnerable to political or other types of rivals by projecting an image of strength. Accusers may also be trying to reach one of several target audiences. Most commonly this will be a nonpartisan voting bloc or loyal party supporters.

Thus, the theory of this book breaks with previous psychological and anthropological trends to focus on the political calculations of legislators and the strength of political parties, noting for now that both of these are related to the rules by which legislators are elected—a point we will return to in detail in Chapter 3. Further, we are less concerned with the cultural context in which legislators' actions take place and more concerned with actors' signaling efforts and the extent to which politics are contentious, disruptive, and ethically challenged. From this theoretical perspective, we can offer insights about who brawls, how brawling affects legislators' careers, and what legislative violence means for democratic representation and democracy more broadly.

The Research Strategy

A book focusing on legislative brawling can be considered, more generally, to be a study of political violence, which, by its very nature and logic of operation, can be difficult to study systematically. As those who study communal riots in India have pointed out, much of the power of this type of political violence comes from the appearance of chaos that it creates. Brass (2003) makes the point that communal riots are recognized by all who participate and observe to be "illegitimate" and are also planned (sometimes very carefully planned) to appear spontaneous (14). It is, in fact, in exhibiting these very qualities that political violence has the power to shock and appall, shaping public opinion along the way. If stripped of this veneer of inexplicable, illicit havoc, political violence would lose much of its power to evoke feelings and influence public sentiment. At the same time, because of this intentional obfuscation, many of the facts or pieces of evidence that a researcher would find useful in understanding why individuals participate in such violence will be intentionally concealed from view. Thus, the researcher is challenged to explain a phenomenon that, by its very nature, is designed to stymie systematic explanation.

Further, there are additional challenges associated with empirical evaluations of the internal motivations of individuals. It is very difficult to know a person's motivations with certainty, both because they may not disclose their true motivations when asked directly and because they might not have a conscious understanding of their own motivations. Our task, then, is as much interpretive as explanatory—making meaning out of what we observe with the assistance of established theories in political science; drawing out the logical, empirical implications of these interpretations; and trying wherever possible to structure our analyses in ways that allow us to establish cause-and-effect relationships.

Our empirical methods are mixed. We focus our research on Taiwan and Ukraine, two countries with extensive experience with legislative brawls. For Taiwan, we have constructed databases that track the legislative and brawling behavior of individual legislators, as well as their performance in subsequent elections for all sessions of the Legislative Yuan between 1986 and 2020. For Ukraine, we have data on media coverage of the Verkhovna Rada and brawls from the most recent full term (2014–2019). With this quantitative data, we seek to identify systematic patterns associated with individuals who choose to brawl in the legislature. In addition to quantitative analyses of brawling behavior and its correlates, we also offer evidence from key actors' opinions and insights. Qualitative interviews of political experts and elites, as well as media accounts of important events, also add to our capacity to draw inferences about individual legislators' participation in brawling. Finally, we draw on survey data from Taiwan to examine attitudes of ordinary citizens toward brawling. These data include survey experiments and panel data collected before and after an actual brawl in Taiwan in 2017, to see how citizens reacted to an actual instance of brawling.

The Taiwanese and Ukrainian political contexts are discussed in detail in Chapter 2. Here, we note that the two cases share many common features but also have differences that are valuable for evaluating our theory. First, both countries are young democracies, which is not surprising because these are the places where we see extensive brawling in legislatures. Further, these are countries whose political systems have undergone periods of extremely contentious politics. Legislative brawling began in Taiwan in the late 1980s as an opposition party strategy to push for greater democratization. Ukraine has seen two intense periods of protest dubbed "revolutions" around electoral politics—with the more recent, Euromaidan protests ushering in a wave of new political faces in 2014. Second, both countries fill the seats of their legislature using a mix of closed-list proportional representation and single-member district electoral rules. What's more, in both countries, party elites' control over who fills their lists is not absolute. Finally, both countries' politics are structured around a single major political cleavage, related to geopolitical tensions with a large, powerful neighboring country.

In terms of important differences, the countries are in completely different regions of the world with distinct political histories and cultures. Furthermore, although party leadership is not iron-clad in terms of ballot access in either country, political parties themselves are very strong in Taiwan and very weak in Ukraine (Herron 2002a; Thames 2007, 2016). We see this difference in terms of who actually influences ballot access in each country. In Taiwan, it is extreme supporters of the political party and key segments of the electorate who influence party leaders' list-making decisions. In Ukraine, by contrast, it is legislators themselves, who can offer resources and voting power that party leaders find attractive as they attempt to help their party persist.

Outline of Chapters

Before we begin to make and evaluate our argument in earnest, Chapter 2 offers a more substantial description of the phenomenon under study. This chapter tells stories of brawls and their relationship to legislative disruption and corruption. This book focuses on the experiences of Taiwan and Ukraine, and this chapter provides background knowledge for those two cases. In addition to providing a brief general political history, it also looks at brawling and some of the key individuals involved in each country. This chapter is meant to acquaint readers with the phenomenon of legislative brawls and our primary cases, and also serves to flesh out further our key definitions and distinctions between categories of brawls and the contexts in which they occur. It then moves outward to a more general look at brawling around the world. In addition to a broad overview of the frequency and distribution of brawls globally, we also look briefly at brawls in several particular countries. In the course of this chapter, we present many varied accounts of brawls, which we hope provide readers with a bit of entertainment in addition to important empirical grounding. After all, we would be remiss if we neglected to pay homage to the origins of most people's interest in brawls.

Chapter 3 offers a more extensive discussion of our theory of legislative brawls. It draws on signaling theory and institutional theories to outline key theoretical premises and offers a discussion in its primary context—opposition disruption. Here is where we argue in detail that individual legislators initiate brawls strategically to improve their career prospects by signaling that they are particularly committed and worthy of support to a specific audience, and that the audience and specific content of the signal vary by the institutional contexts within which legislators are operating. On the basis of this argument, we offer general expectations about (1) who is likely to brawl, (2) how brawling behavior gets communicated to a given audience, (3) who the target audiences for brawls actually are, and (4) what brawls mean for legislative careers. We also discuss the residual category of brawls, brawls over questions of honor, and highlight some of their similarities to, and differences from, brawls in the context of opposition disruption.

Chapter 4 focuses on the question of who brawls. Our theory of individual legislator initiative and signaling, as well as our available empirical evidence, allows us to derive several more specific expectations about who is more likely to brawl. In this chapter, we draw on qualitative data from Ukraine and quantitative data from Taiwan to investigate individual legislator characteristics, as well as contextual factors to understand who is brawling. We are able to demonstrate several patterns consistent with our expectations, such as the fact that more junior legislators, who have more need to develop their reputations, are more likely to brawl.

Chapter 5 takes up the issue of how brawlers can reasonably anticipate their behavior reaching a receptive audience by looking at media coverage of brawls. Interview data with legislators in the two countries suggests that they are acutely aware of the importance of media coverage for their career longevity, and that brawlers are perceived as seeking media attention for their behavior. From Taiwan and Ukraine, we are able to show that brawlers do see increased media coverage relative to nonbrawlers.

Chapter 6 delves deeper into the question of who the intended audience of a brawl is. In this chapter we return to the key point that citizens in general do not like brawls, and thus the electorate writ large is never the intended audience. We employ both quantitative and qualitative analyses to investigate the intended audiences that brawlers are trying to reach. Public opinion data and a natural experiment involving an actual brawl in Taiwan offer compelling evidence of the audience in strong party systems. Further, we present interview evidence from both Taiwan and Ukraine that helps us understand how both political elites and ordinary citizens respond to brawling, and who in each setting is viewed as a sympathetic or receptive audience to brawls.

Stories from South Korea, Mexico, and Uganda offer further empirical support regarding the intended audience for brawls.

Chapter 7 tackles a key empirical question raised by our theory: if legislators brawl strategically, thinking about furthering their legislative careers, how do brawlers fare professionally? Here we offer compelling evidence that some but not all brawlers increase their chances of being re-elected, but only under certain electoral circumstances. In support of this point, we present quantitative evidence across time and electoral systems in Taiwan, as well as an extended discussion contrasting the careers of prominent brawlers in Ukraine.

Chapter 8, the final chapter of the book, takes up questions of the implications of our study both for democratic representation in legislatures and for our understanding of political violence. Our discussion begins with an investigation of the prospects for antibrawling reform, featuring an in-depth look at the story of South Korea, where legislative brawling was prolific until 2012, when legislative reforms successfully brought it to a halt for nearly a decade. However, the recent reappearance of brawling in South Korea suggests that simply changing the rules of the legislative process may not be sufficient unless it is accompanied by a change in how citizens evaluate their brawling politicians. The book closes by considering brawling in relation to general understandings of political violence and returns to an observation we made in this introduction—speculating on how national security issues and salient social cleavages that promote political polarization might relate to brawling.

2
Brawls in Taiwan, in Ukraine, and around the World

We formally defined parliamentary brawls in Chapter 1 to identify essential features of this phenomenon, but parliamentary brawls come in all shapes and sizes. Despite key similarities, each brawl occurs in a unique historical context and institutional setting, and each incident involves a specific political controversy. Brawling politicians behave in unique ways and explain those actions differently. This chapter offers historical background and examples of brawling from the book's two main cases: Taiwan and Ukraine. We then discuss previous research on brawling and provide examples of parliamentary brawls around the world.

Taiwan

Taiwan's Historical Background

At the end of the 16th century, Taiwan was populated almost entirely by Indigenous people, who were divided into many different tribes. Starting in the 17th century, several waves of Han immigrants from southeastern China moved to Taiwan. The various regimes controlling parts of the island—Dutch, Spanish, the Cheng family, and the Qing dynasty—sometimes encouraged and sometimes discouraged this immigration, but it continued nonetheless (Wills 1999; Shepherd 1999). By the end of the 19th century, Taiwan was a predominantly Han society. Geographically, chronologically, and politically, it was on the outer frontiers of China, having only been formally incorporated into the Qing empire in 1684 and upgraded to provincial status in 1887. In 1895, following the Sino-Japanese War, Taiwan was ceded to Japan.

Japan, eager to show the world that it was a full equal to the great Western powers, took the administration of its first colony seriously. During its

50-year rule, Japan built up a modern infrastructure of railroads, a postal system, a police system, irrigation projects, an education system, administrative bureaucracy, and so on, and it invested in factories, modern agriculture, mining, banking, and other parts of a modern economy (Ho 1978; Lamley 1999). During this era, a unique Taiwanese identity started to emerge, especially in the northern urban centers of Taipei and Keelung, where Taiwanese people could see the special privileges being given to the Japanese colonial elite (Dawley 2019). Movements espousing local autonomy emerged in the 1920s, and two local elections were held in 1935 and 1937. Unfortunately, the rise of ultra-nationalism in Japan choked off democracy throughout the empire (Rigger 1999).

Meanwhile, in mainland China, the collapse of the Qing dynasty led to the establishment of the Republic of China (ROC) in 1912. The ROC took inspiration from Sun Yat-sen's call for liberty and democracy, though it consistently fell short of these ideals. Under Sun's doctrine of "tutelage," which held that authoritarian rule was necessary until society was ready for democracy, the ROC was dominated by the Kuomintang (Chinese Nationalist Party, KMT) first under Sun and later under Chiang Kai-shek (CKS) and did not get around to promulgating a constitution until 1946. Under the famously corrupt KMT, the ROC never established full control of the country, and it was forced to flee the mainland and move the official capital to Taipei after the People's Republic of China was declared in 1949. The ROC had controlled Taiwan formally ever since Japan renounced possession at the end of World War II in 1945.

Whereas the Japanese had governed strictly but consistently and predictably according to their laws, KMT rule was much more arbitrary and corrupt. Angered by KMT corruption and skyrocketing food shortages exacerbated by official grain seizures, which often ended up on the black market, on February 28, 1947, mobs surrounded government and police offices in Taipei demanding far more power for local people. A week later, Chinese troops arrived from the mainland and violently put down the uprising, taking the opportunity to target many Taiwanese elites who might organize resistance to KMT rule. The next two decades of harsh authoritarianism are commonly labeled as the "White Terror" (Lai, Myers, and Wou 1991; Roy 2003). The "228 Incident" is widely seen as the founding point for modern Taiwanese politics, as this is the point when many people started to see a fundamental conflict between the people living in Taiwan prior to 1945 ("Taiwanese") and those who arrived from China after 1945 ("mainlanders").

An estimated 1.5 million people, including 600,000 soldiers, moved from the mainland to Taiwan between 1945 and the late 1950s (Roy 2003). These mainlanders accounted for roughly 20% of the total population in the early 1950s, and they held almost all the political and military power. Martial law was declared, and *The Temporary Provisions during the Period of National Mobilization for Suppression of the Communist Rebellion* effectively suspended the regular constitution. Since it was impossible to hold new elections in China, members of national representative bodies were frozen in their positions. In an echo of the earlier tutelage doctrine, the KMT was officially dedicated to the eventual establishment of a liberal democracy in a unified China, but the extraordinary conditions made authoritarian rule necessary. The regime's legitimacy rested on its claims to be the rightful government of all of China, and no challenges to that claim could be tolerated.

When CKS died in 1975, his son Chiang Ching-kuo (CCK) had already taken over as de facto leader of the party-state regime. During the CCK era, Taiwan experienced rapid economic growth, and, as its goal of reconquering China became increasingly farfetched, KMT popularity was increasingly based on its record of governance. Nonetheless, it faced significant pressures to relax its grip on power, and CCK took some steps toward a transition to democracy, beginning with bringing some Taiwanese into high positions in the party and the government, though power was still dominated by the mainlander elite. Some demonstrations were tolerated, and opposition figures started to openly cooperate with each other.

However, there were limits to how much change CCK could tolerate, and the regime violently cracked down on an opposition demonstration in 1979 in what became known as the Kaohsiung Incident. Eight of the leaders arrested were found guilty in a public trial, but this turned out to be a watershed moment for the opposition movement. A group of young, charismatic lawyers, recruited to represent the defendants in the trial, became the core of the opposition movement. In 1986, they founded the first opposition party, the Democratic Progressive Party (DPP), a step that was still officially illegal. A number of democratic milestones ensued. Martial law was lifted in 1987 and the DPP was legalized in 1989. CCK died in 1988, and he was succeeded as president and KMT party chair by Lee Teng-hui, a Taiwanese who had been educated during the Japanese colonial era. The *Temporary Provisions* were rescinded in 1991, and the remaining "senior" legislators were forced to retire. Elections for all seats in the legislature were held in 1992, and the first direct presidential elections were held in 1996 (Tien 1989, 1996).

In the early part of the democratic transition, the opposition was driven by prodemocratic appeals, especially the need to replace the "eternal legislators." However, once most of the constitutional questions had been resolved in the early 1990s, the DPP needed a new focus. It increasingly became centered on Taiwanese identity and sovereignty (Chu and Lin 1996; T. Cheng and Hsu 1996). After the DPP won the presidency in 2000, the KMT ejected Lee Teng-hui, whom many suspected of being secretly in favor of Taiwan independence. Based on its 1992 Consensus (One China, Each Side with Its Own Interpretation), the KMT re-envisioned itself as a party that could fruitfully interact with the People's Republic of China and could thus bring prosperity by integrating the Taiwanese and Chinese markets (Sullivan and Smyth 2018). Since the mid-1990s, questions about identity, sovereignty, and how to deal with China have dominated politics in Taiwan (Achen and Wang 2017). The KMT and DPP, with clear and opposing positions on these issues, have constructed durable coalitions in the electorate, and this has encouraged discipline and cooperation within the parties. Thus, Taiwan's contemporary strong party system is firmly grounded in historical developments, social conflict, and different visions of the future.

Taiwan's Political Institutions

Taiwan has a semipresidential system. Prior to 1997, the premier required a vote of investiture from the legislature. Theoretically, this might have given the legislature primacy over the executive branch. However, the KMT's control of all political institutions, including the presidency, legislature, and executive branch, was never seriously challenged, and, in practice, the KMT party chair, who was usually also the president, dominated the regime. In 1997, the constitution was revised to allow the president to directly appoint the premier while clarifying that the legislature had the right to remove the premier with a no-confidence vote. Under this arrangement, the president has continued to dominate the executive branch. Even during the period of divided government from 2000 to 2008, the premier came from the president's party, not from the legislative majority coalition parties.

Taiwan has a unicameral legislature. The premier has a veto, but this can be overridden by a majority of all members. The government can introduce legislation, but government bills are not granted any special treatment. The exception to this is the annual budget, for which the legislature can cut but not increase individual items and cannot move money from one item to another. The legislature does not have enough power to unilaterally dominate politics, but it has enough that it cannot be simply brushed aside.

The number of legislators and the ways in which they were chosen has varied significantly. The ROC officially promulgated its constitution in 1946, and over 700 people were elected by various means that have not all been rigorously documented. About half of these came with the regime to Taiwan, the overwhelming majority of whom were KMT members. Since they were not able to contest re-election in their districts, the members of the First Legislature were simply frozen in place. These "eternal legislators" who claimed to represent all of China were an important pillar of the KMT's claims to legitimacy. However, as they aged and died, the lack of any mechanism to replace them became a problem. In 1972, the regime began holding "supplemental" elections in the "free areas" of the ROC (i.e., Taiwan) for seats that would have three-year terms. These seats were elected from geographical, functional, and Indigenous constituencies, and some were simply appointed as representatives of overseas Chinese. Importantly, the supplemental legislators were always easily outnumbered by the senior legislators, so the KMT's grip on power was never threatened.

In 1991, the remaining senior legislators were forced to retire, and elections for the Second Legislature were finally held in 1992. Of the 161 seats of the Second Legislature, 119 were elected in geographical constituencies, 6 by Indigenous voters, and 36 from party lists. In 1998, the number of seats was increased to 225, including 168 geographic constituencies, 8 Indigenous seats, and 49 party list seats.

All legislative elections in geographic and Indigenous constituencies until 2004 were held under single nontransferable vote (SNTV) rules. In a multiseat district, SNTV gives each voter one vote to cast for a single candidate. If the district elects m seats, the m candidates who receive the most votes win the seats. When m is large,[1] parties that hope to win a majority must nominate multiple candidates in each district. This forces voters who want to support a particular party to choose a specific candidate within that party (Ramseyer and Rosenbluth 1993; Grofman et al. 1999).

The party lists were chosen by closed-list proportional representation (CLPR), but there was no separate ballot for these seats. The SNTV votes were simply aggregated according to each candidate's party.

In 2008, the legislature was cut in half to 113 seats, and the electoral system was changed to a mixed-member majoritarian system. Currently, voters have two ballots. The first is cast in 1 of 73 single member plurality (SMP) districts or for 6 Indigenous seats elected by SNTV. The second ballot is for political parties and elects 34 legislators by CLPR.

For our purposes, legislators during the brawling era can be divided into three separate groups: those elected by SNTV, those elected by SMP, and those elected by CLPR. SNTV legislators dominated the legislature before 2008, while SMP legislators have held most of the seats since then. Party list legislators have held a minority of seats since their introduction in 1992.

Brawling in Taiwan

Taiwan experienced its first legislative brawl in 1987, and brawls have continued to occur with regularity ever since. Figure 2.1 shows the frequency of brawls in Taiwan's legislature.

The early legislative brawls in Taiwan were an integral part of the democratization process (Liao 1997). By the 1980s, the legislature was divided into geriatric but still numerically dominant senior legislators, who hadn't faced any voters in decades, and young, energetic supplemental legislators, who were well versed in electoral politics. Most of these young legislators

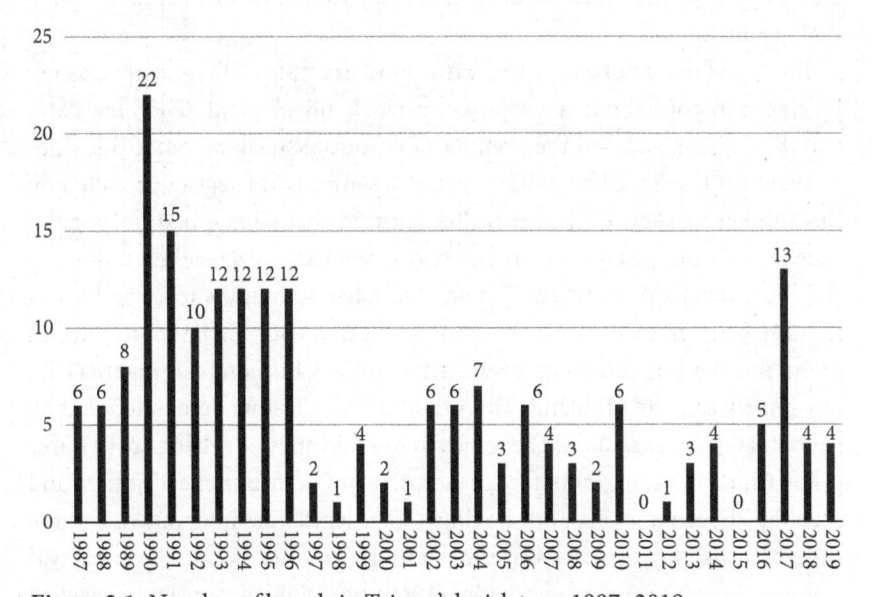

Figure 2.1 Number of brawls in Taiwan's legislature, 1987–2019.

were KMT members, but a handful represented an increasingly vocal opposition.

Most of the early brawls highlighted the illegitimacy of the senior legislators, who were an ideal focal point. Typically, a conflict began when an opposition legislator objected to the participation of a senior legislator, claiming the latter had no right to make decisions and sometimes adding a gratuitous personal insult. One of the senior legislators would indignantly respond that he absolutely had a legitimate place in the legislature, using the same reasoning that had gone unchallenged for decades. However, public opinion was gradually becoming a more important element in national politics, and not many people in Taiwan were particularly committed to the idea that these doddering old codgers whom no one in Taiwan had ever voted for were somehow the embodiment of the ROC's continued legitimacy.

When conflict broke out, a small number of supplemental KMT legislators, often second-generation mainlanders or people in caucus leadership positions, rushed to the aid of their senior colleagues. However, most supplemental KMT legislators' careers were based in patronage and local factional politics rather than strict KMT ideology; they had little reason to stick their necks out for the old geezers and generally remained on the sidelines. After things settled down, the KMT still had an overwhelming numerical advantage and could pass its programs, but the brawling allowed the opposition ample opportunities to communicate the illegitimacy of the old regime to the voting public.

The brawl on October 23, 1987, is a good example of these early clashes. During a report about a proposed petrochemical plant, DPP legislator Chu Kao-cheng accused the premier of cowardly sneaking out a side door to avoid protesters. Chang Hung-hsueh, a senior KMT legislator, called on the Speaker to silence Chu, and Chu retorted that Chang had no popular base and should just sit down. The two screamed at each other, pounding their fists on the desk, when Chu added, "Chang Hung-hsueh, you haven't faced an election in 40 years. Don't you know that you will die soon?" At this point, another senior legislator waved his cane at Chu, complaining that Chu was always causing problems, and other DPP legislators demanded that all legislators with canes should be removed to avoid anyone getting hurt. At this point, Chu and Chang went face to face, screaming insults at each other, and then they began pushing and shoving. Other legislators intervened, and the cane-brandishing legislator was shoved to the ground. Eventually order was restored, but the morning's scheduled interpellation session was cancelled (UDN 1987).

After the senior legislators were forcibly retired and an entirely new legislature was elected in 1992, some people expected brawling to disappear in the Second Legislature.[2] However, brawling would continue to be a common occurrence for another four years. Many brawls in the 1993–1996 period were about substantive issues, such as nuclear power or the annual budget, as people were still figuring out how politics should work in this new era. The legislature was no longer a rubber stamp, and many of the conflicts involved the DPP's attempts to use parliamentary procedures to obstruct the executive branch's agenda. There were also some remaining democratization questions left. Several of the brawls, for example, involved the new rules for direct presidential elections.

The brawls in the first decade tended to be smaller affairs, usually only involving a handful of people. Many featured direct person-to-person physical clashes, such as punching and shoving. However, they also often involved the destruction of items, such as overturning desks or ripping up a bill. One common act was ripping out microphones to highlight the illegitimate nature of the legislature: senior legislators shouldn't have the right to speak, and their presence made a mockery of all speech in the people's chamber.

After the first direct presidential election in 1996, legislative brawling began to become more infrequent. The brawls that did occur were often about personal insults rather than substantive political issues. For a brief period, it seemed as if brawls might slowly be fading out of Taiwan's political fabric.

In 2000, the DPP won the presidency. Though the KMT retained a majority in the legislature, Chen Shui-bian's election marked the first time the KMT had not held absolute power since the end of World War II. Chen tread gingerly for a year and a half, appointing a former general as premier and trying to reassure all sides that the transition would be smooth. However, the gloves came off when the Fifth Legislature took office in February 2002. Chen's green camp, the DPP and the new Taiwan Solidarity Union (TSU), failed to win a majority, and the legislature remained controlled by the blue camp, the KMT and the new People First Party (PFP). As with a decade earlier, some of these conflicts involved figuring out how things would work in this new era of divided government. For example, the two sides clashed over who should control nominations. The blue camp decided to boycott the confirmation of President Chen's slate of judicial nominees, and there were physical clashes as the KMT and PFP tried to block any of their members from entering the legislative chamber to vote while the DPP tried to clear their path (Lin, Wang, and Hsiao 2002).

However, unlike a decade earlier, these clashes would not fade away as the rules of the game became clearer. In the closely balanced and extremely bitter partisan fighting of the 2000s, the two sides took to routinely mobilizing their members to fight out all kinds of partisan disputes. The anecdote opening this book, involving Wang Shu-hui eating a bill, unfolded in this acrimonious environment. This impetus toward legislative violence proved to be lasting, remaining a prominent feature of politics when the KMT won a landslide election in 2008 and again when the DPP won a landslide victory in 2016.

Most of the brawls in the past two decades revolve around podium occupations. These tend to involve large numbers of legislators who try to obstruct the agenda by denying the presiding officer access to the Speaker's chair. We commonly see human walls, as opposition legislators occupy the entire podium. They also often block doors, trying to prevent majority legislators from entering the chamber. However, the majority legislators are usually able to get inside, and a struggle ensues as the majority tries to physically pull the minority off the rostrum so that the presiding officer can take his or her place and pass the agenda. Wang Shu-hui's aforementioned brawl is an example of just such a podium occupation.

In many ways, Taiwan's democratic politics reflect common themes that we continue to see in democracies around the world today: intense partisan disagreements that tend to come back to some core set of issues that divide elites and the electorate alike. What is more distinctive in Taiwan, however, is that over time these disagreements have translated into regular acts of physical conflict in the legislature, which is not as common in other places—even if the expectations of nonviolence in the democratic process are often more theoretical than practical. Though our second primary case—Ukraine—has a distinct political history and faces a very different political reality today, its legislature has similar tendencies to Taiwan's, with policy fights often manifesting physically.

Ukraine

Ukraine's Historical Background

Independent since 1991, most of Ukraine's political life has been characterized by a push and pull between Europe and Russia. Prior to the Polish partitions in the 18th century, the lands that would become Ukraine were divided between the Polish-Lithuanian Commonwealth and the Russian Empire. The second Polish partition (1793) unified much of the land that constitutes present-day Ukraine, while increasing Russia's territorial control. Ukraine's territory spent the 19th century divided between the Austro-Hungarian and Russian Empires, with its territory in Crimea bearing witness to Russia's defeat by France in the Crimean War. World War I spawned a nationalist movement for Ukrainian independence and also pitted Poland and postrevolutionary Russia against each other for control of the territory. Ultimately, Russia prevailed and Ukraine became part of the Soviet Union. Since the dissolution of the Soviet Union in 1991, the country has been divided politically between those who favor closer connections to Russia and those who favor closer connections to Europe—typically individuals who identify more as Ukrainian nationalists. In the broadest sense, then, Ukraine's domestic politics are intimately connected to its geopolitical position, and particularly relations with Russia.

Ukraine has seen two major domestic political crises since independence, both of which reflect the centrality of Russia to Ukrainian politics. The first of these crises erupted around the 2004 presidential election. Then-president Leonid Kuchma, disgraced by a series of corruption scandals, was not seeking re-election. The top competitors were two of his former prime ministers: Viktor Yanukovych, Kuchma's preferred candidate, and Viktor Yushchenko, who had gained a reputation for challenging the oligarchs and was favored by pro-Europe Ukrainians. During the campaign, Yushchenko became violently ill and went to Vienna to receive medical treatment, where it was revealed he had been poisoned with a substance manufactured in Russia. It was widely suspected that the pro-Russia Yanukovych and his supporters were behind the poisoning. When the central election commission declared Yanukovych the winner, contrary to exit polls that placed the now-recovered Yushchenko in the lead, mass protests erupted in the Maidan (the main square of Kyiv). These protests, which became known as the Orange Revolution, forced a re-run of the election. Yushchenko prevailed in this re-run and served one 5-year term as president.

Just as Yanukovych followed Yushchenko in the role of prime minister under Kuchma, so too he followed as president. In 2010, Yanukovych rode a wave of disillusionment with then-president Yushchenko into office. In particular, Ukrainians had tired of ongoing drama between Yushchenko and his former political ally Yulia Tymoshenko, who subsequently became a political target for persecution by Yanukovych.

In 2013, Yanukovych backed out of signing an EU association agreement, and protests once again erupted in the Maidan. While these "Euromaidan" protests, which lasted for months and cost the lives of nearly 130 Ukrainians, were motivated in part by upset over the president's resistance to closer ties with Europe (and the perception that Russia was ultimately behind such resistance), they also reflected continued disillusionment with Ukrainian politics since the Orange Revolution nearly a decade earlier. In yet another connection between domestic and international politics in Ukraine, Russia took advantage of the instability created by the Euromaidan to annex Crimea in February 2014 and to support "rebel" groups in the Eastern Donbas region of Ukraine in the spring of 2014. Active conflict, increasingly more openly identified with Russia, continued in Donbas until Russia's invasion of Ukraine in February 2022.

Whereas Ukraine's extended history highlights tensions with Russia, its more recent political history has created a system of high-level corruption, where a small number of economic elites have an outsized, and illegitimate, influence on politics. These oligarchs were entrepreneurs and opportunists with mafia ties in the early 1990s who took advantage of the economic crisis brought on by independence from the Soviet Union and assumed control of former state-owned enterprises using force and criminal tactics as much as their business savvy (Plokhy 2015, 330). As such, it is no surprise that Ukrainian politics since independence have been infused with corruption—essentially an extension of the ways in which those who currently hold economic influence in the country came by that economic power in the first place. While there is obviously no formal account, given the illicit nature of corruption, conversations with experts and observers of politics reveal a general understanding that oligarchs "own" between one-fourth and one-third of the members of parliament (MPs) in the Verkhovna Rada.

Ukraine's Political Institutions

Ukraine has a semipresidential system dominated by the presidency, where members of the legislature are elected to their seats either by CLPR or SMP districts. Despite the use of CLPR, which is typically thought to give political parties more power, political parties are not strong in Ukraine. They are often formed as vehicles to support individual political figures. Members switch parties frequently and form connections in legislative factions (fractions) that only sometimes correspond to political parties and are equally as fluid (Herron 2002a; Thames 2005, 2007; Slomczynski, Shabad, and Zielinski 2008). For example, of the original eight political parties that won seats in the 1998 election, two dissolved and one split into two parties, and 462 MPs changed party affiliations 527 times (Thames 2007, 224). In countries with strong party systems, party switching is often seen as a sign that legislators don't actually care about their chances for re-election. In a weak party system like Ukraine, however, deputies change parties *precisely because* they care about re-election (Thames 2007). Thames's (2007) analysis of party switching from 1998 to 2002 found that individuals who switched parties tended to move toward parties with demonstrated electoral success and ties to the power of the executive branch.

Legislators are elected to the single-chamber Verkhovna Rada for a five-year term. Ukraine's electoral laws have gradually evolved into the split that is used today: 50% of seats elected by CLPR with a 5% threshold, and 50% of seats elected by SMP. In the legislature's first two elections (1991 and 1994), all seats were elected via a majority runoff system, where any district where a candidate did not receive 50% of the votes in the first round would proceed to a second round of voting between the top two first-round candidates. Elections in 2006 and 2007 employed a purely proportional system with a 3% threshold. The 2012 election returned to a split of list CLPR and SMP, which had previously been used in 1998 and 2002, albeit with a slightly lower threshold for the party list seats (4% instead of 5%).

The mixed-member electoral system of the Verkhovna Rada has interesting consequences for legislative behavior. Beyond the fact that legislators switch parties frequently, research has also found that legislators elected in districts rather than on party lists are more likely to switch legislative parties or fractions (Thames 2016). And while district legislators are generally more independent in terms of how they vote, this behavior is not uniform. It also depends on how safe or competitive the electoral district is. Ukrainian legislators in competitive single-member districts or low on party lists tend to have voted with their party fraction more often (Herron 2002b).

Recent research has illuminated a long-standard practice of "ghost" or "proxy" voting in the Verkhovna Rada. Herron, Fitzpatrick, and Palamarenko (2019) demonstrate that this practice—where individuals do not cast votes themselves but relinquish their card needed to cast their vote so that it might be used as the holder sees fit—is widespread and has been particularly employed for crucial legislation. This practice presents challenges for interpreting voting as a standard legislative activity, since some proportion of a legislator's votes may not reflect any activity on their part.

Proxy voting may arguably represent a valid indicator of party loyalty or cohesion—being so committed to a given fraction that you allow other members of that party to cast your vote for you. Furthermore, while party switching demonstrates both the weakness of Ukrainian political parties and the desire of Ukrainian legislators to seek re-election, it also suggests that legislators may still perceive advantages to being affiliated with a political party, even when parties are not strong. Moreover, it is not just legislators elected via party list seats who perceive benefit in party affiliation. Much as district legislators in the US context rely on party labels for re-election (Cox and McCubbins 1993), district legislators, even those who are elected as independents, often find it useful to join parties in the legislature. Thus, parties are weak in Ukraine, but not entirely irrelevant to legislators.

The general pattern of legislative behavior reflected in research on the Verkhovna Rada is consistent with our impressions in speaking with parliamentarians, staffers, and legislative analysts and paints a portrait of a democracy with weak political parties. Legislators are essentially independent operators, behaving with an eye toward securing re-election. In some cases, they perceive advantage in joining and demonstrating loyalty to a political party. In other cases, they have the resources or the "personal vote coalitions" (Thames and Castleberg 2006) to either maintain a single-member district seat or move into a more advantageous position on a preferred party list, and, as such, they can behave more independently in their legislative activities.

Brawling in Ukraine

Regular brawling in Ukraine's legislature does not have the prodemocratic protest roots seen in Taiwan. In fact, legislative violence from Kuchma to Yanucovych was more notable for being deployed instrumentally by progovernment supporters looking to break up opposition disruptions, not for use as signaling. In December 2003, for example, the issue was a constitutional amendment that opposition parties feared would have enabled then-president Kuchma to stay in office beyond the two terms that were allowed by the constitution. Opposition parliamentarians blocked the Speaker's podium to stop a vote on the amendment, and fighting broke out as progovernment legislators tried to remove opposition legislators and see the legislation passed.

One reporter who covered parliamentary affairs during this era recalled a particularly violent episode in December 2010. In that instance, the Fatherland party of former prime minister Julia Tymoshenko obstructed the Speaker's podium in protest of a corruption investigation that had been opened against her (BBC 2010). Late that evening, as the press had grown weary of covering the stand-off and had largely left, members of then-president Yanukovych's Party of Regions attempted to retake the podium by force, causing injury to at least six opposition MPs, five of whom were hospitalized in the brawl's aftermath. One opposition member was hit over the head with a chair, while others accused members of the government of wielding iron bars and chains.[3]

Even in this era, however, some brawls bore more of the hallmarks that we associated with brawls used for signaling purposes. For example, a major legislative disruption sparked brawling in April 2010. Opposition members had come to parliament to protest the government's recent passage of a controversial piece of legislation that allowed the Russian navy extended access to Ukrainian ports in Crimea. They pelted the speaker's podium with eggs and set off smoke bombs in the chamber, setting off alarms, but the speaker continued his address, shielded from the eggs with umbrellas. Meanwhile, physical altercations broke out around the edges of the chamber between opposition and government supporters.

Observers have noted an uptick in the frequency and intensity of legislative brawls since the 2014 Euromaidan crisis (Sputnik 2017), and these brawls appear to conform more consistently to our understanding of brawls as costly signals, often in the context of opposition disruption. Like Taiwan, Ukraine's brawls often pit legislators on opposite sides of the country's major political cleavage against each other. In March 2013 a brawl broke out as one parliamentarian was booed for giving a speech in Russian and calling those who booed him "neo-fascists" (RFE/RL 2013). In July 2014, MP Nikolai Levchenko was pushed off the podium after he criticized a motion to enlist males under the age of 50 and increase military reserves. Just three months before that, in April, lawmakers exchanged punches after a member of the Communist Party accused his far right colleagues of bolstering Moscow during the early days of the Crimea crisis. And fights broke out again in 2018 when opposition lawmaker Nestor Shufrych called Viktor Medvedchuk, a pro-Russian Ukrainian politician, an "agent" of Russian President Vladimir Putin.

Finally, many brawls in Ukraine revolve around questions of honor. February 9, 2017, saw a brawl where an MP from then-president Poroshenko's legislative bloc, Serhiy Leschenko, was attacked by Serhiy Ivan Melnychuck for comments he made on social media. Leschenko had criticized fellow MPs on Facebook for not attending a meeting of parliament's anticorruption committee, of which he was a member. Although the Facebook criticisms appeared to be aimed at members of Leschenko's own legislative bloc, Melnychuck, who had been elected as a member of the Radical Party but had subsequently declared himself an independent and was not a member of the Poroshenko bloc, took issue. Melnychuck was a former commander of a volunteer military battalion and saw this as an attack on his honor (Ramani 2017). What began as a verbal dispute between the two on the floor of parliament ended with Melnychuck delivering several blows to Leschenko and tearing his clothes.

While there are some similarities, brawls in Ukraine have a noticeably different profile than those in Taiwan. Although Ukraine's party system is much weaker and more fragmented than Taiwan's, its politics are similarly organized around a single cleavage pertaining to relations with a large, neighboring country. As we have seen, many brawls reflect this specific tension. Unlike Taiwan, in which the brawls almost universally feature a showdown between KMT and DPP legislators defending party positions, brawls in Ukraine are not so tightly associated with specific parties. Indeed, some of the brawls are more closely associated with specific individuals pursuing their own goals and questions of personal honor rather than representing their broader parties.

Brawls around the World: How Common Are They Anyway?

While parliamentary brawls are not an everyday occurrence, neither are they as rare as many people assume. In this section, we draw on two pieces of research that have attempted to identify all recent cases of parliamentary violence around the world to present a global picture of the phenomenon.

Christopher Gandrud (2016) was the first scholar to attempt to systematically document all cases of parliamentary brawling around the world.

Gandrud searched several news databases to identify 131 incidents between 1981 and 2012. Eighty-six of these cases occurred in 30 democracies, about three-fifths of which happened in only seven countries: India, Italy, South Korea, Mexico, Taiwan, Turkey, and Ukraine. While this was groundbreaking research, there were a few limitations with Gandrud's data collection. Most importantly, Gandrud only searched English-language sources. For countries in which the primary language was not English, this meant that only incidents that involved issues interesting to international audiences, were particularly salacious, or were otherwise deemed newsworthy by English-language outlets would be identified. This almost certainly biases the data against finding cases in small or poor countries, especially those that do not have a domestic English-language newspaper. It also limited Gandrud to sources found in online databases. Not all newspapers are included in online databases. Even sources that are currently archived may not have put older content online. Globally, Gandrud only finds eight cases of brawling prior to 1990. This is probably not because the 1980s were a golden period of legislative harmony. Rather, it illustrates some of the limitations of this data collection approach. At any rate, Gandrud's work was a valuable first step in describing brawling worldwide and offering preliminary explanations for why brawling occurs (Gandrud 2016).

Moritz Schmoll and Wang Leung Ting (2023) have taken the next logical step. They followed Gandrud's strategy of searching online news databases, but they vastly increased the scope of this search. Rather than limiting themselves to only English sources, Schmoll and Ting searched in seven languages: Arabic, Chinese, English, French, Portuguese, Russian, and Spanish. This ambitious and daunting research strategy reveals a far larger number of cases. They find 375 cases between 1980 and 2018, including 348 since 1990. Again, the data are skewed toward more recent years, with very few cases in the 1980s and roughly 20 cases a year in the 2010s. This is an enormous increase in documented cases, showing brawls to be a more common phenomenon than is generally understood. Their data identify cases in 73 different countries in all parts of the globe. Most countries in South America and South Asia have seen brawls, as have many in the Middle East, North Africa, sub-Saharan Africa, East Asia, and Eastern Europe. Readers should not fall victim to the temptation to believe that parliamentary brawls only happen to poor countries or new or troubled democracies. Schmoll and Ting document several cases in rich, established democracies, including cases in Italy, Japan, France, and New Zealand. While parliamentary brawls are more common in new democracies, they can happen anywhere (Schmoll and Ting 2023).

Schmoll and Ting should be lauded for their effort to be so comprehensive, and yet even their data set probably significantly underestimates the extent of brawling around the world. If we assume that the higher numbers in more recent years are due to the limitations of databases from earlier time periods rather than any sudden surge in the popularity of brawling, then there are numerous cases from earlier years that are still undocumented. If we assume that there are actually about 20 cases a year, as Schmoll and Ting found in the most recent decade, it is reasonable to guess that there may have actually been around 600 cases between 1990 and 2018. Even that estimate may be an undercount. Our research has uncovered 202 brawling incidents in Taiwan alone. It is possible that Schmoll and Ting are using stricter criteria for the definition of a brawl, but it seems likely that their keywords or databases missed a number of valid cases. There are also countries in which most of the domestic media is published in a language other than the seven they searched. Turkey, Japan, South Korea, and Lithuania are obvious examples of countries in which brawling might be undercounted due to language differences.

Schmoll and Ting go beyond the mere frequency of brawling to look at the features of each brawl. One of the most interesting is their classification of the causes of each brawl. Of the 334 brawls since 1994, 27.8% were considered to be power affecting, 17.1% were symbolic, 33.2% involved a policy dispute, and 21.9% were caused by an ad hominem attack (Schmoll and Ting 2023, Table 1). In the parlance of our framework (Chapter 3), we expect the first three categories are largely occurring in a context of opposition disruption, while the fourth category is more likely to be what we think of as honor brawling.

Magical Mystery Tour: Stories of Brawls in Different Places

In this section we describe several parliamentary brawls from a variety of regions, some of which are from much earlier times. The goal of this section is to give readers a feel for what brawls are like on the ground. Each brawl is unique, and yet there are certain themes that recur. This is not meant to be a comprehensive depiction of brawling around the world; rather, these diverse and gripping cases should further underscore the point that legislative brawling is still a topic that is largely unexplored. We hope readers will forgive us for inevitably failing to do justice to the intricacies of politics in each individual context. Enjoy the fun stories!

United Kingdom: Two Swords Apart

In the House of Commons, the two major parties traditionally sit on opposite sides of the chamber. There are two lines on the floor that members are not supposed to cross, which are famously said to be two sword lengths apart to prevent members from fighting, as wearing swords was once common in the British Parliament. We are not aware of any cases in which swords were actually used in violent conflicts, but there are numerous cases in which swords were used to intimidate or physically threaten other members of Parliament. More generally, the threat of violence was often present in the early British Parliament. George Henry Jennings (1881) recounts this history in such wonderful 19th-century prose that we cannot resist directly quoting a few episodes.

On an incident in the midst of the English Civil War, Jennings writes about the threat of physical conflict and even swordplay in Parliament.

> It was Hampden who moved (November 22, 1641) that the Great Remonstrance, which had just been passed by a majority of eleven only, should be printed; it being intended by its promoters to serve, among other purposes, as a declaration from the House of Commons to the people. The proposal roused the opposite party to the utmost, and Hyde and other of its members endeavored to enter a formal protest against the printing. "We had catched at each other's locks," wrote Sire Philip Warwick, "and sheathed our swords in each other's bowels, had not the sagacity and great calmness of Mr. Hampden, by a short speech, prevented it, and led us to defer our angry debate until the next morning." (Jennings 1881, 73)

Elsewhere, Jennings reiterates that the threat of violence in this same incident was widely understood to be present.

> Some waved their hats over their heads, and others took their swords in their scabbards out of their belts, and held them by the pommels in their

hands, setting the lower part on the ground; so, if God had not prevented it, there was very great danger that mischief might have been done. (Jennings 1881, 28)

A few decades later, the threat of violence was still clearly present in Parliament.

In October, 1680, the Parliament met. The Whigs had so great a majority in the Commons that the Exclusion Bill went through all its stages there without difficulty. The whole nation now looked with breathless anxiety to the House of Lords. The assemblage of peers was large. The King himself was present. The debate was long, earnest, and occasionally furious. Some hands were laid on the pommels of swords, in a manner which revived the recollection of the stormy Parliaments of Henry the Third and Richard the Second. Shaftesbury and Essex were joined by the treacherous Sunderland. But the genius of Halifax bore down all opposition. (Jennings 1881, 90)

Such incidents are not merely matters of the distant past. At least two brawls occurred in the 20th century. In 1923, the opposition Labour Party blocked debate on benefits for ex-servicemen by shouting and singing and forced the Speaker to declare a short recess. As MPs left the chamber, Labour MP Robert Murray was hit on the head with Order Papers. He struck out at Tory MP Walter Guinness, whom he assumed had been the attacker. The two were eventually separated, but other fights broke out elsewhere on the floor before order was restored. As *The Times* succinctly put it, "All the time, there was much uproar and confusion" (*The Times* 1923).

In 1931, John McGovern, a Scottish MP upset over the arrests of lay preachers, refused to yield the floor. Eventually the Speaker ordered him forcibly removed by the sergeant-at-arms, but several of McGovern's colleagues stepped forward to resist this. "There was a wild scuffle for some minutes", before McGovern was eventually dragged out of the chamber (*The Times* 1931).

Just recently, facing a proposed ban on fracking raised by the opposition Labour Party, Tory whips Wendy Morton and Craig Whittaker were accused of physically pulling hesitant Conservative MPs into the chamber to ensure that they voted on the measure. After the incident, a Labour MP asked for a formal investigation into MPs being "physically manhandled" (Walker, Allegretti, and Crerar 2022, paragraph 9). While this incident may not rise to the level of a full-scale brawl, it is a reminder that, even today, physicality is not entirely absent from the House of Commons.

United States: Insults and Honor

In the early days of the new republic, there was no established party system in which politicians could build their reputations. Instead, they had to rely on their personal reputations in attempts to build coalitions with other politicians. Maintaining one's honor—and ensuring that other politicians were aware of that reputation—was paramount (Freeman 2001).

The most famous legislative brawl of the 1790s between Matthew Lyon of Vermont and Roger Griswold of Connecticut was fraught with questions of honor. Lyon had privately insulted Connecticut's representatives, so Griswold approached him on the floor and accused Lyon of cowardice, after which Lyon spat in Griswold's face. When the House elected not to expel Lyon for this act, Griswold responded as the code of honor demanded. Beating someone with a walking stick or cane was widely understood as marking the victim as a social inferior, so Griswold purchased a hickory walking stick and attacked Lyon on the House floor. Lyon grabbed tongs from the fireplace and fought back, a scene immortalized in one of the most famous political cartoons in American history. James Madison wrote that Griswold had dishonored himself in this exchange, though not because of the violence. Madison felt that Griswold should not have asked a committee to formally discipline Lyon. A man of honor could not abide such an insult, so Griswold should have reacted to Lyon's spitting by immediately beating him or challenging him to a duel (Freeman 2001, 172–174).

The US Congress regularly saw violence for many decades. During the period before the Civil War, Freeman describes a pattern of Southerners physically bullying Northerners. Southern voters demanded their representatives act as gentlemen of honor, and fighting and dueling were integral parts of establishing and maintaining this reputation. Northern voters, in contrast, tended to look down upon fighting and dueling as barbaric acts unbecoming of modern, civilized gentlemen. This difference in voters' expectations of proper behavior led to an imbalance in Washington, since Southern legislators could expect that voters would reward them for brawling, while Northern legislators expected to be punished. Southerners could constantly escalate disputes to the point of physical conflict, and Northerners had to back down. Many of these disputes played out in the context of the battles over slavery, and having an extra weapon in their arsenal gave Southerners an advantage in these battles (Freeman 2018, ch. 4).

Freeman sees the intensification of violence in Congress in the 1840s and 1850s as deeply enmeshed in the country's descent into Civil War. Tired of endless bullying by Southern politicians and worried that Southern attempts to protect slavery were eroding freedoms such as the right to free speech in the North, Northern voters became increasingly willing to tolerate politicians who fought back. The establishment of the Republican Party as a party based entirely in the North and composed of a new breed of politicians willing to stand up and fight for their issues was the culmination of this escalation. The last three Congresses before the Civil War were the most violent in American history, with perhaps the most famous incident being the caning of Senator Charles Sumner (Freeman 2018, ch. 7; Gandrud 2016).

We are not aware of any studies of brawling in state legislatures, but we would not be surprised to find a rich history in those arenas. One such dramatic case in 1887 was labeled by the local press as the Black Day of the Indiana General Assembly. This case involved a partisan dispute over a US Senate seat, which at the time was chosen by the state legislature. A melee broke out on the floor of the state Senate when Democrats blocked the Republican lieutenant governor-elect from entering the chamber to take his place as presiding officer. That melee was stopped when one legislator fired his pistol in the air, but the gunfire set off brawls in the rest of the capital grounds, including the state House. A mob gathered outside the capitol, and eventually the governor had to call in city and county police to restore order and avoid bloodshed (Clark 2017; Wikipedia n.d.).

Brawling has been much less common in Congress in the post–Civil War era, though it did not disappear entirely. The most recent episode we are aware of took place in 1963, when Henry Gonzalez (D-TX) slugged Ed Foreman (R-TX) on the House floor after Foreman called him a "pinko" (Russell 1992). And while we certainly would not characterize the events of January 6, 2021, as a parliamentary brawl, it is worth noting that violence could be poised to make a comeback in the US Congress.

Japan: Racing against the Clock ... or Not

Japan has a long history of parliamentary brawls that continues to the present day, though contemporary brawls in the Japanese Diet are perhaps not as large or dramatic as some of those seen in the immediate postwar period. Japan has traditionally had a powerful influence on other countries in East Asia, especially former Japanese colonies Korea and Taiwan. While no one in either South Korea or Taiwan told us that their own brawls were inspired by Japan, it is hard to believe that they were unaware of events in Japan.

Japan's peak period of brawling lasted from the 1954 brawl over police reform to the 1960 brawl over the US-Japan Security Treaty. Prime Minister Yoshida's 1954 police reform bill proposed changing the organizational basis of the police bureaucracy from regions and municipalities to one based on prefectures. This was vigorously opposed by the progressive bloc, led by the Japan Socialist Party. An article in *Yomiuri Shinbun*, one of Japan's main newspapers, provides a detailed, evocative, and dramatic account of the parliamentary struggle over police reform in which no fewer than 20 MPs are mentioned by name (*Yomiuri Shinbun* 1954).

On the last day of the session, all the other important legislation had passed. Only the police bill remained, and it had to pass by midnight. From 8 p.m., both sides were keenly focused on the midnight deadline. The opposition blocked several doors to the chamber and formed a human wall to prevent Speaker Tsutsumi from reaching his chair. Around 10:30 p.m., around 200 government legislators and 10 parliamentary guards charged the opposition lines and slowly began to push them back. The opposition then deployed several female legislators to sit in the Speaker's and cabinet ministers' chairs so that those people could not take their required positions. The government MPs were not deterred by this ploy and attempted to forcefully remove the occupiers. The news story dwells on this part of the brawl, breathlessly recounting the women's screams and injuries, including one particularly lurid tidbit in which MP Daisuke Yoshie's dress was torn, completely exposing her chest.

With only 10 minutes remaining, the Speaker again attempted to take his position and was again rebuffed. He then called for outside police forces to restore order. Dozens of Tokyo Metropolitan Police plunged into the fray, but they were kicked and punched just like everyone else and failed to gain control of the situation. As the midnight deadline arrived and the opposition prepared to celebrate its victory, the government parties suddenly announced that the Speaker had extended the session by two days. The opposition protested that the deadline had already passed and that the extension was invalid, but the extension effectively cancelled the deadline. Without the advantage of a ticking clock, the opposition was unable to continue its resistance, and the police reform bill was duly passed (*Yomiuri Shinbun* 1954).

The brawl was both lengthy and violent, with participants repeatedly pushing, pulling, kicking, and punching each other over the course of several hours. At least 50 people were injured. After the brawl, both the politicians and the police tried to distance themselves from the violence. The five largest parties issued a joint statement criticizing themselves for the incident and promising to avoid any future brawls. The police released detailed lists of all the injuries and losses they had suffered (broken wristwatches and fountain pens!), and a police spokesman claimed that they played only a subordinate role to the politicians in the conflict and had only entered the chamber when they were pulled in by other combatants or went in to retrieve their police hats, which had been knocked off their heads (*Yomiuri Shinbun* 1954; Modern Japan in Archives). These public displays of remorse, condemnations of violence, and promises to eschew such behavior in the future did not prevent the Japanese Diet from engaging in other intense, large-scale brawls over the next few years.

South Korea: Whatever It Takes to Get in the Room

Brawls have played a prominent role in Korea during the postwar period. Early major brawls occurred in 1952, 1954, and 1969, when presidents tried to amend the constitution to change the electoral system or relax term limits. These early brawls were between the opposition and the police rather than between the opposition and legislators from the governing majority. The opposition was not well represented in the legislature in the 1972–1988 period, so there were few brawls. However, following the transition to democracy in the late 1980s, brawls became a frequent occurrence. Most of these involved the governing party trying to force through its agenda by using controversial parliamentary tactics. There were several particularly intense brawls between 2008 and 2011 over the US-Korea Free Trade Agreement (FTA) and a media reform bill. The shocking violence of two brawls in particular led to legislative reform in 2012 that halted brawling for several years. We will return to the topic of this reform in the concluding chapter. Here we present the events surrounding the FTA, which provoked several brawls between its introduction to the legislature in 2008 and its passage three years later. Two of these, one at the beginning of the process and the other at the end, were particularly dramatic.

The FTA was introduced in the National Assembly in 2008, shortly after the conservative Grand National Party (GNP) won the presidency and a majority in the legislature. The progressive Democratic Party (DP), which had negotiated the treaty but were now in opposition, argued against a quick passage. They felt that conditions in the US had changed with the election of Barak Obama, and they hoped to renegotiate several provisions. Moreover, they argued that the National Assembly should take its time to thoroughly review such an important agreement (*Hankyoreh* 2008a).

Two days before the FTA was introduced to committee, the GNP demonstrated that it was willing to use strongarm tactics—the committee chair exercised his power to bar any legislators who might destabilize proceedings from the committee hearing, effectively barring the entire opposition (Kang 2008). On the day of the hearing, GNP lawmakers occupied the committee room and barricaded themselves inside. A four-hour brawl ensued as the opposition tried to force its way into the room.

The struggle was intense by Korean or, indeed, any standards. GNP lawmakers tried to repel the opposition by spraying them in the face with fire extinguishers, while opposition legislators tried to break down the door with a sledgehammer and an electric chainsaw. Windows were shattered, furniture was smashed, and the door was eventually broken down. However, by the time the opposition lawmakers reached the conference room, the GNP had already passed the motion to formally introduce the FTA, adjourned, and left the room (Kang 2008; *Hankyoreh* 2008b; Glionna 2009).

The opposition proclaimed that its actions, while extreme, were justified. As an aide to the chair of the Democratic Labor Party said, "We had to get inside that room.... For us, democracy was on the line" (Glionna 2009, paragraph 35). Within the GNP, reactions were more mixed. Some legislators argued that it was necessary to pass the FTA and called for punishment of brawlers. Others argued that they had tried to prevent violence inside the hearing by barring the opposition from entering the room (Glionna 2009). A conflicted GNP Foreign Affairs Committee member said, "It's embarrassing and complicated. I could feel the thirst for blood within the standing committee" (*Hankyoreh* 2008b, paragraph 3). After the brawl, Speaker Kim Hyong-o issued a statement of apology, writing that the GNP "needs to reflect and retrace whether it was necessary to present the bill so one-sidedly and to engage in such extreme obstruction efforts" (*Hankyoreh* 2008c, paragraph 2).

Nearly three years later, the US Congress passed the FTA and the GNP prepared to make a final push to ratify it in the Korean National Assembly. After the intense 2008 brawl and another brawl in 2009 over media reform that was nearly as violent, politicians did not want to further anger the public by appearing eager for a fight. A group of 87 opposition legislators signed a pledge to refrain from physically blocking the ratification if the government promised to renegotiate a key provision over dispute resolution after ratification (E. Kim 2011a). A group of 21 GNP legislators pledged to give up their seats if the GNP used violent tactics to pass the FTA (E. Kim 2011c). One of them, Jeong Tae-Keun, went on a hunger strike, which he pledged to continue until the FTA was passed using normal procedures and the parties agreed on a reform to prevent future brawls (Yonhap 2011a). President Lee then made a rare visit to the parliament, in which he offered to seek a revision to the key provision after passage. After extensive internal discussions the DP rejected this offer, insisting that renegotiation should precede ratification (J. Chang and Kim 2011; E. Kim 2011a). This refusal gave the GNP a rationale to change from conciliation to confrontation. GNP party leader Hong Joon-pyo said, "We have accepted the DP's demand 100% and can't wait any longer. There is no other option but to put (the bill) to a vote" (E. Kim 2011b, paragraph 7) GNP floor leader Hwang Woo-yea, who had been part of the group of 21, asked, "Is the DP trying to drive this matter to a dead end? The time has come for a resolution" (E. Kim 2011b, paragraph 9).

The GNP surprised everyone by occupying the National Assembly chamber several days before they had been expected to act. Police were ordered to seal off the National Assembly compound and the doors were locked, sealing the GNP legislators in and almost all of the opposition legislators out. With an overwhelming majority in the chamber, the GNP quickly went through parliamentary procedures to move to a final passage vote. During one of these votes, Kim Sun-dong, a legislator from the Democratic Labor Party who had managed to get inside the chamber before it was sealed, threw a tear gas bomb at the presiding officer in an attempt to stop the process. While the air in the chamber cleared, Kim was detained and Speaker Park Hee-tae issued an emergency order to further lock down the chamber. When things resumed, the FTA was put to a final vote and passed 151 to 7, with 12 abstentions (Yonhap 2011b, 2011c; E. Kim 2011c).

Public reaction to the brawl was mixed. Surveys showed disapproval of the GNP's heavy-handed tactics, but the use of tear gas was even more unpopular and may have dulled the backlash to the GNP (Chung 2011). In the aftermath of the brawl, the opposition expressed remorse that it had failed. DP party leader Sohn Hak-kyu lamented, "It was absurd and shameless the (GNP) rammed through the bill in a closed session. (I) apologize for not being able to block it" (E. Kim 2011d, paragraph 5). In contrast to the DP's message that it should have fought even harder, some in the GNP expressed regret over having resorted to hardline tactics. Foreign Affairs Committee Chair Nam Kyung-pil offered to resign his post, explaining, "I had hoped to make an advanced, beautiful parliament that works on dialogue and negotiations in the process of ratification, but my wish ended up unfulfilled. My efforts were insufficient" (E. Kim 2011e, paragraph 3).

Turkey: Women Take the Lead

Like Taiwan, Ukraine, and South Korea, Turkey has seen frequent parliamentary brawling in recent decades. Brawling began with a transition to democracy in the 1950s. Parliamentary brawls do not usually cause serious injury, but a Turkish brawl in 2001 led to the death of a legislator when Mehmet Fevzi Sihanlioglu suffered a fatal heart attack in the aftermath of a brawl (*Irish Times* 2001). Many Turkish brawls have revolved around the basic rules of the democratic system. Here, we present the story of one such recent incident over amendments to the constitution.

In the wake of a failed coup in July 2016, Turkish president Erdoğan pushed forward constitutional amendments that would greatly enhance presidential powers. Proponents argued that the amendments would rationalize government by doing away with the prime minister and creating clear lines of authority, while critics charged that it would lead to one-man rule and an end to democracy. Erdoğan's Justice and Development Party (AKP) and the smaller Nationalist Movement Party (MHP) together held 355 seats in parliament, more than the 330 votes necessary to send the amendments to a referendum. They were opposed by the Republican People's Party (CHP) and the People's Democratic Party (HDP), which combined for 192 seats, though 11 HDP deputies had been jailed. The initial stages of the parliamentary process involved marathon sessions lasting late into the night and led to brawls featuring punches, bleeding deputies, a broken nose, and claims of being bitten (*The Guardian* 2017; Kizil 2017; Nordland 2017; Fox 2017).

During the critical second reading on January 19, opposition lawmakers again tried to disrupt proceedings. While most Turkish parliamentary brawls are male dominated, this time the women on both sides took the lead. Aylin Nazlıaka, a female MP, handcuffed herself to the lectern, explaining, "I wanted to give a message to the nation by handcuffing myself to the parliamentary lectern. It also represents how the parliament has been handcuffed.

While the door of the parliament has been chained, it is important that we have chained ourselves" (*Hürriyet Daily News* 2017, paragraph 3). This action forced two recesses and a delay of two hours. After failing to convince Nazlıaka to abandon her protest, ruling party legislators tried to unscrew the microphone and remove the handcuffs, leading to shoving, slapping, hair pulling, kicking, and punching. Several lawmakers were injured in the brouhaha. One who received extra attention was Şafak Pavey, a wheelchair-bound CHP deputy, whose prosthetic leg was detached and damaged when she was pushed to the ground. Several lawmakers were wounded and three were sent to the hospital (Fraser 2017; Nordland 2017; *Deutsche Welle* 2017; *Hürriyet Daily News* 2017). During all this, the ruling party kept holding votes to push each clause through. The final vote was taken two days later and passed 339 to 142, with 5 blank votes (France24 2017).

Neither side expressed regret over their role in the clash. Prime Minister Binali Yildirim congratulated MPs for successfully passing the amendments, saying, "We have done our job. Now we convey the issue to its real owner, our people" (BBC 2017, paragraph 19). In contrast, the CHP leader Kemal Kilicdaroglu lamented that the parliament had "handed over its own authority" and vowed to continue the struggle against the amendments in the coming referendum (France24 2017, paragraph 12). Şafak Pavey, the lawmaker who had been pushed out of her wheelchair, described the fury of the ruling party legislators: "[The AKP lawmakers] all attacked us, blinded with anger" (*Hürriyet Daily News* 2017, paragraph 5), adding darkly, "This attack shows what awaits us once the (reform of) the constitution is passed" (*Deutsche Welle* 2017, paragraph 6).

Mexico, Guyana, and South Africa: Symbols and Speeches

Recent brawls from North and South America as well as sub-Saharan Africa highlight a couple of common brawling patterns in recent years: opposition objection to election results, the chief executive, or both, as well as the centrality of ceremonial objects in the legislative process.

Mexico

Even though Mexico's parliament, with its strong party system, was prone to opposition disruption in the late 1980s and 1990s, a military presence in the chamber kept all those outbursts at a level of mere disruption, with only occasional, incidental physical contact. After the presidential election of 2006, however, Mexico saw its first significant, multiday legislative brawl. With the long-dominant Institutional Revolutionary Party (PRI) in decline since the late 1990s, animosity between the National Action Party (PAN) and the Party of the Democratic Revolution (PRD) had grown. So when Felipe Calderon (PAN) narrowly beat Andres Manuel Lopez Obrador (PRD) in the 2006 presidential election, the stage was set for a showdown in the Mexican House of Deputies.

In September, in an escalation of previous disruption tactics (during which deputies had characteristically stayed in or near their seats, shouting and drawing attention to themselves in various ways), PRD members took the Speaker's podium to prevent outgoing President Fox (PAN) from being able to deliver his State of the Union address. There was minimal violence associated with this incident, and the government subsequently passed a law that the president could simply send the address to congress and did not need to appear in person—thereby undercutting the power of podium occupation.

The incident emboldened PRD deputies, however, and they staged another podium occupation on November 28, in advance of Calderon's December 1 inauguration, which was set to take place in the chamber. Physical fights between PRD and PAN members ensued, as PRD members attempted to block the podium and abscond with ceremonial items such as a mace that were necessary for inaugural proceedings. Over the course of several days, the partisanship of this particular brawl ultimately spilled out of the single chamber of deputies, with PAN senators stopping by to join the fray, attempting to remove PRD deputies from the podium. Ultimately, after days of altercations, leadership for both the PAN and the PRD came together to secure the podium so that Calderon could be inaugurated.

Guyana

In December 2021, more than a year had passed in Guyana since a contested election in which the incumbent government had attempted to claim victory but was found to have lost. The contentious election continued a long-standing rivalry between the country's two major ethnic groups (Black and Indo-Guyanese), which has played out through partisan politics since before the country's independence from Britain in 1966. Against this backdrop, on December 29, Guyana's parliament had just passed a landmark piece of legislation, the National Resource Fund (NRF) bill, meant to govern the country's emerging oil wealth. After the bill's passage and a recess, parliamentarians had returned to debate amendments to the bill.

Before the government's finance minister could begin his presentation on amendments, however, opposition members began to disrupt proceedings, approaching the speaker's podium to halt the minister's reading. After some scuffling, MPs from the government physically surrounded the senior minister at the podium so that he could continue his presentation. At this point, an opposition MP, Annette Ferguson, attempted to steal the chamber's ceremonial mace—considered to represent the authority of the parliament. Ferguson's actions set off another round of scuffling as members of the government and opposition fought for control of the mace, and members of the government also fought to retain control of the speaker's podium (News Room 2021). A member of parliamentary staff ultimately secured control of the mace and recounted being dragged from the chamber, assaulted, and subject to racial slurs (*Guyana Chronicle* 2021). Overall, eight members of the opposition were identified as central to the brawl, four women and four men MPs, and recommended to receive disciplinary action.

South Africa
In February 2017, South Africa's president Jacob Zuma was scheduled to address parliament in South Africa's equivalent of a State of the Union address. Amid antipresident protests in the streets surrounding parliament, members of a small opposition party called the Economic Freedom Fighters disrupted the president's address, accusing him of corruption and calling him a "scoundrel." It was as security forces attempted to remove the disrupting opposition that the brawl occurred. While most members of the Democratic Alliance (the country's main opposition party) refrained from brawling, they did stage a walkout following the brawlers' removal from the chamber.

Uganda: Bringing in Security Forces

South Africa's was not the only sub-Saharan parliament to see violence in 2017. In September 2017, a multiday brawl occurred in the Ugandan parliament. This brawl happened amidst an ongoing fight over a constitutional amendment that would allow President Yoweri Museveni to run for reelection despite having reached the limit of his constitutionally mandated terms. Not surprisingly, opposition parliamentarians were opposed to the proposed amendment, which ultimately passed. And while opposition to a proposed constitutional change is a common reason for opposition politicians to initiate a brawl in any country, the actual causes of brawling in this case were much more immediate and specific.

Though brawling was billed in the media as occurring over the course of September 27 and 28, most of what occurred on September 27 amounted to threats of violence and disruption. On this day, progovernment parliamentarian Ronald Kibuule entered parliament with a firearm. Opposition member Ibrahim Ssemujju Nganda alerted the chamber to Kibuule's firearm possession and said the MP had threatened him with the weapon. Despite early denials by Kibuule, CCTV review eventually confirmed that he had, in fact, brought a firearm into the chamber (Okello 2017). Prior to this confirmation, however, opposition members disrupted parliamentary proceedings on Nganda's word, filling the aisles and chanting that Kibuule had a gun.

On September 28, Speaker of the House Rebecca Kadaga confirmed that Kibuule had carried a gun into parliament and suspended him along with 24 opposition MPs who had been involved in the previous day's disruption, making parliament "ungovernable." The named opposition members refused to vacate the chamber as instructed. As security forces came into the chamber to remove the suspended MPs, the brawl erupted. At the moment the tussling began, media footage showed a full parliament, shaped very much like the British House of Commons, with all benches on the opposition side emptied and opposition members spilling into the aisles, much as they had been the day before, while members on the government side begin to appreciate what is happening and rise to meet a potential oncoming challenge.

In media coverage of the scrum, MPs could be seen standing on top of the table that holds the government's speaking podium, wrestling one another to the floor, launching chairs, and wielding microphone stands as weapons. Two women MPs were reportedly injured in the brawl. The amendment in question was tabled at that time by the government but subsequently advanced by Speaker Kadaga. Perhaps most interesting, a cabinet minister we interviewed who was present for the brawl suggested that MPs had learned about parliamentary brawling by observing YouTube videos.[4]

Conclusion

While we see many unique and distinctive dynamics reflected in these stories of legislative brawls from around the world, it is the task of a project like this one to focus readers' attention on some of the commonalities. One way to do this is to look at what legislators were fighting over. For example, Schmoll and Ting (2023) sort brawls into four big categories: power affecting, symbolic, policy disputes, and ad hominem attacks. All four categories are well represented in this chapter. However, while it is natural to gravitate toward the substantive issue at stake, this might not be the best entry point for understanding legislative brawls. If one focuses on the issues at hand, it is easy to see those political fights as so contentious that they inevitably provoked a brawl. Indeed, participants in a brawl frequently portray their struggle in near-apocalyptic terms: democracy itself is at stake. However, controversial issues usually do not produce a brawl. Moreover, not every brawl involves an existential issue; some brawls erupt over fairly minor questions. There is no simple causal arrow running from controversial issue to parliamentary brawl. Someone has to initiate and escalate the physical conflict, and we argue this is a complex strategic decision firmly grounded in the logic of political communication.

We think that one of the most important points about the brawling stories presented in this chapter is that almost all our knowledge of them comes—either directly or indirectly—from the mass media. Traditionally, one of the most important roles of the mass media is to decide what is and what is not newsworthy. Plenty of what goes on inside parliament is overlooked because the media deems it too boring, opaque, arcane, technical, unimportant, or otherwise unsuitable for the news. The brawls presented here crossed this threshold. The media not only reported on them but also did so in quite a bit of detail. We are able to describe the twists and turns of the Korean brawl over the FTA, for example, because the mass media decided these were details readers would be interested in.

It is significant that the media reports on parliamentary brawls. It is critical that these reports often identified individual legislators by name. In this chapter, we have hit readers with a barrage of names. For most readers, the names Viktor Medvedchuk, Kim Sun-dong, and Şafak Pavey will mean almost nothing. However, there may be a few readers who are intimately familiar with Ukrainian, Korean, or Turkish politics and will think about those individuals differently now that we have focused attention on their brawling behavior. Likewise, when individual legislators are named in media reports about brawls, it is possible that various audiences will use that information to change their evaluation of the legislator.

Another commonality that we wish to draw to readers' attention is the prominence of opposition disruption in most of these brawls. It was not that the issue was so contentious that a brawl was inevitable. Rather, the opposition, for whatever reason, decided that this was an issue that it would take a stand on. When the opposition chose to do that—and it specifically chose to do that by physically disrupting legislative proceedings—brawling became much more likely. There are, of course, certain issues that are more likely to drive the opposition to disruption. For example, relations with the president, especially efforts to increase executive power relative to legislative power, sparked brawls in South Korea, Turkey, Ukraine, Uganda, Mexico, and South Africa. Other brawls were set off when an obviously weak opposition tried desperately to delay the passage of legislation it opposed. This has been a recurrent theme in brawls in Taiwan, South Korea, and Japan. Tactically, many brawls feature the opposition's attempts to occupy specific locations or to remove ceremonial objects. While these may seem to be different tactics, the underlying rationale of the opposition disruption is quite similar: if the presiding officer or the ceremonial mace is not in the proper place, any actions undertaken will be viewed as illegitimate. The common thread in this diverse array of brawls is not the issue at hand or the dilatory tactic employed; rather, it is the opposition's choice to disrupt. As such, opposition disruption is the context for our theoretical understanding of most parliamentary brawls.

Not all brawls occur due to opposition disruption. We have seen personal insults and provocations spark numerous brawls, including in Taiwan, Ukraine, the US, and South Africa. While such brawls may be deeply embedded in the grand political schisms that divide a society, as was often the case in brawls between Northern and Southern congressmen in the US Congress before the Civil War, these brawls were more immediately about legislators defending their personal honor. Questions of honor thus demarcate a separate class of brawls.

While brawls around the world and in our two case studies for this book all have unique features, we do see common themes emerge in the dynamics of parliamentary brawling. It is from observing some of these commonalities and employing strong deductive logic that we move on to construct a general theory of brawling, asking and answering the question: why would any elected representative choose to brawl?

3
An Individual Theory of Parliamentary Brawls

In this chapter we develop a theory to explain why legislators brawl by incorporating insights from literatures not generally associated with legislative behavior, including signaling theory, typically employed in international relations, and the logic of contentious politics from the social movements and the nonviolent protest literature. Further, although brawling is a behavior that takes place inside legislative institutions, our theory explicitly considers the broader institutional context in which legislators are embedded. Within any given institutional setting, actors are simultaneously considering the constraints of that specific institution and other associated institutions (Mainwaring and Shugart 1997; Hicken 2009; Batto et al. 2016). Thus, brawling legislators are not only considering the institutional constraints of the legislature but also sensitive to and motivated by their electoral system and political parties. Here, we see individual legislators' decisions to disrupt orderly legislative proceedings with violence as directly related to their broader political ambitions. In light of those ambitions and important contextual factors, we identify a chain of logic to explain the brawling behavior of individual legislators. This general logic allows for brawlers to emerge in a variety of contexts, signal to various audiences with their brawling, and communicate a general set of messages with legislative violence.

The chapter begins with a discussion of the concept of brawls as costly signals and highlights an important contextual factor for many brawlers: opposition disruption. Next, we discuss the importance of institutional variation within the context of opposition disruption, namely the strength of political parties, which ultimately shapes the intended audience of brawls and provides nuance to the message being sent. Finally, we discuss brawling outside the context of opposition disruption, what we call "honor brawls."

There is a basic logic behind almost all individual legislators' decisions to engage in a brawl: they want to use violence to send a costly signal about their type to a target audience that can help them pursue their political career.

While the precise manifestation of this logic varies in different contexts, three consistent themes are worth noting. First, the electoral rules play a fundamental role in shaping legislative behaviors. Elected officials who want to be re-elected are sensitive to the rules that shape how elections are determined, and, more broadly, electoral rules influence the strength of political parties. Second, the brawler's intended audience must find the signal useful. They must be attentive and interested enough to receive the signal, but they must also be lacking just enough information for the signal to tell them something meaningful about the individual. Third, it is very clear from our research that the general electorate as a whole is never the intended recipient of the signal. In fact, the general electorate's reaction to brawls lays bare the costs involved in signaling via brawling.

Brawls as Costly Signals

Legislators perceive value in signaling their type to actors who (1) will influence their future career ambitions—which usually involves a desire for re-election—but (2) may not have sufficient information to know that the legislator in question is worthy of their support. Signaling theory has been used to explain circumstances where actors' types are unobservable and they need some way to communicate their true type to other actors. This state is truly prepared to go to war, but how to make sure other states recognize it as such? This mafia foot soldier is extremely loyal to the organization, but how to differentiate himself from other individuals who will, of course, claim the same level of loyalty?[1] Costly signals provide a means by which actors can attempt to demonstrate they are of a type that might otherwise be unobservable.

A costly signal is some act that an individual of a true type can undertake but which other actors who might make similar claims will not be willing or able to perform (Morrow 1999, 88). The loyal mafia foot soldier will serve a lengthy jail sentence rather than cooperate with law enforcement. Serving the jail sentence, then, is the costly signal that distinguishes this individual from others who might claim loyalty but will instead turn state's witness at the first sign of personal cost. The state that wants to distinguish itself as committed to war may send the costly signal of deploying troops and military resources to its border, thereby distinguishing itself with the expense from states that simply claim a readiness to fight.

Costly signals often involve violence—sometimes because of a specific institutional context, and sometimes because of the effect it creates. A leader who wants to demonstrate a readiness for war may choose to test chemical weapons on his own citizens. This test not only demonstrates a readiness others might simply claim but also produces a horrific image in most people's minds, making it entirely plausible that this individual is ready for war, no matter the cost. When mafia leadership want to make sure that individuals are actually committed to the organization and not undercover law enforcement, they will direct the individual to commit murder. This is an act that a true mafioso should be willing and able to commit but that an undercover agent, by virtue of legal prohibitions, will not be able to. How should we think about the value of violence as a costly signal in a legislative context? Similar to the contexts described above, legislative violence signals extreme resolve and commitment, above and beyond what any given legislator may claim in their rhetoric.

The costs associated with some of the acts of violence described above may be evident, but what are the costs of legislative violence? First, violence always carries an inherent risk of harm to self. The individual who begins punching or shoving risks incurring the same. There are instances of legislative brawling where individuals have required medical attention in the aftermath. One of the last major brawls in South Korea involved a member of the opposition wielding a chainsaw to cut through locked chamber doors at great risk of harm to self and others. Second, some legislatures attach legal penalties to brawling. These can range from disciplinary penalties such as formal censure, fines, removal from positions such as committee positions, and suspension from parliamentary privileges to an extreme of expulsion from office. These penalties are rarely doled out, but brawlers must remember that they do exist. Finally, and most importantly, brawling carries reputational costs in the electorate. Ordinary people almost always hate brawling. Evidence from Taiwan demonstrates that the general public does not like brawls, and those who are identified as brawlers can face a sharp decline in voters' willingness to support them (Batto and Beaulieu 2020). One brawler in Ukraine, Yehor Soboliev, captured the "risky" nature of brawling as a strategy, citing the fact that even his wife did not approve of his physical altercations.[2] Granted, partisan loyalties will also shape citizens' attitudes toward brawling, as we will discuss in greater detail below, but a brawler who uses violence as a signal may have to face broad reputational costs in the form of general disapproval of their actions. These costs are substantial, and most of the time legislators

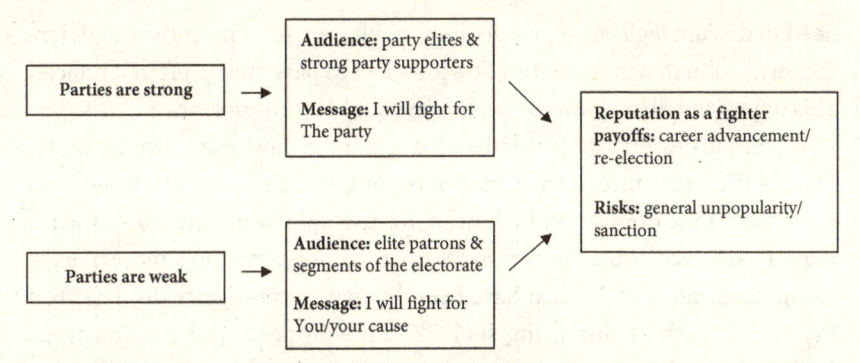

```
Parties are strong  →  Audience: party elites &
                        strong party supporters
                        Message: I will fight for
                        The party                   ↘
                                                        Reputation as a fighter
                                                        payoffs: career advancement/
                                                        re-election

                                                        Risks: general unpopularity/
                                                        sanction
Parties are weak   →   Audience: elite patrons &    ↗
                        segments of the electorate
                        Message: I will fight for
                        You/your cause
```

Figure 3.1 Brawling amidst opposition disruption.

conclude that they outweigh any potential benefits. It is worth remembering that legislators almost always choose not to brawl.

Given these costs, why, then, would legislators want to use violence? Another key premise of this theory is that individual legislators are looking to further their careers. In this quest, individual legislators want to stand out as worthy representatives. In their desire to stand out, a career-minded legislator may try to distinguish themselves from other legislators by signaling their resolve with a legislative brawl. The specific signal, as well as the intended audience for the signal, however, will depend on the broader context of legislative activity. Figure 3.1 offers a basic outline of the signaling logic at work for a legislator, in the most important contextual factors for legislative brawling—opposition disruption.

The Context of Opposition Disruption

Legislative contexts where the opposition is particularly weak vis-à-vis the government invite disruptive behaviors, initiated by parties and individuals in the opposition. This is consistent with Gandrud's (2016) finding that brawls are more likely in majoritarian political systems—that is, systems where a clear majority wields the power of government, and the opposition has little to no influence over the crafting and passage of legislation. Hence, opposition parties in the legislative minority, which cannot defeat the government's agenda via votes, may resort to some forms of disruption, either as a delay tactic or as a means of publicizing objection to a particular piece of legislation, or both. Parties in government are less likely to perceive a need to disrupt legislative proceedings and have strong incentives to defend the institution that is currently allowing them to pass their preferred policies. This opposition disruption is not, however, inherently violent.

When parties initiate legislative disruption, it most often occurs on the floor of the legislature, during the course of normal legislative proceedings. Members of the opposition in Taiwan, for example, routinely storm the podium in advance of the Speaker arriving to call for a vote on a piece of legislation. Legislators in Mexico have been known to coordinate displays from their seats, such as displaying spoiled ballots in protest of election fraud. Legislators in Ukraine have unfurled national flags and banners with protest slogans, often accompanied by chanting and singing songs.

In some contexts, such disruptive acts themselves can serve as costly signals without even involving violence. In Mexico, for example, during the decades that the Institutional Revolutionary Party (PRI) controlled government and placed a military presence in the legislative chambers, simply standing up in one's seat and shouting at the government was considered costly enough to earn a legislator a reputation for fighting against the government. Former Mexican president Vicente Fox, of the conservative National Action Party (PAN), began his political career in just such a way. Marco Rascon, of the liberal Party of the Democratic Revolution (PRD), gained similar notoriety during the same era for disrupting legislative proceedings wearing a pig mask.

In fact, we often see such opposition-initiated disruption in authoritarian or competitive-authoritarian regimes. From their position of perpetual weakness vis-à-vis an authoritarian government, opposition parties may simply wish to express frustration at their continued lack of influence, or they may recognize legislative disruption as an opportunity to press for greater democratization or oppose degradation of the system. The use of disruption in Taiwan, for example, began during the long period of undemocratic Kuomintang (KMT) rule. Similarly, opposition legislators in Mexico's chamber of deputies would stage coordinated walk-outs during the 70-year period when the PRI controlled government. This observation is also consistent with Gandrud's (2016) finding that brawls are more frequent in younger democracies, which, since the end of the Cold War, are more likely to be electoral- or competitive-authoritarian regimes (Flores and Nooruddin 2016).

Even within democratic legislatures, however, opposition parties can use disruption to counter legislation they dislike but lack the votes to stop from passing. Podium occupation is the most common form of legislative disruption used to this end. Members of the opposition will position themselves on and around the Speaker's podium, often focusing on controlling the microphone there, with the idea that the Speaker will be unable physically to take the podium and/or call for a vote. While such occupation usually fails to stop an item from passing (though it may delay its passage by a few hours or days), this disruption has the advantage of drawing media attention, which allows the opposition to communicate with citizens about objections to the government's legislative agenda.

The perceived utility of disruptive tactics in politics has been explored at great length in the literature on contentious politics. The logic of contentious politics has gained the most traction in the study of state-society relations, to understand how groups and individuals lacking formal power inside the state can nonetheless influence the state's actions. While this perspective is most often associated with the activities of social movements, such as protests, its theoretical insights are helpful to understand why actors inside a legislature might choose to employ these kinds of disruptive tactics. It makes sense to think of parties in government, who wield more legislative power than the opposition, as analogous to the state, and to consider the opposition as similar to actors within society, lacking (at least some of) the formal channels of influence afforded to those in the government.

Tarrow (1998) offers three points of emphasis when considering what such acts of disruption can accomplish. First, contentious political action is "the concrete performance of a movement's determination" (Tarrow 1998, 96). Legislative disruption demonstrates that the opposition is determined to fulfill its role opposing the government. Political opposition may be hoping to communicate its strength or resolve directly to the government, in the hopes of enhancing their ability to effect change directly. Alternatively, the opposition may be hoping to communicate to citizens, in the hopes of building support and applying indirect pressure to the government. In the course of such disruption, political parties may also be communicating to their own members about what the party stands for. Thus, disruptive legislative tactics allow parties to communicate their identity, which may serve to strengthen solidarity among the group. Legislative disruption serves both external, signaling functions for the opposition and internal, cohesion-building functions for opposition parties.

Second, because legislative disruption "obstructs the routine activities of opponents, bystanders, or authorities" and "forces them to attend to protests' demands" (Tarrow 1998, 96), this disruption has a potentially more instrumental purpose of attempting to produce some desired outcome of the disruptors. Here we can think of the typical instance where the government is about to pass legislation that the opposition does not want to see passed. By occupying the podium, pushing, and shoving, the opposition is forcing the government to acknowledge that the opposition is not in agreement with the legislation and is effectively delaying the passage of the legislation.

To the extent that this incident also receives media coverage, that same reckoning may be imposed on the electorate (Tarrow's "bystanders"). But because this disruption is contained within the institution itself, citizen bystanders will not experience the same level of disruption that they might with contentious political action in society. Contrast a legislative brawl, on the one hand, and protesters blocking a highway to protest police violence, on the other. Clearly the drivers on the highway are affected in ways they cannot ignore. A voter learning that the opposition party stormed the podium, unfurled a banner, or sang the national anthem can choose to consume as much news coverage as possible or can change the channel or click to a different website entirely. In other words, citizens' daily lives need not be disrupted in any meaningful way by legislative violence.

Here it is important to note the possibility of another key group of bystanders—other members of the legislature. Legislative disruption often involves some degree of coordination between members of a party.[3] Multiple individuals are required to make and hold signs, to take the podium, and to sing the requisite songs. At the same time, such disruptions rarely consume all members of the legislature, even of the disrupting party. Thus, another important group of bystanders will be those individual legislators who are witness to the disruption and whose legislative activities *are* directly impeded. In many cases, these may be precisely the bystanders that the disrupting party is hoping to reach—either more moderate or reticent members of their own party or moderate or reticent members of the governing party.

Third, contentious political actions are important because "disruption broadens the circle of conflict" (Tarrow 1998, 96). Actors causing disruption in the legislature are not merely attempting to shore up internal cohesion within a party or influence the governing party in some way; they are using a tactic that is meant to draw more actors into the conflict. When opposition parties disrupt legislative proceedings, they nearly always provide a rationale for the disruption, which is typically picked up by the media and communicated to the broader public. Thus, if a party is particularly opposed to a narrow piece of legislation, it can use disruptive tactics within the legislature to influence public opinion on that policy.

There are clear parallels between nonviolent parliamentary disruptions and nonviolent civil disobedience. Nonviolent civil disobedience involves a group lacking the formal institutional power to block an action, refusing to obey legal structures in order to highlight the conflict between that action and higher ideals. The authorities might deal with nonviolent protesters by portraying them as law-breaking rabble rousers and trying to discredit them. However, authorities often must resort to coercion, and when they do this, they risk "backfire." Backfire is "a public reaction of outrage to an event that is publicized and perceived as unjust" (Hess and Martin 2006, 249). That sense of injustice is often created when the authorities use excessive force to repress a nonviolent movement that is considered to have some degree of legitimacy. As such, it behooves the authorities to remove nonviolent protesters with as little coercive force as possible (Gandhi 1938; Sharp 1973; Hess and Martin 2006; Nepstad 2013). This logic of nonviolent protest reveals reasons that both minority and majority parties tend not to encourage violence during disruptions. The former want to focus on the injustice of the proposed policy, while the latter want to avoid inciting a backfire.

In our extensive investigations in countries where brawling has practically become a norm, we have not uncovered any systematic pattern of party leadership directing its members to engage in violence. Expressed reactions toward legislative violence among senior legislators and party leadership seem to range from disapproval to agnosticism. It is interesting to note that even in countries where some political parties were born out of violent protest movements (Sinn Fein associated with the Irish Republican Army in Ireland, or Herri Batasuna associated with Basque separatists in Spain), those parties never advocated violence within the legislature—they would engage in disruption such as coordinated walkouts or boycotts of parliamentary seats but kept their disruptions within the legislature decidedly nonviolent.

At the same time, while the parties' legislative leadership (who might organize or have to contend with opposition disruption) do not appear to advocate use of violence explicitly, it is accepted that legislators may incur or initiate some incidental physical contact in the course of disruptive activities. Some mild pushing, pulling, or shoving is to be expected, as members jostle for position or attempt to diffuse the disruptive situation. For individual legislators, there is an opportunity in the context of opposition disruption to escalate beyond these accepted levels and use violence as a costly signal, to distinguish oneself from others participating in the disruptive activities. Furthermore, once disruption begins, violence is a signal available to individual legislators in both the government and opposition—members of parliament on both sides now have an opportunity to signal extraordinary resolve, either in sympathy with the position of the opposition or on behalf of the government seeking to maintain order.

Logically, violence as a costly signal should be more useful to individual legislators than to political parties as a whole. Recall that costly signals allow actors to differentiate themselves from other, similar actors. Opposition parties are already distinct from the government. They are in opposition. Further, in the context of opposition disruption, it is not clear that any one party is trying to distinguish itself from any otherwise similar party in opposition. If the opposition is composed of a single strong party, for example, there is not any signaling value to the *party* from sending a more costly signal of violence.

Individual legislators, however, are always one of many and need ways to differentiate themselves from all the other legislators. And while party leadership may be undoubtedly interested in learning about legislators' types, they are not eager to see too much violence. Party leaders care about the party's general reputation, and brawling both is unpopular with most voters and has the potential to paint the party image as being violent, irrational, and even antidemocratic. Parties want the public's focus to be on the issue and the partisan disagreement, not on the violence. This sets up a conundrum: Parties want to engage in disruption and may also welcome the opportunity to obtain information about legislators, while individuals want to distinguish themselves from one another (and may choose to escalate to intentional violence to do so), and yet parties do not want the violence to get out of hand. Strong parties should be able to thread this needle, tacitly endorsing a low level of violence for disruption purposes, looking the other way when violence escalates to moderate levels, and actively discouraging the most extreme acts of violence.

Thus, opposition disruption—often motivated by political parties in the opposition—offers a clear opportunity for individuals to use violence as a signal. But what they are signaling and to whom will depend on other contextual factors that we discuss next. Critical to shaping the content of a given violent signal is the strength of political parties, which, in turn, depends on the electoral system.

We should note, however, referring back to Figure 3.1, that individual legislators can choose to brawl in cases of opposition disruption in both places where political parties are strong and places where parties are weak. Where parties are strongest, we tend to see cohesive, party-led, opposition-initiated disruption. In systems where parties are weaker, individual legislators in the opposition can still come together to engage in disruption in protest of government actions, though this will take greater organizational effort than in systems with strong opposition parties. Such coordinated disruption may occur less frequently where parties are generally weak, though if the country's politics are polarized around a particularly salient issue, this can often provide a kind of coordinating power for disruptive actions even where parties are weak. For example, while political parties are weak in Ukraine, ongoing conflict with Russia and the country's pro-/anti-Russia divide offer the necessary polarization to spark opposition disruption even without strong parties to coordinate such activities. Finally, while opposition disruption is possible both where parties are strong and where they are weak, party strength will determine the potential target audiences and may add some nuance to the general sense of the message that is being communicated through a brawl.

Strong Party Systems and Disruption Brawling

In strong party systems, parties are institutionalized—meaning they enjoy the regular support of political elites and connections to the electorate more broadly—and parties have a great deal of influence over legislative careers (Barnes 2016). Legislators who care about career advancement need to gain favor with influential party members who can direct resources and support their future career. The intended audience for a would-be brawler in this situation, then, will be influential actors within the legislator's party. These potential audiences can generally be characterized as individuals in party leadership and/or extreme supporters of the party in the electorate. In the case of either of these audiences, the signal being sent is that the legislator resolves to fight for the party and its policies.

For an individual legislator wanting to signal that they are the type of legislator who will be loyal to (and fight on behalf of) the party, violence can be a way to differentiate themselves from legislators who just say they are loyal, particularly when party leadership does not know ex ante how party members will actually vote or how much energy they will devote to pursuing a particular policy. In the context of opposition disruption in particular, party members who are willing to engage in the disruptive acts will demonstrate a greater commitment to the party than those who refrain from participating. But if disruption is widely embraced among legislators, then one cannot distinguish themselves simply by engaging in disruption. Hence, there is a need for a kind of signal that carries a higher cost—violence. If most party members are chanting or occupying the podium, engaging in violence allows an individual legislator to further differentiate themselves from among those party members willing to engage in disruption.

What we tend to observe, then, empirically, is that disruption always precedes violence and that disruption can be collective or individual. Individual party members may first use disruption as a way to distinguish themselves and signal greater commitment or loyalty than other copartisans, particularly if partisan coordination has been lukewarm in a given case. Once sufficient party members are also engaged in this initial disruption, however, the need for a stronger differentiating signal arises.

Hyde's (2011) work on international election observation is a nice illustration of the type of signaling initiation and escalation that we observe in these circumstances. Toward the end of the Cold War, democracy promoters demanded electoral democracy but did not necessarily insist that elections be monitored by independent third parties. Early democrats began holding elections to demonstrate a commitment to democracy, but soon even leaders not committed to democracy were also holding elections. Wanting to differentiate themselves from other would-be democrats, true democrats then escalated and began inviting international observers to monitor elections as a more costly signal that revealed their type. Because it ostensibly cut off opportunities for election rigging, the invitation to outside observers was seen as a costly signal that only true democrats would be willing to send. Democracy promoters were happy to have this additional signal of actors' types, but since it would have been inappropriate for them to demand that sovereign states invite monitors, they were not the driving force behind the adoption of the practice.

Analogously, party leaders who want disruption do not demand violence from their individual party members. Some individual legislators, wishing to signal their commitment to the party, however, see it as advantageous to send this additional costly signal of commitment to their party, and some influential actors within the party are glad to receive this additional signal. In the case of election observation, using monitors to signal a democratic commitment eventually became a norm such that *not* inviting observers today is a clear sign that a country lacks a true commitment to democracy. In a similar but less positive way, there is a risk that legislative violence can become normalized and chronic, and the risks of *not* using violence in some contexts will be explored further, later in this chapter.

Strong Party Systems and Target Audiences

When parties are strong and opposition disruption is occurring, brawlers are sending signals to individuals associated with their party, either to influential party leaders or to loyal party supporters. Recall that there are two primary conditions that must be met for a signal to be useful to send: First, the target audience must be unsure of the legislator's type. Second, the target audience must be appropriate to the ultimate goals of signaling in the first place.

Two factors will shape the target audience for a brawl where parties are strong: (1) the amount of information party leaders have about ordinary backbenchers from their party and (2) the extent to which party leaders or loyal party voters can influence electoral outcomes. Note that while the two audiences need not be mutually exclusive, in practice we find that one audience may have greater need of the information or be more influential in a legislator's re-election calculus. In some systems, for example, party leaders know their members very well, so they do not need more information. In other systems, loyal party voters carry outsized influence over nominations and re-election and, as such, become critical for legislators.

Regarding the first condition—uncertainty and need for information—loyal party voters rarely have universal and fine-grained political knowledge, so sending a signal to them about one's type is almost always informative. In contrast, the degree to which party leaders have information about individual legislators depends heavily on three institutional factors. First, the size of the legislature matters. With more legislators, it is harder for party leaders to know exactly what motivates each individual. Second, the electoral system can produce a more or less anonymous group of legislators. If electoral rules encourage individualistic campaigns in which legislators describe themselves in detail to voters, party leaders may learn quite a bit about their type. Alternatively, if legislators are elected simply by their party label, they may enter the legislature without making such potentially differentiating statements. This most obviously applies to legislators elected on closed party lists, but it can also apply to legislators elected from safe seats in single-member districts, especially if the party "parachutes" in an outsider. Third, and related, party leaders will have better information if most legislators are careerist politicians. If legislators have spent decades in politics, party leaders will have had ample opportunities to learn about them. However, if most legislators are political newcomers, party leaders might not know much at all. The electoral rules influence careerism, most notably if they prohibit re-election. However, the extent to which political parties cultivate and guide the careers of individual members, sometimes across many different elected and appointed offices, also matters.

The second condition for effective signaling is potential influence—in this case, that is the extent to which party leaders and loyal party supporters can influence electoral outcomes. In cases where nominations are tantamount to winning the election, the critical question is the degree to which nominations are open or closed (Rahat and Hazan 2001). If nominations are determined by a small group of party insiders, in the extreme case unilaterally by the party leader, legislators have a strong incentive to ensure that a small group of decision-makers understands their type. If nominations are decided by a wider group of party members, loyal party supporters can have an important impact on the outcome. Even in the extreme case in which the entire electorate is allowed to participate in the nomination decision (such as an open primary), loyal party supporters tend to participate at much higher rates than other voters and play a disproportionate role in determining outcomes. If nominations are not tantamount to winning, loyal party supporters in the general electorate become the backbone of a legislator's electoral coalition. Again, even though all voters can participate, loyal party supporters punch above their weight by participating at higher rates, contributing donations, serving as volunteers, and mobilizing other voters. In such cases, their enthusiastic support is critical.

One possible alternative to our logic is that brawlers are trying to send signals to ordinary voters back in their districts rather than to specific party actors. In electoral systems with single-member districts, the moderate, nonpartisan voters in the middle of the partisan spectrum may have the final say over who is elected and who is defeated. However, it is unlikely that legislators are trying to communicate with these voters by brawling during opposition disruption. For one thing, brawls in strong party systems are, by nature, partisan, and these voters are not receptive to partisan appeals, a fact that politicians have been shown to be sensitive to in their communication (Hemphill and Shapiro 2019). Recall also that most voters react negatively to physical conflict in the legislature, which is likely to be true whether we consider a district constituency or the electorate as a whole. Finally, if legislators want to communicate with these voters, they have other tools, such as constituency service, promoting local development projects, and draping themselves with local symbols and culture, to make more effective and nonpartisan appeals to their constituency in general and the median voter within that constituency in particular. While brawling is unlikely to be targeted at moderate, nonpartisan voters, there may be exceptions. Brawling for constituency appeal is something that we will take up again, along with potential costs to not brawling, when we discuss honor brawling at the end of this chapter.

Taiwan, Mexico, and South Korea illustrate the signaling logic of brawls in strong party systems nicely. All three have strong party systems. In Taiwan the Kuomintang (KMT) and Democratic Progressive Party (DPP) have been far and away the two most influential parties since the DPP was founded in 1986. In Mexico the same three parties have dominated politics since the PRI began to lose its near-absolute grip on power in the 1990s, with both the PAN and PRD having controlled the presidency since, along with a return of the PRI. Korean parties are organized around presidential candidates and are not as institutionalized as Taiwanese or Mexican parties. Nonetheless, from legislators' point of view, Korean parties are very powerful since voters tend to vote primarily on the basis of the party label.

Brawling in Taiwan appears to be aimed primarily at party supporters rather than party leadership. Taiwan has a small legislature with only 113 seats, so even a majority party caucus only has around 60 to 80 members. Taiwan allows members to run for re-election, and most members eventually serve multiple terms. Further, most "new" Taiwanese legislative candidates are veteran party politicians or children of party stalwarts. In interviews, Taiwanese legislators and party leaders repeatedly scoffed at the notion that party leaders could learn anything new about their caucus members from brawling behavior, insisting that they already knew their legislators quite well.

At the same time that party leaders know a great deal about legislators in their party, their control over nominations varies depending on the electoral rules. Of note here, nominations for single-member district seats are highly decentralized, with contested nominations typically determined by telephone surveys (Yu, Shoji, and Batto 2016). Moreover, most of these seats are reasonably competitive in general elections. This all points to a clear target audience in Taiwan: brawling legislators are trying to send signals to the loyal party supporters who can help them win nomination fights and general elections.

By contrast, party leaders in Taiwan have much more influence over the construction of party lists. In recent elections, the two major parties have exercised centralized control over the lists, with a central party committee, often heavily influenced by the party chair, determining the makeup of the lists. With just 34 list seats, the parties usually have ample information about each individual on the list, so there is not as much need for list legislators to communicate their type. Prior to electoral reform in 2008, most seats were elected in multimember districts by the single nontransferable vote (SNTV)—an electoral system where voters select a single preferred candidate to fill a seat in a multimember district, with the m seats being distributed to the m candidates who get the most votes.[4] Since large parties usually nominated multiple candidates in each district, it was rarely a challenge for incumbents to secure renomination. However, since each voter can only vote for one candidate, even loyal party supporters who just want to support the party have to choose from among several nominees. To put it bluntly, there are no safe seats in SNTV elections. In this context, a credible signal that a legislator is a loyal party soldier can be extremely valuable.

The idea of party leadership representing a meaningful audience for brawling gains more traction in the cases of Mexico and South Korea. Mexico and South Korea both have much larger legislatures, with 500 and 300 seats, respectively. Recall that prior to 2018 deputies in Mexico were not eligible for consecutive re-election, so each entering cohort of deputies had no recent immediate legislative reputation to precede them—and a very small proportion of legislators ever pursued nonconsecutive re-election. Korean district legislators could run for re-election, but winning re-election was highly dependent on the whims of the party leader. Party leaders, often just the president or party chair, tightly controlled nominations, and since most seats were not competitive, nomination was usually tantamount to election itself. With far more legislators to worry about and less available information about each, the signals sent by brawlers would have been much more useful to Mexican and South Korean party leaders than to their Taiwanese counterparts. Indeed, in private interviews, several South Korean legislative experts expressed the view that brawling legislators were trying to communicate with their party leader and not with ordinary loyal party supporters. Likewise, the 2006 brawl over the Mexican president's inaugural address to the legislature offered an opportunity for legislators to signal their commitment to party leadership, which experts on the Mexican legislature have agreed is a reasonable way to understand what brawling legislators were trying to accomplish in that instance.

Strong Party Systems and the Content of the Signal

Given that brawlers are trying to send signals to party actors in strong party systems, it makes sense that the content of the signal should be related to the party. We believe that in most cases, legislators are trying to signal simply that they are loyal party soldiers who are willing to fight for the party's ideals and positions. Both party leaders considering which legislators to cultivate or elevate and loyal party supporters trying to decide whether to throw their energy and resources completely behind a particular legislator should be receptive to this message. Leaders want to make sure that they have a solid set legislators they can count on. Loyal party supporters likewise want to ensure that they do not elect a representative who will take positions against the party. In both cases, brawlers are signaling that they will continue to energetically support the party even when those actions require doing unpopular things.

It is possible that legislators try to send a finer-tuned policy-oriented signal. That is, by participating in a particular brawl, the legislator might try to present himself or herself more as committed to that particular policy than to party goals in general. It is possible that a particular legislator could build up a reputation as the person who always leads the fight against higher taxes, or for marriage equality. While possible, we think it is rather unlikely in cases of brawling during opposition disruption in strong party systems. Legislators have many other tools to cultivate this type of reputation. They can ally with social groups, appear on television media programs, base their election campaigns around this issue, serve on relevant committees, introduce bills, hold public hearings or press conferences, and so on to ensure a steady stream of information painting them as the leader on one particular issue. Moreover, brawling is a crude action, and target audiences might not perceive a nuanced message. Media coverage tends to focus on colorful fighting rather than dry policy debates, so audiences are unlikely to discern precisely why an individual is brawling. This, however, is another point to which we will return in our discussion of honor brawls at the end of the chapter.

Weak Party Systems and Disruption Brawling

Brawlers in weak party systems are similar to brawlers in strong party systems in several ways. First, they are operating in the context of opposition disruption, where a weak opposition has insufficient tools or resources to stop the policy agenda of the government. Unlike the brawler in the strong party system, however, this brawler is operating in a context where parties are weak, which changes the nature of the audience to whom the brawler is signaling. Though the audiences differ, they do share another similarity with brawlers—there are potential target audiences to be found among both elites and citizens. In contrast to the party leaders in a strong party system, the elite audience for a brawler in a weak party system tends to be the elites who control resources that the legislator needs to further their political career, whom we might call patrons. The citizen audience is made of narrow segments of the electorate, who constitute a specific, extreme ideologically based voting bloc. In Ukraine, for example, brawlers were frequently appealing to voters characterized as "radicals." Rather than trying to present themselves as loyal party soldiers, brawlers in weak party systems try to cultivate an individual reputation of loyalty to and a willingness to fight for those audiences who can help them advance their political careers—a message that is not terribly different from that of the more partisan brawlers, but not tied to a specific party. Ultimately, these brawlers want to acquire fungible resources that can be used for political purposes, regardless of their party affiliation.

By definition, weak parties are less influential than strong parties in several important ways. They do not structure the political environment as thoroughly, so voters often make their decisions on the basis of criteria other than the party label. Localism, constituency service, pork-barrel projects, specific issue stances, ideology unrelated to party cleavages, mobilization networks, personal connections, and vote buying are all likely to be more powerful determinants of the vote when parties are weak. Weak parties are also less able to cultivate and structure politicians' careers. Individual politicians have to look out for themselves. The party organization will not see to it that capable politicians rise through the ranks, and it is unable to deter challengers from either inside or outside the party. Because of this, politicians are less beholden to the party. Being expelled from a party is not necessarily a death sentence, since politicians can simply take their personal resources to another party or go it alone as an independent. In fact, one hallmark of weak party systems is that legislators often switch parties between elections, during legislative sessions (Herron 2002a; Thames 2007). Inside the legislature, party caucuses have much less leverage over their members. Even if the chamber rules give party leaders a high degree of formal control over the agenda, that power can easily evaporate if party unity breaks down.

There are several key ways that the target audiences for brawlers in weak party systems look different compared to strong party systems. First, we note that even in weak party systems actors connected to political parties will have some desirable resources to distribute, such as party list seats, so some brawlers may be trying to communicate with them. However, most legislators will need nonparty resources and appeals to secure their political futures. In fact, some parties expect the individuals they invite to join the party to bring financial resources to the party.

Second, some legislators will appeal to specific segments of the electorate that are not necessarily identifiable by their support for a given party. This goal here is to create a vanguard of highly motivated supporters (aka a voting bloc) for any future political endeavor. Many democracies identify small segments of the voting public who either favor more extreme and confrontational political tactics, for example, due to a recent history of contentious political action in the country, or are so attached to a specific issue position (think single-issue voters in the US) that they appreciate extreme actions undertaken with respect to that issue. Several of the members of Ukraine's parliament such as Volodymyr Parasyuk and Yehor Soboliev, who were elected to the legislature following the Euromaidan protests and ended up as brawling, had connections to some of these groups in the electorate through prior protest involvement. While these brawlers tended to characterize their own brawling motivations as a sincere reaction to issues they felt strongly about, one might interpret these same behaviors as an attempt to signal a continued commitment to the voters who had been active in supporting the Euromaidan protests.

Third, what politicians need to sustain their careers in weak party systems, above all else, is money. Successful politicians in such systems are experts at converting financial resources into political power. This may involve building roads, schools, or hospitals; it may involve constructing and motivating enormous mobilization networks; it may involve sponsoring a local sports team or festival; it may involve setting up a think tank or a nonprofit organization to promote a specific policy; or it may involve outright vote buying or bribery. Money is usually the lifeblood of a personal vote. And since money is often used to build networks, some legislators might appeal to elite actors or patrons who can directly provide mobilization networks. Some such actors might include labor union leaders, leaders of ethnic or religious minorities, business interests, more powerful politicians, and organized crime bosses. Ideally, the actor would be able to provide both financial and organizational resources.

In Ukraine, the relevant nonpartisan economic elites are generally known as "the oligarchs," a handful of super-wealthy individuals whose ties to organized crime allowed them to capitalize on the economic openings that came with the collapse of the Soviet Union and Ukrainian independence. These individuals are known to make money in particular business sectors and to dominate particular geographic localities within the country. In some instances they become involved in politics—such as President Poroshenko during Ukraine's 8th convocation of the Verkhovna Rada, a billionaire from southwest Ukraine whose business interests include candy-making and media, or Ihor Kolomoysky, a billionaire from Eastern Ukraine with business interests in finance, media, and petroleum who was appointed governor of the Central-Eastern Ukrainian Dnipropetrovsk Oblast in 2014, and in 2019 ranked third-most influential Ukrainian by the publication *Focus* magazine ("100 Most Influential Ukrainians" 2019). While oligarchs' formal involvement in politics tends to be more local—focusing on the geographic region where they exercise the most power—their primary involvement in politics is to finance others' political careers. Conservative estimates put the proportion of legislators in the Verkhovna Rada who depend on financing from oligarchs at one-third, while some legislators within the parliament suggest the actual proportion may be closer to two-thirds.

Whereas the brawler in a strong party system sends a message that he or she is an energetic and loyal soldier, for the brawler in a weak party system, the intent is for the target audience—either citizen or elite—to interpret the signal as indicating that the legislator will fight energetically for that audience's interests, even if this involves incurring significant costs.

Brawling over Questions of Honor

The great majority of brawls involve opposition disruption, but there are exceptions. Almost all of these other brawls involve questions about an individual legislator's personal character or honor. While these incidents represent a fraction of the universe of legislative brawling and tend to have more idiosyncrasies, their underlying logic is usually similar to that of disruption brawls: brawlers are trying to send signals that convey the same types of messages to similar target audiences. Honor brawls begin with one legislator leveling an accusation of dishonor at an accused; if the accused wants to be perceived as honorable, they may brawl to refute this charge. In other cases, however, the accused may actually be dishonorable and may need to fight to resist being perceived as weak. Figure 3.2 outlines these dynamics. One important distinction to note for these brawls is that there are distinct signaling opportunities (with associated payoffs and risks) for both the accusers and the accused.

Honor brawls can take place in countries with strong party systems or weak party systems, because they are grounded in nonpartisan logic. Indeed, the idea has been best described in the context of a nonpartisan political system, devoid of any mature political institutions. Joanne Freeman (2001) argues that in the US of the 1790s and 1800s, the lack of a robust institutional context meant that the first challenge for everyone—politicians and voters alike—was figuring out who to cooperate with and trust. Political actors could not rely on partisan cues to effortlessly mix in with a ready-made band of like-minded fellow party members. In this vacuum, reputation was paramount. Members of the new Congress went to great lengths to cultivate a reputation of republican virtue, even if no one quite knew exactly what this meant. For example, it was unclear whether it was better to dress in finery, thereby displaying sophistication and worthiness of public trust, or to dress

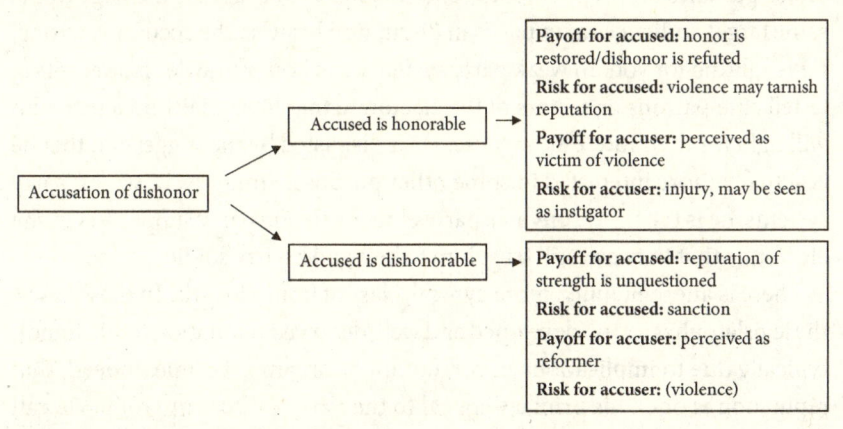

Figure 3.2 Honor brawls.

plainly, thereby displaying common values and worthiness of public trust. Nevertheless, politicians fretted endlessly over questions like this in their efforts to portray themselves in the best light.

If a good reputation was the key to power, then, conversely, one of the primary ways to conduct a political struggle was to undermine another person's reputation. Freeman writes, "Given the importance of reputation, an attack on a man's honor was the ultimate trump card.... When honor was at stake, all else fell by the wayside" (Freeman 2001, 28). Freeman tells of multiple instances in which members of Congress went to extreme measures to defend their reputations from attacks against their character, including physical conflicts inside the chambers of Congress, as well as outside. This was, after all, the era of the duel.

In our terminology, a character attack is an accusation that the legislator has other priorities. The accusing legislator may claim that rather than working on behalf of a party, group, or cause, he (the accused, and those accused in honor brawls are overwhelmingly male) is actually working for something else such as personal wealth, sex, a corporate patron, a crime gang, and so on. You cannot trust him; he is dishonorable.

If the umbrage taken by the accused is because he believes himself to be honorable or wants to be perceived as such, then an honor brawl can be interpreted as an effort to refute the charge of dishonor. The impugned legislator directly confronts the person who maligned his character, taking extreme actions to show the world how repugnant these slanderous accusations are. In light of the heavy damage these attacks on his reputation could inflict if allowed to stand, throwing a few punches is hardly an extreme reaction. Those punches are an attempt to send a signal with a similar message to the same target audiences as in partisan disruption brawls: The accuser is wrong; I *am* fighting for you. In weak party systems, the honor brawler is attempting to tell elite patrons or sectors of the electorate that he *is* a faithful agent who will fight for their interests or cause. He is disgusted by the suggestion that he is actually more interested in some other purpose. Similarly, in strong party systems, he is trying to convince party elites or strong party supporters in the electorate that they *can* still trust him to be a good party soldier.

There is another, much more cynical, class of honor brawls. In these cases, the legislator has a well-developed and well-deserved reputation for dishonor, typically due to implications in corruption or organized crime. Indeed, that reputation is often his primary appeal to the party, patron, or group. He can spread cash around, can crack some skulls, and will not shy away from dirty work, should the need arise. Such an accused may need to brawl because he cannot let these accusations stand. In the abstract sense, for such an individual to allow someone to call him out publicly may be perceived as weakness. More practically, the accusation could potentially get the legal system involved, and that might neutralize his power base. By fighting back and publicly insisting on his innocence, he wards off the legal threat while also reminding his target audience that he can be a potent soldier for the cause. In such cases, the individual may feel compelled to respond to these public insults with violence, because *not* to do so would send a signal of weakness, which could undermine the reputations he has developed. Violence is not being used to send a costly signal but rather to avoid a potentially costlier signal that might be communicated with nonviolence.

Here, then, is another point to which we promised to return at the end of the chapter—for these honor brawls, the target audience of brawlers who have been accused of corruption may, in fact, be a distinct constituency. Recall that we argued that legislators brawling in the context of opposition disruption have more effective ways to communicate with and perform service for their constituencies—and tend to avoid making partisan appeals to that audience. These residual brawls, by contrast, tend to have very little partisan content. Furthermore, if they are aimed at avoiding sending a signal of weakness through nonviolence, then the primary concern may be perceived weakness among members of a constituency. Not only does this sort of representative's constituency likely understand well their representative's ties to organized crime, but also they most likely live under a system of control that requires the representative (boss) to maintain a reputation of strength to be effective.

The signaling intent of the accuser is worth considering. Recall that we also consider individuals who are on the receiving end of legislative violence to be involved in the brawling, which makes particular sense in these honor brawls where they are in many cases provoking the attack. We have argued that specific policy commitments are not likely to be part of the signal that brawlers are sending during opposition disruption, but in some honor brawls that involve personalistic attacks and corruption accusations, the accuser may be looking to establish a reputation for fighting corruption or organized crime. These provocateurs, then, are attempting to signal information about themselves to a target audience, such as a commitment to fight corruption.

Finally, there is an interesting gender imbalance in honor brawls. As mentioned earlier, the accused is almost always male. Gender stereotypes tend to portray honor to be a more masculine quality. This makes establishing and maintaining an honorable reputation a higher priority for men. Further, women are generally perceived as more honest and are thus less likely to be accused of being dishonorable. Even if such an accusation were leveled, standard gender norms make it less urgent or acceptable for an accused woman to defend with violence as an accused man might. Accusers, in contrast, can be either women or men. A woman who is on the receiving end of a physical attack from a male legislator defending his honor is likely to communicate even stronger resolve and commitment. This gender dynamic is illustrated quite nicely in the two honor brawls presented in Chapter 4.

Honor brawls look different than disruption brawls. They take place in more varied locations. Disruption brawls tend to center around the Speaker's podium, the places where legislators speak formally, ballot boxes, entrances to the chamber, or other sites of formal processes. Honor brawls, by contrast, can happen on the floor of the legislature, when one individual is making a formal speech at the podium, for example, but these brawls are equally likely to happen at individual legislators' seats, in a committee room, or in the corridors of a legislature. Unlike brawls during opposition disruption, which almost always occur when the legislature takes up a controversial agenda item, these residual brawls may erupt while the legislature is engaged in mundane business or even when the chamber is in recess.

Honor brawls are smaller in scale. The typical honor brawl is centered on two individuals who come to blows after trading insults, and may then also involve a few other individuals who intervene to separate the fighting individuals.

Finally, the pretext under which such brawls occur is rarely about differing policy positions or opposition to legislation. These fights grow out of personal insults. This does not mean they are apolitical or even nonpartisan. It might seem a bit unexpected for a nonpartisan idea such as honor to feature in a strong party system, but in fact this is precisely how many partisan and intraparty battles are waged. By discrediting a legislator, you can also weaken their faction and policy agenda. If they are corrupt, everything they supposedly stand for can be questioned. Strong parties can almost always prevent factional fights from spilling into open pugilism on the chamber floor, so almost all honor brawls in strong party systems involve legislators from different parties. Even in weak party systems, there is almost always a political undertone.

We offer this discussion of honor brawls to acknowledge that not all legislative violence takes place in the context of opposition disruption. Further, while we can point to some regularities within this small subset of instances of brawling, we want to acknowledge that small skirmishes can, in fact, be quite idiosyncratic in nature, whereas brawling around opposition disruption tends to exhibit clearer patterns. Where we do identify regularities, it is interesting to note the extent to which they conform to the general logic of signaling theory. Nevertheless, most of the implications and expectations, as well as the empirical investigations throughout the book, focus on brawling in the context of opposition disruption.

Implications and Expectations

Based on the above explanation of brawling, we offer the following set of expectations and potential implications, which will be formally investigated in the empirical chapters that follow.

Who Brawls and How

This theoretical framework, that legislators use violence in the legislature to send costly signals, offers clear implications for the kinds of legislators who are likely to brawl—those who are more likely to find such costly signals useful. First, age and length of service in the legislature should matter—those who lack an existing reputation should be interested in cultivating one. It has been observed in Taiwan that older legislators don't fight as much. And while colloquial observations that this is because older legislators are friends and know each other may be valid, it is also certainly true that younger legislators have not established a reputation and are likely looking for more opportunities to send signals about their type.

Second, members of the political opposition should be more prone to brawling than members of the government. Unlike opposition members who are interested in disruption, majority legislators want to clear away disruption so that the legislature can operate smoothly and pass their agenda. Too much physical conflict has the potential to throw the chamber into chaos and prevent any business from being conducted, so majority party leaders and supporters may not look as forgivingly on brawlers from their party as their counterparts in the opposition will. Moreover, the two sides evaluate outcomes differently. Majority party actors can look directly at the policy outputs to determine whether the party caucus has done a good job. Brawlers may get some credit for passing legislation, but credit also goes to other actors, such as policy specialists, committee chairs, and floor leaders. Opposition party actors do not expect to pass their own legislation, so their focus is much more heavily on obstruction. If brawlers play the biggest role in obstruction, they will get a disproportionate amount of the credit for their party's success. Majority legislative parties presented with nonviolent disruption face a similar conundrum. They need to clear away an obstruction, but heavy-handed tactics risk inducing backfire among the general public. However, if moderate tactics prove insufficient, hardliners will inevitably demand using any means necessary, just as outnumbered police are often tempted to pull out the billy clubs, tear gas, and water cannons. Nonviolent disruption, especially by a large minority party, can force the majority party to choose between bad and worse options. The disruption exposes its illegitimacy—in this case its stance in opposition to public opinion. The best-case scenario is to force through its proposal with a minimal amount of coercion, the equivalent of gently carrying away protesters one by one. In this case, the cost of the unpopular stance is mitigated by the benefit of getting the desired policy outcome. However, if the majority does not have sufficient manpower to do this, it must either use more violent methods and risk an intense public backlash or admit defeat, a particularly galling choice after it has paid the price of publicly taking an unpopular stance. Though some members of the government might see opportunities to differentiate themselves via brawling, we expect these to be less frequent than for opposition members, particularly in the context of opposition disruption and brawling.

Third, as discussed previously, how individuals get elected should matter for whether they choose to brawl. All else equal, individuals elected in districts, rather than on party lists, likely have more incentive to engage in brawls, with individuals elected in multimember districts under rules such as SNTV perhaps having the most incentive to brawl. We should also expect to see more honor brawling in single-member districts where the accused attempt to reinforce a particular style of corrupt or patronage politics in the district. Whether party list members brawl will depend on the strength of the party system. In strong party systems, candidates on party lists don't have as much need to cultivate a personal reputation, but in weak party systems, even party list legislators might see value in building a personal reputation as a resource they can trade for better list placement or a future single-member district candidacy. The logic of delegation, which abstractly assumes strong and cohesive parties, helps us understand this logic. Unlike district legislators, who act as agents of both district voters and their parties, list legislators are only responsible to a single principal: their parties. If those parties are strong, leaders should have quite a bit of confidence in the loyalty of their list legislators because they will have been effectively screened during the selection process and the party is likely to retain effective tools to impose sanctions on any disloyalty (Carey 2007; Batto 2012). In this case, there is not much need for list legislators to reassure party leaders by sending a message that they are fighting for the party. Strong party list legislators may feel a need to participate in moderate disruptions to meet party goals, but there is very little incentive to go beyond that with any deliberately visible violence. In weak party systems, leaders do not have as much control over the selection of list legislators or their future career prospects. To put it another way, while party leaders may be list legislators' most important principal, they are not necessarily their only significant principal. Since weak party list legislators have to worry about multiple principals, they might find it quite useful to send a message to a nonpartisan elite ("I'm fighting for your interests") or to a voting bloc of citizens ("I'm fighting for your issue"). Thus, while list legislators in weak party systems may still have weaker incentives to brawl than their single-member plurality counterparts in weak party systems, they may have stronger incentives to brawl than list legislators in strong party systems.

Transmission of Brawling Signals

If our theory of brawls as strategic signals is correct, then legislators should reasonably expect that the costly signals they are sending with brawls will be transmitted to their intended audience. If the intended audience were internal to the legislature, then transmission would most likely be guaranteed, but as previous discussions and the following section highlight, most of the actors that brawling legislators could be trying to signal are unlikely to be present at brawls themselves. Even in the case of brawling where actors are trying to signal party leadership, there may not always be perfect overlap between legislative leadership of a party caucus and leadership of the party as a whole. As such, we expect to be able to find evidence of the strategic nature of brawling in media coverage of the legislature.

In general, two types of evidence might lead legislators to develop reasonable expectations regarding transmission of their signals in the media. First, we should be able to observe indications that the media cover brawls. Research on media coverage of politics and legislative politics in particular has typically revealed a bias toward focusing coverage on large political parties and the government in particular (Helfer and Van Aelst 2016; Vos 2016). Nevertheless, media have also shown preferences for covering unexpected events and events and activities that are critical of the government (Helfer and Van Aelst 2016). While we do not expect members of the legislative majority or government to be prime brawlers, brawls are conducted in such a way as to appear spontaneous and unexpected. As such, they likely draw media attention.

Second, we should be able to find that brawlers increase their own personal media coverage. This was, in fact, the primary perception of the motivation for brawling among nonbrawling Ukrainian legislators. When asked why her colleagues would brawl, for example, first-time member of parliament Oksana Yurnyets responded with a shrug and wave of her hand: Oh, they're just trying to get on the news. Thus, beyond indications of a media preference for covering brawls, brawling legislators should be able to have some confidence that if they participate in a brawl, it will boost their own media exposure, thereby alerting the intended audience of their costly signal.

Intended Audience of Brawls

If our assertions regarding the intended audience of brawls are accurate, we should be able to find two types of evidence in this regard. First, we would expect legislators and legislative experts to be able to identify the kinds of individuals who are most important for furthering legislators' careers. Second, we would expect to be able to find evidence of brawling signals being received by members of these audiences. Recall that in strong party systems we expect the intended audiences to be connected to parties themselves, whereas in weak party systems we expect the intended audience to be either specific individuals who can offer financial support and resources or select segments of the electorate that are not tied to a given party. Finally, and perhaps most importantly, what we do *not* expect to find is a general resonance in the electorate at large. On the contrary, we have strong expectations that most voters, especially those with no or only very weak partisan leanings, will express disapproval of brawling.

Career Prospects

If we are correct that brawlers are sending these costly signals to further their careers, then we should be able to find evidence that it actually works. Here our systematic investigation will focus on re-election prospects, recognizing that there may be paths to career advancement outside re-election. Where parties are stronger, we should see those brawlers who are elected under electoral rules that demand more partisan support to improve their re-election prospects. These expectations are tempered, however, by the acknowledgment that brawling carries both potential payoffs and risks and may not be a magic bullet for career advancement in light of all the factors that affect legislators' political careers.

Additional Questions to Explore

Here we have suggested a theoretical framework and empirical implications, which we will investigate throughout the remainder of this book to improve our understanding of legislative violence. At the same time, the above theory also raises several questions that we will explore further throughout the book. In general, given the framework we have laid out, we might wonder if all legislators will have the ability or need to send signals via violence. First, are women legislators going to be able to use violence as effectively as a signal? In part this depends on whether signaling is to party leadership or some segment of the electorate. Whose attitudes matter? We know that voters hold different expectations for male and female politicians, and that sexists in particular hold women politicians to different standards (Barnes, Beaulieu, and Saxton 2020). In such case, what may be seen as acceptable behavior for a man in the legislature may be perceived as unacceptable for a woman (Brooks 2011). Whether the same holds true for party leaders, however, is a more open question. A somewhat different possibility is that parties may place different demands to participate in disruption on men and women. In that case, women may face different definitions of what it means to be a good party soldier, so the need to send a signal and the credibility of that signal might be different.

Second, in strong party systems, are the effects of brawling specific to a given party? Just as some legislators develop reputations as brawlers, perhaps some parties come to be seen as more disruptive. If supporters of a given party are less disturbed by violence, we might expect that party to be more prone to brawling regardless of its status in the majority or minority.

Finally, and perhaps most importantly, what are the consequences of brawling for democratic representation more generally? Recall that Freeman's work on violence in the antebellum US House of Representatives connected such acts to the eventual severing of the Union and Civil War. If some legislators are willing to use violence in the course of democratic deliberations, it does suggest the erosion of civility and a possible slide toward democratic breakdown. In particular, we are curious about the consequences of brawls on democratic representation. One of our foundational assumptions, supported by systematic evidence, is that the electorate in general does not like brawling. We have made this point to underscore that the electorate in general are not the intended audience for brawlers' signals. At the same time, given general media exposure, they are an audience who will learn about brawls when they occur. The impact of an unpopular legislative activity such as brawls on the long-term health of the democratic regime is an important issue that we will grapple with throughout the book and return to in our conclusions.

4
Who Brawls

Francisco Dominguez Servien was one of the most prominent brawlers in the Mexican Chamber of Deputies' days of opposition disruption and brawling following the 2006 elections. He is, in fact, precisely the type of legislator we would expect to find brawling. This brawl occurred in the aftermath of the presidential candidate for the Party of the Democratic Revolution (PRD), Mexico's main leftist party, narrowly losing the election and accusing the victorious candidate from the National Action Party (PAN) of perpetrating widespread fraud. In Congress, PRD legislators disrupted proceedings and occupied the podium in the Chamber of Deputies to prevent President-elect Calderon from being sworn in. Dominguez, 39 years old, was newly elected[1] to Congress from a district in Central Mexico as a representative of the National Action Party (PAN). Dominguez was thus young, junior, elected to his legislative seat from a single-member district, and a member of a major political party. As we will explain below, these characteristics are all consistent with the choice to brawl.

Our theory of the individual logic of legislative brawls offers some very straightforward implications for who, in a given legislature, would brawl. Recall that legislators are using brawls as a signal to communicate to specific audiences, in the hopes that these audiences will positively affect their chances for re-election. We will turn to questions of signal transmission, audiences, and ultimate consequences of brawls in subsequent chapters, but in this chapter, we focus on the question of which legislators would find brawling a useful means of communication. In thinking through the implications of our theory for who brawls, we will connect general insights of signaling theory with the specific circumstances facing legislators who want to be re-elected. The expectations we derive are then investigated with data from 2014 to 2019 in Ukraine and from 2005 to 2019 in Taiwan.

Review of Theory and Empirical Expectations

We divide our expectations about who brawls into two categories: individual characteristics and contextual factors. Individual characteristics vary by legislator, while contextual factors refer to the context within which different legislators are operating and depend primarily on institutional arrangements. Contextual factors can vary within a country, and thus within the legislature, but they are not specific to the individual legislators themselves.

Following the logic of brawls as costly signals, the fundamental question when considering who is likely to brawl is: who most needs to send costly signals? Note that this is not the same as asking who *can* send the costliest signals. It is the relative costliness (cost relative to expected benefit) rather than the mere ability to pay the cost of those signals that is critical. We expect that legislators in need of the signaling opportunity—and only those legislators—will be willing to bear the cost of brawling.

Individual Characteristics

From the general premise that brawls are used by individuals as a costly signal and that costly signals are used to reveal a type that is otherwise not known, we develop several expectations about individual characteristics of legislators that are more likely to be associated with brawling. The first characteristic we expect to be associated with brawling is age—we expect younger legislators to be more likely to brawl. Younger legislators are more likely to be agile and adept at physical altercations than older legislators, though this is not necessarily why they are more likely to brawl. Indeed, this observation suggests that the higher physical toll of brawling might imply a costlier signal for older legislators and the signal might thus be more beneficial for them. However, the important question is whether the individual needs to send a signal, and the important point here is that young legislators are less likely to have established reputations either inside or outside the legislature. Brawls, then, are a useful reputation-building tool for younger, unknown legislators. Older legislators might be able to send similar, or even stronger, signals, but because they are more likely to have established reputations, they simply have less need to send such signals. Their type is likely already known.

Low levels of seniority should be associated with brawling for similar reasons. Senior legislators generally have more established reputations than their junior colleagues since they are more likely to have experience as policymakers and to receive media coverage (Cox 1987). Senior legislators thus have less need to send signals. In addition, senior legislators may find the cost of brawling prohibitively high since they may have forged working relationships with members of other parties that could be damaged by brawling. It might be harder to sit down and strike a bargain with someone next week if you punch them today, especially if they felt your actions had betrayed their friendship. To wit: the Ugandan government minister we interviewed about the 2017 brawl there confirmed that senior members of parliament largely abstained from brawling.

The final individual characteristic we consider is gender. In contrast to our expectations about age and seniority, it is not obvious that either gender has significantly stronger incentives to brawl. While both genders have the same opportunities to participate and send signals through legislative violence, the extensive research on sexism and gender stereotypes in politics provides reasons to suspect gendered differences in the costs and benefits of these actions. In particular, research has emphasized the gendered nature of both norms of parliamentary behavior and decisions to violate those norms (Ilie 2013). Shukan (2013), for example, notes that women's participation in brawls in Ukraine is rare because this is typically viewed as a masculine activity. Thus, we must consider seriously whether the same signaling needs and opportunities are equally available to men and women.

The gender literature has repeatedly demonstrated that the same actions by men and women can be interpreted quite differently. For example, men and women are punished differently for different types of scandalous behavior (Barnes, Beaulieu, and Saxton 2020). More generally, women are punished more for engaging in conflict. While agentic men are often seen as strong leaders, women who eschew consensus and collaboration are often seen as bossy, hard to get along with, and less socially skilled (Rudman and Glick 1999; Eagly and Karau 2002; Williams and Tiedens 2016; Brescoll, Okimoto, and Vial 2018). Thus, it is not obvious that audiences will perceive the same content in a signal sent by a brawling woman legislator compared to the message a man sends when he engages in a legislative brawl.

The message communicated by brawling is one steeped in masculine imagery. At the heart of the signal that both partisan and personalistic brawlers want to send is that they are loyal and willing to fight either for a party and its positions or for some elite interest or voting bloc. In other words, the legislator is a good soldier for the cause. This image of fighting soldiers is inherently associated with violence, and violence is generally associated with masculinity.[2] When women brawl, they might violate social norms about proper female behavior, which can provoke backlash from citizens (Courtemanche and Green 2020).

If stereotypical gender roles suggest that women should avoid conflict, they also suggest that women should embrace compromise. Women are thought to be more compassionate (Huddy and Terkildsen 1993; Kahn 1994; Holman, Merolla, and Zechmeister 2016). In legislative politics, this propensity to consider the needs and desires of others can lead female legislators to seek compromises that everyone can accept rather than ramming through their ideal policy (Rosenthal 2000; Schneider et al. 2016). While many voters see seeking compromise as an attractive trait, strong partisans or specific interests may not. Compromise is great when the other side yields. When representatives from your side make concessions, they are often seen as selling out their supporters' interests (Harbridge and Malhotra 2011). If this logic is correct, women are particularly vulnerable to suspicions that they are not dependable fighters for the cause, whether that is a partisan or particularistic cause. They may have more need to send a signal of their reliability to reassure their supporters of their fidelity.

Thus, depending on the pressure of prevailing norms, women may be wary of appearing overly combative and incurring backlash by brawling. Alternatively, if the baseline assumption is that women are less likely to be violent, brawling women might be able to send a signal that they are even more serious and committed than their male counterparts. That is, brawling men might send a signal that they are soldiers for their party, while women who do the same thing might send a much costlier signal implying that they are *very resolute* soldiers for their party.

In addition to thinking about men and women in isolation, we must consider how the signals are affected when men and women interact in a brawl. It is one thing for a man to punch or grab another man or a woman to shove or kick another woman. It is quite something else if the two actors are a woman and a man. There are usually much stronger negative reactions to seeing a man attack a woman than when a woman attacks a man. As a result, when a woman is involved, the most critical difference may be in the signals that men send. The man's intended signal of being a good party soldier might suddenly transform into one of being a chauvinistic brute who doesn't understand basic ideas of how to treat women. Even worse, if he makes contact in an inappropriate place, he might suddenly become a lecherous sexual predator who takes advantage of a brawl to grope women. Needless to say, most male legislators do not want to send this sort of signal. This might not help the woman burnish her image or get re-elected, but it can do a lot of damage to the man she is opposing. Gender could thus be used as a strategic weapon, especially in partisan conflicts.

Individuals might not care very much about damaging another legislator's image, but parties are very interested in damaging the images of legislators from other parties. When parties have a concrete objective, such as occupying a specific space, they can create an advantage if their women are pitted against the other side's men. The obvious counter to this is for the other party to also deploy its female members so that women are responsible for dealing with other women. In other words, parties have an incentive to encourage their female members to take active roles in partisan disruptions. Thus, it might be that women are less likely to brawl because violence violates norms of femininity. It also might be that women are more likely to brawl since there might be more demands from their parties for them to brawl and brawling might send a more powerful signal for them.

Overall, the incentives for men and women to brawl are complicated. Relative to men, women may have more need to brawl since voters may be more likely to doubt their commitment and since parties may put more pressure on them to engage in disruptions. However, brawling may also subject them to a harsher backlash, since such intense conflictual behavior is an overt violation of typical gender norms. For women, brawling appears to be a high-risk, high-reward enterprise, where the reward is far from guaranteed. Furthermore, research on women's political behavior in office has emphasized their general aversion to risk (Barnes and Beaulieu 2019; Esarey & Schwindt-Bayer 2018). As such, it is unclear whether women legislators will be inclined to pursue the potential rewards associated with brawling. Furthermore, we have argued that the context in which fighting occurs may matter for brawling along lines of gender. In the next section we explore other contextual factors that might lead some legislators to brawl.

Contextual Factors

There are several institutional and contextual factors that will shape an individual legislator's propensity to brawl. First, and arguably most importantly, the way that legislators are elected will affect their brawling propensity. Because brawls offer individual legislators a chance to send costly signals to distinguish themselves from their counterparts, legislators in electoral systems that encourage personal vote seeking are more likely to see value in brawling. It is well established that systems in which a voter cannot vote for a specific candidate are not conducive to personal vote seeking. For example, closed-list proportional representation, in which a voter simply votes for a party list, does not allow the voter to favor any specific candidate on that list. On Election Day, the candidate's fortune depends entirely on how many votes are cast for the party list; how much voters like the candidate relative to other candidates on the list does not matter. This does not mean that personal popularity is meaningless in a closed-list system. Depending on how the list is constructed, politicians with a bloc of personal support within the party or in the electorate might be able to secure a higher ranking on the list. In general, though, the payoffs for personal votes are much lower in closed-list proportional representation than in other systems. In single-member districts, voters vote for a specific individual. They may wish to support a particular party, but they may also want to support a particular individual in spite of his or her party. To the extent that candidates can build up support across party lines or simply inspire heightened mobilization among voters who are predisposed to support their party, there are clear incentives to construct a personal vote in single-member district systems.

The strongest incentives to cultivate a personal vote are found in systems that require voters to choose from multiple candidates from the same party. In the single nontransferable vote (SNTV) system, for example, there are multiple seats in each district and voters must cast one vote for a specific individual. Since parties might be able to win more than one seat in the district, they often nominate multiple candidates. This forces voters, even party supporters who don't care which party nominees win, to choose. Unlike in single-member districts with only one nominee per party, the party label is not sufficient to win votes since there are other candidates who have the same party label. A personal factor, such as a reputation as a loyal party soldier, might be extremely valuable in differentiating one nominee from the others (Carey and Shugart 1995). In general, we expect legislators elected by closed-list proportional representation to be less likely to brawl than legislators elected by systems in which voters can support a specific individual on their ballot.

The position of specific political parties and of the overall party system constitutes a second contextual factor. Even though most brawls are explicitly partisan in strong party systems, the payoffs to brawling are not equivalent for legislators in the governing party and legislators in the opposition. Opposition parties generally initiate disruptions because they want to block, or put a spotlight on, the government's agenda. This gives opposition legislators clear incentives to escalate disruption and brawl. Incentives for representatives from government parties are more mixed—precisely as we saw in stories of brawling in Japan and South Korea in Chapter 2. They generally just want to pass their agenda, and they usually prefer to do so by nonconflictual methods. While they may need to mobilize their members to ram their agenda through, this is usually a last resort rather than a first option. To put it another way, it is difficult for government legislators to send a signal that they are good party soldiers when it is not clear what the behavior of a good party soldier in the majority should be. In general, we expect opposition legislators to be more prone to brawling than government legislators.

The size of a party also matters. To the extent that smaller parties are more extreme, it might be argued that legislators from small parties are more likely to brawl. Schmoll and Ting (2023) find that brawling is more common in more fragmented legislatures. Since fragmented legislatures have smaller, more extreme parties, this implies that extremism might be associated with brawling. If important audiences want to see evidence of extremism, these legislators might have a clear need to engage in extreme behavior. However, not all small parties are extreme, and sometimes extremists can be found in a faction of a big party. In fact, we argue that legislators from big parties are more likely to brawl. For one thing, big parties are usually the main protagonists in situations of opposition disruption where most brawling occurs, while the small parties are left to side with a position that they may not wholeheartedly endorse. It is hard to send a signal of fighting for party ideals when your party only somewhat agrees with the position you are fighting for. For another, legislators from large parties may have a stronger need to send a signal via brawling simply because larger parties have more members. Legislators from larger parties have to differentiate themselves from a bigger crowd, and they are less likely to be prominent party leaders in their own right. Thus, it is large party legislators who have stronger incentives to brawl, especially in a highly partisan context.

Who Brawls in Ukraine and Taiwan

To evaluate these expectations, we rely on profiles of prominent brawlers in the 8th convocation of Ukraine's Verkhovna Rada (2014–2019) and a systematic analysis of television newscast coverage of brawls in the 6th through 9th Terms of Taiwan's Legislative Yuan (2005–2019). These data sources provide both qualitative and quantitative investigations of individual and contextual factors that influence who brawls.

Qualitative Evidence from Ukraine

Ask any Ukrainian about legislative brawling during the era of the 8th legislature and invariably one or more of the following four names would come up: Volodymyr Parasyuk, Yehor Soboliev, Oleh Liashko, or Andriy Teteruk. Parasyuk and Soboliev were known to be frequent brawlers, Liashko was understood as someone who had already established a reputation as a brawler, and Teteruk was noted for involvement in a very specific brawl that was largely seen as out of character with who he was as a representative. Profiles of these individuals reveal individual and contextual factors that are largely consistent with our theoretical expectations.

Volodymyr Parasyuk was an independent freshman legislator in the 8th convocation of the Ukrainian legislature. Prior to winning a seat from the western city of Lviv, Parasyuk had fought as a soldier in the Donbas and had also been a prominent figure in the Euromaidan protests. Parasyuk's political career was really jump-started toward the end of the Euromaidan protests, when he made a very public, very impassioned speech opposing the peace agreement that leaders of the Euromaidan protests signed with then-president Yanukovych. Reuters described the speech as "electrifying," referring not only to the reaction of the crowd in the Maidan but also to the fact that President Yanukovych fled the country the very next day (Reuters 2014). Parasyuk described his subsequent decision to run for office as stemming from this position of increased popular recognition, saying, "are you simply left a popular person, or [do] you use it to achieve certain goals and certain ideas."[3]

Parasyuk brought this same image of an impassioned fighter for Ukraine to his legislative duties and augmented it with physical violence. He was critical of the legislature as "theater," where most of his colleagues were corrupt, and lamented that the legislature was not more respected in Ukrainian society. At the same time, he expressed a keen awareness of the ways that these very criticisms limited his media access—media being largely controlled by oligarchs who would not air legislators leveling such criticisms.[4] In the legislature, Parasyuk quickly earned a reputation as a brawler (Romanenko 2017). In one such incident in a meeting of the corruption committee, he accused a fellow committee member of tolerating corruption and injured a security officer in the ensuing scuffle (Interfax-Ukraine 2015). Thus, brawling presented Parasyuk with opportunities to gain media coverage and build his reputation.

In terms of individual characteristics, Parasyuk is exactly who we expect to see brawling. Elected at 33, he was significantly younger than the average Ukrainian legislator at this time (48 years old), and as it was his first term, he lacked seniority. In terms of contextual factors, Parasyuk also conforms to most of our expectations—he was elected from a district, where we would expect personal reputations to matter more, and although he was not formally affiliated with any large party, he definitely identified as part of the political opposition to the government at the time.

Yehor Soboliev was another freshman legislator elected at the same time as Parasyuk. Similar to Parasyuk, Soboliev had been involved in the Euromaidan protests and sought to build a reputation fighting political corruption once in office. Unlike Parasyuk, however, Soboliev's career prior to the legislature was not spent in the military, but rather in journalism. Soboliev had worked for print, television, and online media and specialized in political and investigative journalism. In fact, in the early 2000's, Soboliev anchored a very popular television show on a station owned by Petro Poroshenko (who would be president during the 8th convocation of the legislature) but ended up resigning over disputes with Poroshenko about the coverage of controversial political topics—which Soboliev favored, while Poroshenko did not. During his involvement in the Euromaidan protests, Soboliev worked with others to found a small political party made up of activists, which was then given slots on the party list of Self-Reliance, another small party based primarily in Lviv. Soboliev was 13th on the list for Self-Reliance and was subsequently seated in parliament.

Soboliev was a very active parliamentarian. He chaired an anticorruption committee and caused enough trouble for the government (including leading popular protests) that the legislature took the unusual step of removing him from this post during the term. He claimed to be rated among the top 10 in the entire parliament for being present to cast votes in the legislature. He placed a great emphasis on communicating with voters, both directly and through speeches in parliament where, notwithstanding the lack of official metrics, he believed he was rated as the top speaker in his fraction. Soboliev's opposition activities within parliament often took him outside as well. He organized a tent encampment outside the parliament for several months to pressure the government to allow a vote on anticorruption legislation, and he participated in a physical blockade of railroads to block trade with Russian-occupied territories.

Soboliev also brawled. In February 2015, for example, he took part in a heated fistfight with Vadim Ivchenko over a bill on land ownership that touched on issues of corruption, at a time when Soboliev was the chair of the legislature's anticorruption committee. When interviewed, Soboliev was happy to present pictures of himself where he can be seen holding the microphones of the Speaker and Deputy Speaker of the legislature in a brawl leading up to the government vote regarding trade with the occupied eastern territories of Ukraine. In fact, he was so well known for brawling that he had even been featured in memes. In one image that made the rounds on social media, his head was superimposed on a Ukrainian boxer's body with the words "Beat Him!" as a play on words. In another image he was characterized as the Terminator (the character from the famous Arnold Schwarzenegger movie of the same name) when dismissed from his committee chairmanship with the slogan "I'll be back."[5]

In terms of individual characteristics, Soboliev fits our expectations regarding who brawls. Though older than Parasyuk, at 37 when he was elected, he was still far younger than the average legislator. Moreover, he was a first-term legislator with no previous political career. In terms of contextual factors, the fit with our theoretical expectations is less clean. Soboliev was elected by closed list as part of a small political party. And though small, it should be noted that the Self-Reliance Party was understood to be a pivotal member of the opposition during this time. In terms of opposition status, however, not only was the Self-Reliance Party clearly an important part of the opposition, but also Soboliev himself, with his history of conflict with Petro Poroshenko, unambiguously identified as a member of the political opposition.

The third brawler we profile here, Oleh Liashko, already had an established reputation for brawling by the time he was elected to the 8th convocation of the Ukrainian parliament. At the time of the 2014 elections, Liashko was a seasoned politician, who had twice been elected to the parliament on party lists for Yulia Tymoshenko's bloc in 2006 and 2007 and had won the 2012 parliamentary election in a single-member district, as the head of a political party that bore his name—the Radical Party of Oleh Liashko (often called the Radical Party for short). In 2014 he ran as a presidential candidate for the Radical Party (coming in third with 8% of the vote), won a seat on the Kyiv city council (which he declined to fill), and went on to top his own party list, which won 22 seats in that year's parliamentary election.

Liashko was involved in brawls during the 8th convocation of the legislature, but by then his reputation as a brawler was already well established (Herszenhorn 2014). In fact, most of his involvement during this era was on the receiving end of punches that he provoked. An August 2014 YouTube video, for example, showed him exchanging words with a colleague in the halls of the legislature and receiving a punch that sent him reeling. In March 2015 Liashko wound up in a fight with Serhiy Melnychuk, a former member of the Radical Party, after accusing Melnychuk of accepting bribes—an act Melnychuk claimed was meant to provoke him (Vakulyuk 2015). And in November 2016, Liashko was on the receiving end of several punches thrown by Opposition Party leader Yuriy Boyko after he accused Boyko of traveling to Moscow to receive orders from the government there.

At first glance, Liashko's individual characteristics as a brawler in the 8th convocation appear as though they do not conform neatly to our theory. He was 42 when elected to the 8th convocation—older than both Soboliev and Parasyuk, though still younger than average. Also, he was a seasoned politician, with a senior rank in his political party—literally the leader of the party. It is important to remember, however, that Liashko's reputation as a brawler preceded his election to the 8th convocation of the legislature. When he first started brawling, he was younger and had less political experience, more in line with our theoretical expectations. In terms of contextual factors, Liashko, like Soboliev and Parasyuk, does not conform neatly to our expectations. He was not a member of a large political party, and although his party was technically part of the opposition, this was more by default—the *New York Times* reported, prior to the election, that Liashko anticipated the possibility of being asked to join a government coalition (Herszenhorn 2014).

Qualitative Evidence of Who Brawls over Honor

The fourth brawler of note that we profile from Ukraine is a bit different from the first three. Andriy Teteruk was not a prolific brawler; he was involved in a single incident. More importantly, his brawl was not a case of opposition disruption. Rather, he was trying to defend his assiduously constructed reputation as an honorable legislator. While Teteruk's personal characteristics align with our expectations of who brawls—a young first-term legislator—we do not have the same systematic expectations about brawls concerning honor, as they tend to be more idiosyncratic. Nevertheless, we profile him here not only because his brawl made an impression that Ukrainians remembered but also because he represents an archetype of an individual accused of dishonor, who brawls to defend his honor. His accuser and victim in the brawl also represents an archetypal honor brawler.

Teteruk was a decorated war hero when he ran for the 8th convocation of the Ukrainian legislature. While he was a member of the prime minister's party, elected on the party list, and part of President Poroshenko's legislative fraction, he sought to portray himself as a political outsider who would be different than corrupt career politicians.[6] Unlike Parasyuk and Soboliev, however, the freshman Teteruk sought to cultivate a more low-key reputation as someone who was a quiet, patriotic, hardworking, honorable legislator.

In a committee session, senior legislator Oleksandra Kuzhel directly called Teteruk's reputation into question by questioning his commitment to the country. Teteruk responded by assaulting her with a water bottle, an action for which he was widely criticized in the media. Kuzhel's role was largely ignored in the media, but our interviews suggested that many insiders thought she had intentionally goaded him. Kuzhel had served since 1994 and was a member of the main opposition Fatherland Party at the time of the incident. No one disputed that Teteruk had assaulted Kuzhel, and he was the one to receive negative media attention from the incident. The sense from observers who weighed in on the incident, however, was that Kuzhel had deliberately provoked Teteruk by openly expressing skepticism about his loyalty to Ukraine.

Teteruk represents one archetypal honor brawler, an individual drawn into a physical altercation in an attempt to refute charges that he is dishonorable. Kuzhel too represents an archetypal participant in an honor brawl, a seasoned politician who levels such an accusation somewhat cynically anticipating that if she could induce a violent response, it might bolster her partisan credentials as a relatively new member of the Fatherland Party. No doubt, part of Kuzhel's calculation was that as a woman being assaulted by a male legislator, she stood a better shot at discrediting a political opponent and/or creating sympathy for herself personally.

Since Teteruk and Kuzhel so nicely represent two honor-brawling archetypes, we take this opportunity for a brief digression to Taiwan to look at two other common archetypal honor brawlers. Unlike Teteruk, Lo Fu-chu most definitely deserved any charges of dishonor leveled at him, and while Lee Ching-an may not have been as direct in her accusation as Oleksandra Kuzhel, she did not shy away from the opportunity to take some blows and build her reputation as a reformer.

Lo Fu-chu was not an ordinary Taiwanese politician. Almost all successful candidates are nominated by one of the major parties, but Lo was elected twice, in 1995 and 1998, as an independent. Most media reports danced around his background, saying something to the effect that he was widely regarded as the spiritual leader of one of Taiwan's biggest organized crime gangs. This tiptoeing was necessary since Lo did not like being referred to as a crime lord, and people who publicly called him a gangster often received thinly veiled threats. Legislators were not immune, and Lo threatened many and beat up a few in brawls.

Lo's most famous legislative brawl came in 2001, when he tangled with Kuomintang (KMT) legislator Lee Ching-an. In a committee hearing, Lee raised the issue of organized crime members on the board of a college, and the education minister mentioned Lo's name. The next morning, while Lee was waiting for a committee hearing to start, Lo barged in and started cursing her for having called him a gangster on the floor of the legislature. In response to his cursing, she tried to throw a cup of water on him. He rushed at her, grabbed her hair, pushed her against a wall, and took several swings at her. At one point, he hit her and her head banged against the podium. Her aides tried to step in, but his aides restrained them. Eventually the combatants were separated, and Lee and her aides were taken to the hospital, where she was treated for a mild concussion (C. Chang 2001; Y. Chen 2001).

These two honor brawls offer profiles of four typical types of individuals who appear again and again in such instances of legislative violence. In terms of accusers, we have the sincere reformer (Lee) and the more strategic career politician (Kuzhel), both anticipating benefit from reactions of the individuals they accuse of dishonor. In terms of the accused, we have the sincere fighter, who cannot allow claims of dishonor to stand because he is building a reputation as honorable (Teteruk), and the cynical thug (Lo), who cannot allow claims of dishonor to stand because to do so would convey weakness. We do not necessarily find the systematic demographic or partisan characteristics in honor brawlers that we expect in cases of opposition disruption, and, although we highlight four typical participants in honor brawls, we want to stress again that these instances tend only to involve two individuals and can have many associated idiosyncrasies.

By contrast with honor brawlers, the examples of other prominent brawlers from this era in Ukraine, individuals who brawled frequently in the context of opposition disruption, offer evidence that is more consistent with our theoretical expectations of who brawls. In all cases the more prolific brawlers, Parasyuk, Soboliev, and Liashko, are young and members of the political opposition. While we observe some variation regarding the means by which they were elected and the kinds of political parties they belonged to, if any, this is largely to be expected given the weakness of Ukraine's party system. What we will see in the systematic evidence from Taiwan, with its strong party system, is empirical support for both the individual and contextual factors that our theory predicts regarding who is likely to brawl.

Quantitative Evidence from Taiwan

While profiles of brawlers from Ukraine's 8th parliament offer evidence that suggests support for our theoretical expectations, the use of video allows us to characterize the behavior of Taiwanese legislators more precisely and draw more systematic conclusions. Taiwan has many 24-hour news channels,[7] and, since about 2010, it has become increasingly common for them to post content on YouTube. We supplemented news clips of brawls obtained from YouTube with news clips obtained directly from China TV (CTV). Between these two sources, we were able to obtain video evidence for 47 of the 58 brawling incidents that occurred from 2005 to 2019.

We coded the behavior of each legislator in each brawling incident in terms of how disruptive and/or violent it was. We then constructed an index of individual brawling intensity with six levels ranging from doing nothing to physically attacking another legislator. More detail on the construction of this index is in Appendix 4.1.

Table 4.1 Intensity index categories and frequencies by legislator-event in Taiwan

Level	Behavior	Frequency	%
0	Does not participate in event	6,433	76.6
1	Stands on the chamber floor	285	3.4
2	Occupies the rostrum or lectern	721	8.6
3	Jostles a member of another party	825	9.8
4	Throws or destroys something	47	0.6
5	Attacks another legislator	85	1.0

We assume that each legislator makes a choice whether to participate in each event. It is true that not all legislators are in attendance at every session. However, anecdotal evidence suggests that legislators generally know when a brawl might happen and that being absent on a contentious day is a concrete choice. Table 4.1 shows the distribution of behavior for each legislator-event. Most legislators refrain from participating altogether. Those who do participate in an opposition disruption overwhelmingly opt for a lower-intensity action. The most colorful and violent acts, levels 4 and 5, account for fewer than 2% of choices.

Table 4.2 presents mean values of this brawling intensity index for various relevant groups of legislator-incidents. Because several of the variables we are looking at are correlated with each other, it is necessary to use a regression model to look at the various influences simultaneously. In Table 4.3, we present a multilevel ordered logit model of the brawling intensity index, with the cases grouped by the 47 brawling incidents.

Age and Brawling
Because they are less likely to have an established reputation within the legislature and deep ties to other legislators, we expect to see younger politicians brawling more than older ones.

Table 4.2 shows that legislators under 50 brawl more than those over 50. The average brawling intensity index for legislators aged 40 to 49 is 0.689, while that for legislators in their 50s falls to 0.536. This negative correlation between age and brawling is confirmed in Table 4.3. Thus, the data from Taiwan show clearly that when opposition disruption and brawling occur, younger legislators are more likely to be engaging in violence.

Table 4.2 Descriptive statistics for brawling intensity index in Taiwan, 2005–2019

Variable	Category	Mean	N
Age group	Under 40	.628	624
	40–49	.654	2,540
	50–59	.505	3,461
	60 and up	.573	1,771
Seniority	1st term	.618	3,680
	2nd term or more	.539	4,716
Gender	Male	.540	5,816
	Female	.648	2,580
Electoral system	Closed-list proportional representation	.516	2,333
	Single-member plurality	.750	3,650
	Single nontransferable vote	.362	2,413
Party size	Large party	.636	7,272
	Not large party	.169	1,124
Government or opposition	Majority bloc	.474	5,023
	Minority bloc	.722	3,373
Term	6 (2005–2007)	.265	2,750
	7 (2008–2011)	.436	1,122
	8 (2012–2015)	.579	1,249
	9 (2016–2019)	.878	3,275
All cases		.573	8,396

Seniority and Brawling

As with younger legislators, we expect junior legislators to engage in brawling more often, as they lack the kind of prominence and media exposure that come with more legislative seniority. Table 4.2 presents a comparison of legislators in their first terms and their colleagues who have served

Table 4.3 Multilevel ordered logit model of brawling intensity in Taiwan

	B	SE	Sig
Age: Age in years	−.015	.004	***
Seniority: Not first term	−.195	.070	**
Gender: Female	.100	.072	
Electoral rules: Closed-list proportional representation	−.348	.087	***
Electoral rules: Single nontransferable vote	.302	.129	*
Party size: Large party	1.344	.132	***
Majority or minority: Opposition bloc party	.633	.065	***
Term 7 (2008–2011)	.854	.441	$
Term 8 (2012–2015)	1.239	.456	**
Term 9 (2016–2019)	1.982	.354	***
/cut1	3.101	.369	
/cut2	3.292	.369	
/cut3	3.890	.370	
/cut4	6.138	.380	
/cut5	6.607	.386	
event	.806	.189	
Wald	257.7		
Log likelihood	−4,825.8		
Pr(chi2)	.000		
N(obs)	6,706		
N(groups)	47		

Notes: The dependent variable is the six-level ordinal brawling intensity index described in Appendix 4.1. * $p < .05$, ** $p < .01$, *** $p < .001$, $ $p < .10$.

multiple terms and finds that that first-term legislators (index = 0.645) are indeed more likely to participate than legislators in their second or higher terms (index = 0.569). Given the obvious correlation between age and seniority, it is reasonable to wonder if these two variables are actually capturing the same thing. In fact, they are not. In the multilevel ordered logit model, both variables produce significant coefficients. That is, even controlling for age, more senior legislators are less likely to brawl.

Gender and Brawling

We did not make an unambiguous prediction about gender. On the surface, there is no obvious reason to think men need the signal brawling provides more than women or vice versa, and there are arguments to be made both for why brawling might hurt and for why brawling might help women legislators' reputations. We did note that gender might interact with the party system to create some interesting incentives, so that women might have stronger incentives to brawl in systems with strong parties than in those with weak parties. Unfortunately, the strength of the party system is relatively constant within a given country, so it is difficult to test this expectation with our data. Nonetheless, our data offer some preliminary insights into gender and legislative violence.

Taiwan has much stronger parties than Ukraine, so we might expect to see women play a more prominent role in brawls. In fact, the data suggest that women in the Taiwanese legislature are at least as likely to brawl as their male counterparts. Table 4.2 shows that the mean brawling score for women is quite a bit higher than for men (0.699 to 0.561). However, this gap may be spurious. In the multilevel ordered logit model, the coefficient for women is positive but not statistically different from zero at conventional levels of significance, suggesting that much of the observed gender gap is actually due to other factors. It might be too bold to claim that women brawl more than men, but what we can say with quite a bit of confidence is that, in Taiwan, women have not been less likely to brawl than men.

This quantitative evidence that women feature prominently in Taiwanese brawls fits with our theoretical expectations about the interaction between gender and strong parties. It also fits with other brawling anecdotes presented in this book. For instance, in the 1954 Japanese brawl recounted in Chapter 2, the opposition party deliberately sent its female members to the front lines of the conflict, and the government party responded by sending its female members to deal with them. The strong Japanese parties thus made specific demands on their female members, requiring them to act in clear ways if they wished to avoid being seen as lousy party soldiers. This is a story we see playing out again and again in systems with strong parties, and it is probably one of the driving forces behind the prominence of women in Taiwanese brawls.

Electoral Systems and Brawling

In general, we expect that legislators who rely more on personal vote seeking will have more need of the kind of differentiation that comes with brawling behavior. At first glance, the data from Taiwan appear to contradict our expectations. While single-member plurality (SMP) legislators have a higher average brawling intensity index (0.883) than list legislators (0.524), the average value for SNTV legislators (0.353) is actually the lowest of all. However, recall that almost all SNTV legislators come from the 2005–2007 term, which had far less intense levels of brawling than later terms. Once we control for this in Table 4.3, we find that the coefficient for SNTV is positive and significant. That is, SNTV legislators are more likely to participate in brawls than SMP legislators. Overall, the Taiwanese data clearly show the expected relationship between electoral rules that incentivize cultivating a personal vote and brawling. List-tier legislators brawl less than nominal-tier legislators. Among nominal-tier legislators, SNTV legislators brawl more than SMP legislators.

Parties and Brawling

In general, we expect members of large parties as well as members of parties not in government to be more likely to brawl. The parties in Taiwan are commonly divided into two large camps, the KMT-led blue camp and the Democratic Progressive Party (DPP)-led green camp. Each camp is dominated by one large party and also has a handful of legislators from smaller parties. Thus, we can divide the parties by size, classifying the KMT and DPP as large parties and all others as small parties. We can also classify them by government and opposition status.[8] The blue camp controlled a majority in the legislature in the 6th, 7th, and 8th Terms, while the green camp controlled a majority in the 9th Term.

We expect legislators from large parties to brawl more frequently than those from small parties. In the Taiwanese data, this estimated coefficient shows the strongest association of any we investigate. The gap between the two groups in Table 4.2 is larger than any other gap, and the estimated coefficient for large parties in Table 4.3 is also the largest. In Taiwan, legislative brawls are a game played by legislators from large parties.

We also expect opposition legislators to be more enthusiastic participants in brawls, and the data confirm that this is indeed the common pattern in Taiwan. While the gap between government and opposition legislators is not quite as large as that between large and small parties, Table 4.3 reveals it to be one of the more powerful variables in our model. As befits a party-dominated polity, the natures of individual parties have sizeable impacts on the legislative behavior of their members.

Conclusion

In this chapter we have evaluated a set of expectations about who brawls derived from our theory of legislative brawling as an individually motivated strategic attempt at signaling. We offer expectations based both on characteristics of the individual legislator and on the context within which those legislators are operating, and the evidence we show here is largely supportive of those expectations. Across both the weak and strong party settings of Ukraine and Taiwan respectively, we see younger and less senior members of the legislature associated with more brawling. From Taiwan we get some evidence that women are actively involved in brawling, which makes sense given our assertion that women's brawling behavior is likely motivated more by pressure from parties and attempts to tarnish the reputation of opposing male legislators.

In terms of contextual factors, we see strong evidence from Taiwan and more mixed evidence from Ukraine regarding the influence of electoral systems and parties. In both countries there is some evidence that individuals who gain their legislative seats through more personal vote-seeking electoral rules are more likely to be associated with brawling, though the evidence from Taiwan is stronger in this regard. Similarly, while we see a strong association between brawling from members of large opposition parties in Taiwan, brawlers from Ukraine are not from large parties—and the only brawler from a large party was Teteruk, not a serial brawler but an individual provoked into an honor brawl. Thus, we should note that our expectations about the impact of political parties are most relevant in settings with strong political parties and may be less likely to have an effect in weaker partisan systems.

Not only does this chapter offer support for our theory of the strategic nature of legislative violence, but also it suggests several important implications for democratic representation. First, high legislative turnover through limits on re-election, for example, may incentivize more brawling behavior, as legislators lack other reputation-building tools. Second, electoral systems that cultivate personal vote seeking are likely to enhance brawling incentives, at least where parties are strong. Thus, brawling-prone countries looking to curb this behavior might consider the extent to which current institutions encourage career politicians to invest in careers in the institution rather than needing to quickly build a personal brand and move on.

These results also offer some interesting implications where strength of parties is concerned. Where parties are strong, we can reliably expect members of large, opposition parties to have incentives to fight. Here is where we might also see women called upon to serve as loyal party soldiers in attempts to discredit opponents by provoking violence. Weak party systems make the perpetrators of legislative violence less predictable.

Appendix 4.1 Legislative Behavior Coding for Video Coverage of Taiwan's Legislative Yuan

Before discussing how behavior is coded, some background on the physical layout of the chamber is useful. Legislators' seats are at the back of the chamber. In the middle of the chamber, there is an open space with three lecterns. The two on the sides are used for interpellation of government ministers. The legislator asks questions from the lectern on the right, and the minister answers from the lectern on the left. The lectern in the center is used when the legislature is considering a bill or the budget. Any legislator who wishes to speak must speak from this lectern. At the front of the legislative chamber on the left and right sides are three rows of seats. These seats are for cabinet ministers waiting to be called to the lectern during interpellation, and they are usually empty. Finally, the Speaker's rostrum is in the center. The Speaker's seat is in the center of the top row, and the other seats in these two rows are reserved for professional staff. The committee rooms are rectangular and much smaller than the main chamber, but, for our purposes, the layout is similar.

For each incident and each legislator, we created a number of binary variables. One way to disrupt proceedings is to stop the Speaker or professional staff from conducting business by preventing them from taking their places. Legislators standing on any of the three steps at the front of the legislature were coded as being on the Speaker's *rostrum*. This activity was usually concentrated in the center of the rostrum, but when the rostrum was full, people might spill out into the two side areas (for cabinet minister seating).

Another way to disrupt proceedings is to refuse to allow someone to speak. During interpellation sessions, legislators could occupy the two side lecterns, and during regular business, they could occupy the central lectern. Legislators standing behind the relevant lectern were coded as occupying the *lectern*.

When a disruption takes place, there are typically several legislators who move out to the open area on the floor, where they hold protest signs and shout slogans for the TV cameras. By itself, such conduct does not constitute a disruption or a physical conflict since it does not disrupt proceedings. Indeed, during mundane roll-call votes, it is common for a party floor leader to walk out into this space with a sign indicating how his or her caucus members should vote. However, in the context of a brawl, legislators in this space are doing more than nothing. They are standing up to be counted as supporting or opposing the disruption, even if they are not personally engaging in disruption or even breaking the rules. People in this space are coded as standing on the *floor*. Note that in every case of someone coded as standing on the floor, there is at least one legislator who is engaging in some more intense form of physical disruption. If the only thing happening is that legislators are standing on the floor, it is not considered an event and is not included in our data set.

Next, there are variables to code forms of violence. The most common form of violence involves contact, such as bumping, pushing, and shoving. We do not attempt to distinguish between different levels of intensity. We also do not try to distinguish who initiated the exchange. Any legislator who makes contact with a legislator from a different party is coded as engaging in *jostling*. Note that if one legislator makes contact with another, both are considered to be engaged in jostling.

Another form of violence involves destroying public property in order to produce disruption. Examples of this include ripping out microphones, overturning tables, and seizing, scattering, or even eating necessary documents. Legislators who engage in this behavior are coded as *destroying* public property.

A different tack involves throwing things. Over the years, legislators have thrown shoes, teacups, water balloons, flour bombs, and chairs. Sometimes these projectiles are thrown at specific people, but sometimes they are just thrown in the air. Such behavior is classified as *throwing* objects.

Finally, some behavior is physically aggressive. We code *attacking* as behavior in which one legislator clearly and intentionally engages in potentially harmful violence toward another. Punching, kicking, biting, slapping, wrestling, and clubbing someone with an object are examples. We do not include inadvertent actions such as an off-balance person reaching out and incidentally slapping someone or dragging the other person to the ground as they fall. Unlike jostling, the person who is attacked is not automatically coded as engaging in attacking. However, if that person fights back, he or she is also coded as attacking.

These binary variables are used to construct the brawling intensity index. Legislators who are not recorded as doing any of these are given a zero. Legislators who are present on the *floor* are scored one. Lawmakers who occupy a *lectern* or the *rostrum* are given a score of two. *Jostling* implies a score of three. A four is given for legislators who *throw* or *destroy*. The maximum score of five is reserved for legislators who *attack* a colleague. The index is hierarchical, so legislators who engage in multiple behaviors are scored as the most intense of those behaviors. The distribution of values is shown in Table 4.1.

5
Media and Signal Transmission

The day after Uganda's parliament erupted into a brawl in September 2017, in the context of a proposed constitutional amendment that would extend then-president Museveni's eligibility to pursue re-election and events surrounding a member of parliament (MP) from the government coalition bringing a firearm to the legislative chambers, Uganda's communications commission issued a notice banning television and radio stations from broadcasting the legislative violence live (Biryabarema 2017). The rationale was that such broadcasts might fuel broader societal violence and instability—characterized as "inciting the public"—but critics argued this was simply a way to silence criticism of the proposed amendment. What is clear from either the stated rationale or more cynical interpretations is that all parties involved (government and opposition) appreciated that by broadcasting the brawl live, the media was a critical actor in connecting brawlers to some audience.

The previous empirical chapter gave readers a sense of who is brawling and provided evidence consistent with our theory of brawls as signaling tools. If legislators are using brawls as signaling tools, the signal needs to reach the intended audience. The media have been reporting on legislative activities and motivating legislators to behave in ways that capture media attention at least since the Victorian era (Cox 1987). In our signaling story of brawling, the media have an important role to play—and it is a role they are happy to play. Arguably, if legislators were just trying to signal to other actors within the legislature, they would not need a transmission device such as the media. However, when parties are weak, the key audiences for brawlers are outside the legislature itself. Even where parties are strong, the key partisan actors that legislators are trying to reach may be members of the electorate, party leaders, or other figures outside the legislature. Thus, the role of the media in transmitting brawling signals to the intended audiences becomes crucial. Our empirical evidence from Ukraine and Taiwan shows that the media are eager to report on brawls and that individual brawlers do, in fact, receive more media coverage.

Review of Theory and Empirical Expectations

Recall from Chapter 3 that we argue brawls are the result of individual legislators taking strategic action to send signals to an intended audience rather than spontaneous outbursts of emotion. If brawls are indeed being used strategically to send signals, then the legislators who engage in such acts must reasonably be able to expect that the violence they commit will be communicated to their intended audience. Evidence of legislators being sensitive to what legislative activities might be reported to the public dates to the advent of mass print media and its coverage of legislative activities. Cox (1987) showed how press coverage of the British House of Commons drove increased demands for access to talk time during the Victorian era, and Freeman (2018, chap. 6) argues that members of the US Congress in the antebellum era were sensitive to what was published about their activities and able to shape the media coverage of those media that received congressional funding.

Thus, legislators are undoubtedly aware of the media's ability to transmit signals. At the same time, for brawling to work in a way that individual legislators could reasonably be thought to be sending signals, the following would logically have to be true: (1) *brawls would need to be the type of legislative activity that the media will report on*, and (2) *media reports of brawls would need to provide coverage of the specific individuals involved*, rather than simply reporting on a general scrum, which would confer no signaling advantage to any one individual and would not motivate brawling for signaling purposes. Finally, for legislators to prefer brawling as a means of signaling rather than normal legislative activities such as bill introduction or floor speeches, we should observe that (3) *brawling earns individual legislators more media coverage than nonbrawling activity*.

Media Coverage of Legislatures

We address the first point of logic above by drawing on the literature on media coverage of legislatures. Research on media coverage of legislative politics offers some insights into how the media decides what to report to the public. The implications of this research are that brawls should be likely to receive coverage. Quite a few authors have argued that the media favors stories about conflict, scandals, controversies, charismatic figures, drama, and other sensational topics rather than less exciting issue-based stories. Ranney (1983) argues that "show horses" received more attention than "work horses" in the US Congress. Sabato (1991) characterizes press coverage as a feeding frenzy whipping up a frothy but superficial coverage of scandals. Fallows (1996) decries the media's focus on sexy stories rather than substantive coverage. Rozelle (1994, 110–111) cites several prominent journalists recounting pressure to find stories about colorful personalities, graft, and sin and above all to avoid tedious MEGOs: stories that make "my eyes glaze over."

Subsequent research, however, has painted a much more nuanced picture of how the media covers legislatures. For one thing, it is not necessarily correct that scandals and sensationalism represent the mainstream of media coverage. Studying both print and television coverage of the US Congress, Morris and Clawson (2005) found that most coverage was quite substantive and only a very small proportion was focused on individual personalities or political scandals. More importantly, while the press is inclined to cover conflict, the conflict is generally framed as part of legislative maneuvering in which parties or institutions are the main actors. While individuals are often mentioned, they are usually discussed in the context of acting on behalf of their parties or institutions rather than as interesting topics in their own right.

Thus, while scholars of political media have identified a trend toward personalizing political news in recent decades (Vos 2014), one common finding is that media coverage tends to be disproportionately focused on legislators in powerful positions, such as party leaders or committee chairs, rather than on ordinary rank-and-file members (Cook 1986; Morris and Clawson 2005; Tsfati et al. 2010; Vos 2014). Further, parties with more legislative power (typically larger parties) see their messages reflected in the media more often, and recent experimental work has found the information coming from large parties is more likely to be deemed newsworthy by political journalists (Helfer and Van Aelst 2016; Vos 2016). Finally, all of the large party advantages are amplified if the party in question is in government.

Given the media's bias toward legislative reporting that prioritizes large parties, party elites, and parties in government, individual legislators, particularly those in the opposition, are at a disadvantage if they desire media coverage for themselves. This is particularly challenging given that extensive parliamentary activity—of the more traditional, nonviolent variety—has little to no effect on ordinary legislators' recognition in the media (Tsfati et al. 2010; Vos 2014). However, since the media finds conflict compelling, one way for rank-and-file legislators to grab media attention is to combine conflict and party politics. The media are inclined to cover messages where the government is criticized or blamed—such as those that often emerge during parliamentary question times (van Santen, Helfer, and Van Aelst 2015). Thus, the disruptions that precede partisan brawls, which demonstrate a clear and physical criticism of the government by the opposition, should be expected to motivate media coverage. As we argue throughout this book, many brawlers are trying to send a signal that they are literally fighting for their party's ideals and positions, connecting these individual actions to political conflict and party politics—favorite topics for media coverage.

Even when it does not conform to the partisan patterns described above, there is reason to believe that brawling is the type of activity that media may like to cover. For one thing, the media generally finds conflict compelling (van Santen, Helfer, and Van Aelst 2015; Auel, Eisele, and Kinski 2018), and brawls are nothing if not conflictual. For another, brawls that are not carefully planned partisan events are often sudden and unexpected legislative events, which tend to receive more media coverage owing to their shock value (Helfer and Van Aelst 2016). In addition, as a senior Taiwanese media figure explained to us, TV cameras reflexively follow dynamic scenes, and, unlike most events in the legislature, brawls have movement to look at.[1]

For these reasons, we expect that the media both cover brawls and identify the individuals involved. In the context of partisan disruption, the media are predisposed to cover partisan conflict and to frame that conflict in partisan terms. Prominent participants in the brawl can be neatly folded into that narrative, presented as partisan brawlers fighting for their party, precisely the way in which they hope to be perceived. Outside of partisan brawls, the element of conflict is still present and should be sufficient to attract media attention, and if a clear partisan narrative to the conflict is lacking, then the media may be even more likely to report on the individuals involved.

Is this coverage always good for individual legislators? Some might wonder if the crucial factor is not the amount of coverage but whether the content conveys a positive or negative message. In this chapter, we do not worry about the tone of the coverage. Different voters have different ideas of what is positive and what is negative news. Voters tend to consume information through a "perceptual screen," which often leads them to understand the news in a way that casts their favored party in a positive light or other parties in a negative light (Campbell et al. 1960). Moreover, legislators may be particularly interested in appealing to a small group of critical supporters who may have decidedly nonmedian preferences. This is especially true in single nontransferable vote elections, where some legislators can rely heavily on nonmedian voters (Cox 1990). What might appear to be a negative slant to most voters might be interpreted as a very positive message to the legislator's target audience. As a result, we assume that, more or less, all news coverage is good news coverage, and so we consider only the raw number of news stories.

Brawling Coverage and Individual Mentions

In this section, we present evidence that brawlers get more coverage, consistent with the second point of logic outlined in the introduction. From analysis of Taiwanese media coverage, we see that brawlers get more media coverage than nonbrawlers. Moreover, brawlers get much more coverage when they brawl than when they do not. From text analysis of Ukrainian media coverage of the legislature online, we find that individual legislators tend to receive more individual mentions in articles about brawling than articles about other legislative activity.

Quantitative Evidence from Taiwan

To evaluate our expectations in Taiwan, we turn to the *United Daily News* (UDN) online database.[2] We examine one year of coverage from each term. Historically, brawls were most frequent in the first year of the term. However, since the new electoral system began operation in 2008, brawls have been more frequent in the second year of the term. As such, we study the first year of the term for Terms 1 through 6 and the second year for Terms 7 through 9.

The first task is to investigate whether brawlers generate more news coverage than nonbrawlers. We record the total number of UDN articles mentioning each legislator's name in a given year. For the entire period, legislators generated an average of 103 stories in a given year. However, not all legislators were equal. The 250 legislators who played a prominent role in a brawl that year got nearly twice as much coverage (167 stories) as the 1,210 who did not (90 stories). Figure 5.1 shows that this pattern of brawlers receiving much more media attention is replicated in each year we looked at. From this data, we cannot say conclusively that the brawling itself was the

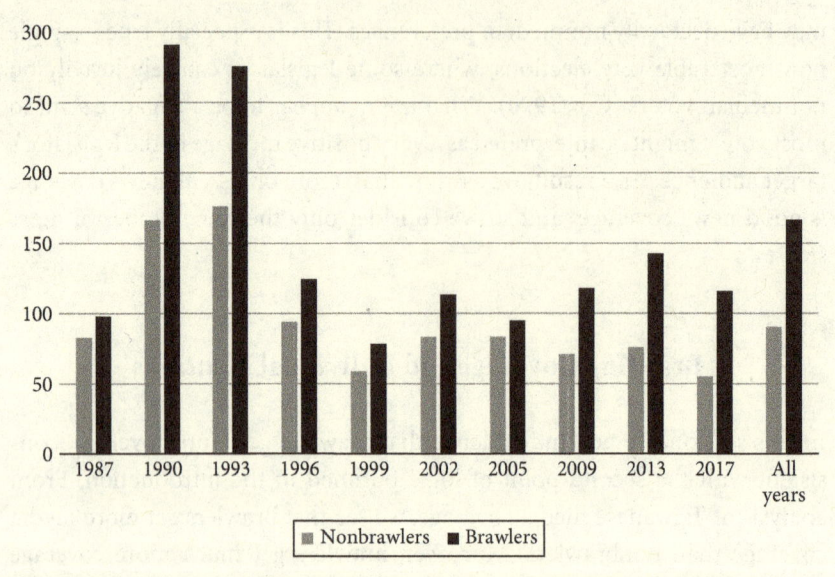

[Figure: bar chart comparing average number of UDN stories for Nonbrawlers vs Brawlers across years 1987, 1990, 1993, 1996, 1999, 2002, 2005, 2009, 2013, 2017, and All years.]

Figure 5.1 Average number of UDN stories for nonbrawlers and brawlers.

critical difference, but it certainly is the case that the media preferred to write about legislators who brawled than those who did not.

To better understand the impact of brawling on media coverage, it is helpful to look more carefully at the 250 legislators who brawled in the given year. We recorded the number of stories that mentioned each legislator day by day so that we could compare how much coverage they got when they brawled and when they did not. Since the news cycle surrounding a brawl may be longer than one day, we considered a brawling window to be a period of three days, starting with the day of the brawl and continuing for the next two days after the brawl.

Figure 5.2 demonstrates that, in fact, media attention increased dramatically during the brawling window. Normally—that is, when they didn't brawl—the 250 legislators got an average of 0.44 stories a day. However, during a brawling window, this figure shot up to 1.68 stories a day—nearly four times as much! Since the brawling window is defined as three days long, this means that each brawl earned a legislator an average of 3.7 extra UDN stories. Legislators routinely hold events such as press conferences or activities back home in an effort to get just one additional news story, so an extra 3.7 stories is a substantively significant boost. Moreover, while we do not have hard data, we suspect that news coverage of brawling is more likely

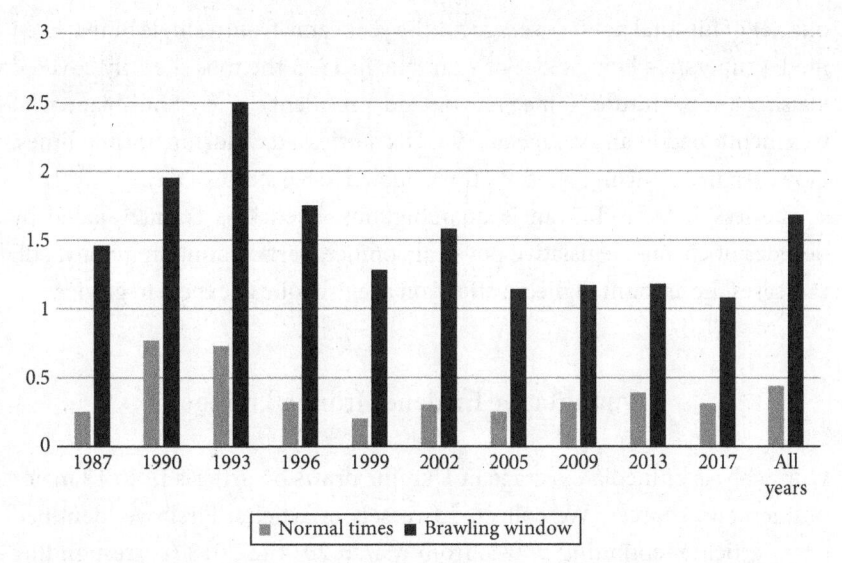

Figure 5.2 UDN stories each day for brawlers during brawling windows and normal times.

to be in a prominent place in the newspaper, perhaps on the front page or in the national news section, than a story about the legislator visiting farmers in an effort to promote local mangos, which is likely to be buried deep in the local news section. Even more importantly, UDN is only one of several newspapers. The total amount of extra news generated by a brawl would also have to account for increased coverage in other newspapers, TV and radio news, magazines, and in-depth discussion on one of Taiwan's many nightly political talk shows. In other words, the 3.6 extra UDN news stories that we have been able to quantify probably significantly underestimates the actual impact that brawling has on media coverage of an individual legislator. In short, this is direct evidence for the connection between brawling and media attention. It was not merely that brawlers were more interesting to the media than nonbrawlers—they were specifically more newsworthy precisely when they brawled.

Some brawlers got a bigger boost in news coverage than others, but nearly all received a positive bump: 238 (95.2%) experienced an increase, while only 12 (4.8%) saw their individual average go down. For ordinary legislators struggling to get any attention, this could be a major boon. For example, in 2002 Lin Nan-sheng usually only averaged 0.11 stories a day, but that shot up to 3.67 a day in a brawling window. To put it another way, more than a quarter of his total news coverage for the year came from a single brawl. Even media superstars benefited. For example, in 1993 the most heavily covered legislator was (future Taipei mayor and president) Chen Shui-bian, who was mentioned in an average of 3.9 UDN stories a day during normal times. However, in a brawling window, this doubled to 8.0 stories a day.

The lesson from Taiwan is unambiguous. Even in a country jaded by decades of chronic legislative physical conflict, participating in a brawl still increases the amount of media attention a legislator can expect to garner.

Quantitative Evidence from Ukraine

Our analysis of media coverage in Ukraine draws on articles from 12 major online news sources. We collected two sets of articles. First, we identified every article mentioning brawls from March 2014 to 2018 (corresponding to the 8th convocation of the Ukrainian parliament). Second, we selected a random sample of all articles covering parliament but not mentioning brawling for the same time period. Online media coverage of parliament in Ukraine is best described as shallow, with few mentions of individual legislators. Nevertheless, its availability makes it useful, relative to other media that feature coverage of the legislature but are more difficult to access, such as more traditional television and print media. Despite providing only a surface picture of media coverage of legislative brawling, we have several reasons to believe that what we observe from these sources is consistent with what we would observe to a greater extent in other media. The 12 most widely accessed Ukrainian news sites analyzed here (Figure 5.3) represent a range of political orientations, from pro-Russian to neutral to pro-Ukrainian. Further, Figure 5.3 also clearly shows that outlets reporting more on the parliament's activities also report more on brawling. This pattern is supportive of our expectation that media want to cover brawling.[3] Figure 5.3 shows that from among the 12 most widely accessed Ukrainian online news sources, 222 articles about the legislature during its eighth convocation were about legislative brawling.[4]

Interviews with Ukrainian legislators underscored the fact that members of the legislature are aware not only of the importance of media coverage but also of the media's desire to cover conflict such as brawls. One legislator, for example, remarked that brawls receive disproportionate coverage on TV, which does not show the boring day-to-day activity of legislating. Further,

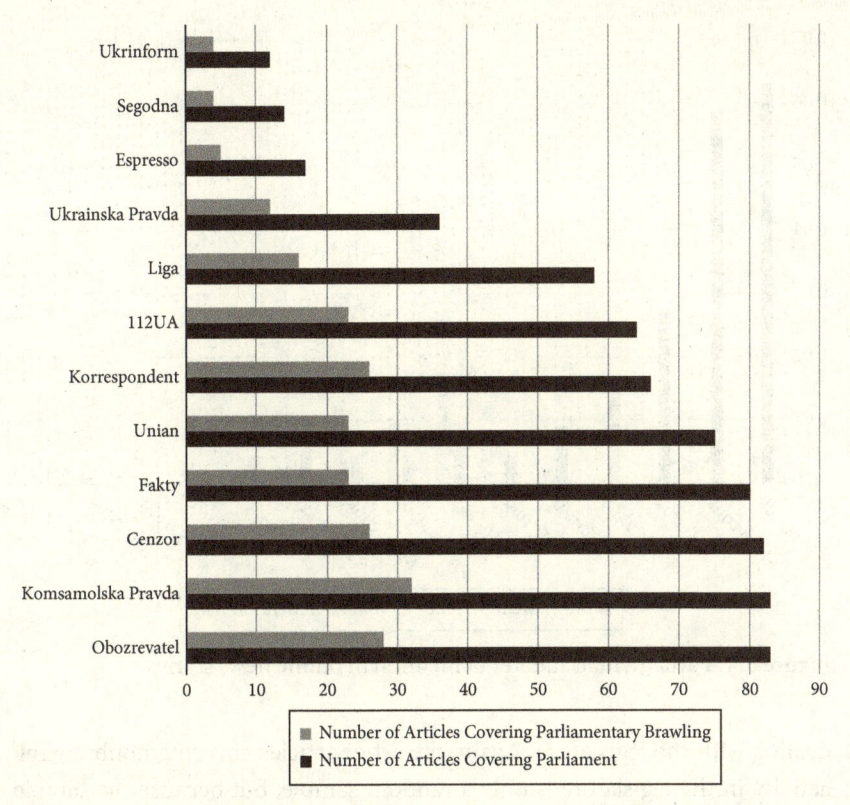

Figure 5.3 Online media coverage of the Verkhovna Rada (2014–2018).

she hinted at the individual incentives to brawl. She characterized legislative activity as involving a great deal of work to collaborate and compromise, but according to her, participating in legislative conflict like a brawl was "instant and free publicity . . . you don't have to work."[5]

Regarding the coverage of individuals in media reports of brawling, we can compare mentions of specific legislators in those 222 news articles about brawling to a random sample of 448 online news stories from the same sources covering the nonbrawling business of the Verkhovna Rada. Figure 5.4 compares the rate of mention for all individual legislators who were named in these two datasets.

The first two points to observe from Figure 5.4 have to do with overall rates of mention in brawling and nonbrawling coverage. First, it appears here that individuals are rarely mentioned in online media coverage of the legislature in Ukraine. Only 15 legislators were identified by name in 678 online articles

112 MAKING PUNCHES COUNT

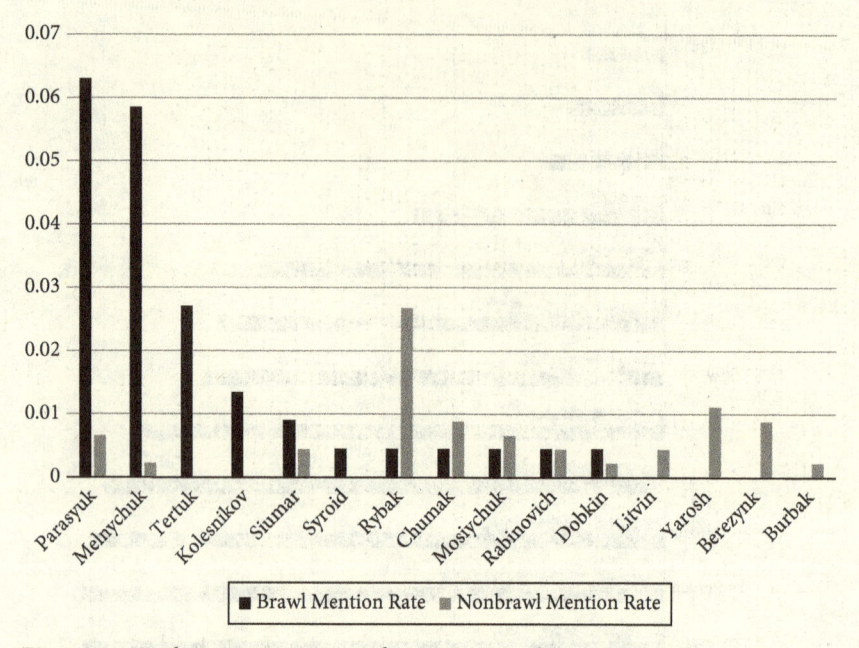

Figure 5.4 Parliamentarian rates of mention in online news stories.

dealing with the legislature. Again, the set of articles covering nonbrawling activity in the legislature is only a random sample, but because the sample is random, we can infer that the rates of individual mention in the sample should be consistent with overall rates of mention in all media coverage—at least online. Second, individual mentions are more than twice as common in brawling coverage as nonbrawling coverage of the legislature. Forty-four total mentions of individuals in brawling coverage amounts to mentions in nearly 20% of those news stories. By contrast, 40 mentions in 448 randomly selected articles suggests a rate of coverage of less than 9% of nonbrawling media coverage.

The second set of observations we can make from this figure have to do with individual rates of mention. Here we see that individuals' average rates of mention are somewhat higher in brawling than nonbrawling coverage—a rate of .018 for brawling coverage and .013 for nonbrawling coverage. However, this trend is driven by much higher coverage for a few prominent brawlers. Nonbrawling coverage, by contrast, is more evenly distributed. These different patterns of coverage produce one group of legislators who receive more brawling coverage and another group who receive more nonbrawling coverage. To illustrate this point, consider that the four individuals who were not mentioned in any brawling articles were mentioned in an average of six nonbrawling articles. In contrast, Volodymyr Parasyuk, who among individuals mentioned for brawling has the most mentions both for brawling and for nonbrawling mentions, only has three nonbrawling mentions.

To understand this difference in how the media covered different legislators, it is worth considering the case of Volodymyr Parasyuk more closely. Recall that prior to being elected as a freshman legislator in the 8th convocation, Parasyuk gained extensive media coverage for an impassioned, impromptu speech delivered at a critical moment of the Euromaidan protests. Further, recall from Chapter 4 that Parasyuk expressed a clear appreciation for how the political positions he took might limit his media exposure. Parasyuk is, thus, an example of someone who was quite successful in securing online media coverage by engaging in conflict.

Our analysis of individual mentions in online media coverage of Ukraine's parliament suggest that individuals are twice as likely to be mentioned by name in stories covering brawls as in stories about nonbrawling legislative activities. And while this observation should motivate legislators seeking media attention to brawl, we see that individual mentions for brawling are not evenly distributed among those individuals mentioned in brawling coverage. Two legislators receive extensive mention in the brawling coverage, while many more legislators only receive a single mention. Moreover, even though many of these legislators receive mention in both brawling and nonbrawling coverage, it appears as though legislators generally receive mention either for brawling or for nonbrawling activity—suggesting that legislators tend to pursue media attention either with more conventional legislative behaviors or with more unconventional tactics such as brawling.

Conclusion

The signaling theory of strategic brawling suggests that individual legislators seek to communicate with specific audiences outside the legislature and anticipate that media will cover their brawling, thereby enabling them to send the desired signals to the desired audiences. This should produce two observable patterns: (1) media should be prone to cover legislative brawling and (2) individuals should expect to receive increased media coverage that mentions them by name. In this chapter we show not only that media cover legislative brawling extensively but also that individual legislators are frequently mentioned by name in this coverage. Furthermore, our analyses in both Taiwan and Ukraine show that individuals can expect to receive more coverage for brawling than for normal, nonbrawling legislative activity.

Interestingly, in Ukraine multiple legislators explicitly acknowledged the expectation that legislators brawl to gain media coverage, while in our interviews in Taiwan, legislators were far more hesitant to spell out this incentive quite so crassly. This may well reflect the difference between a system with weak parties and one with strong parties. Although we argue that all brawlers are seeking to differentiate themselves and communicate with audiences that can further their careers, the types of messages that partisan brawlers are looking to communicate—namely that they are loyal to the party—may work against them acknowledging a desire to be identified as an individual. By contrast, brawlers building an individual brand in a weak party system may be much more willing to acknowledge a desire for personal attention in the media. As Liashko explained in his *New York Times* interview, "There are two ways to get on TV, either for money or to create events.... As we do not have money, and we didn't have it, that is why I had to choose the kind of politics that create events" (Herszenhorn 2014, paragraph 30).

Appendix 5.1 Media Coverage of Brawling in Taiwan—Data Collection and Analysis

We use very different approaches to studying media coverage in Taiwan and Ukraine. This is due partly to the nature of available data and partly to the desire to use different strategies to avoid making the same mistakes in different data sets.

Legislative brawls have been a regular feature in Taiwan since 1987, when the country was just emerging from decades of authoritarian rule. Media sources were severely restricted under martial law; there were two major newspapers and only three TV stations. After martial law was lifted, there was an explosion of media sources. By the late 1990s, there were usually more than a dozen national newspapers and half a dozen 24-hour cable news stations at any time. Many of these outlets failed over the next two decades under pressure from various financial crises and the rise of the internet. This constant reshuffling of Taiwan's media landscape means that very few sources are useful for studying the entire 1987–2019 period. There is, happily, one major exception. The *United Daily News* (UDN) has been one of Taiwan's two or three major newspapers throughout the entire period, and it has not experienced a change of ownership. It also maintains a very good online database, which serves as our primary source for the Taiwan data in Chapters 5 and 7.

The UDN has a clear partisan position in favor of the Kuomintang and against the Democratic Progressive Party. However, we do not think the UDN's slant biases our data. We do not consider the tone of the article or any positive or negative phrases; we only record who was involved in each incident. Several senior media figures—who now represent all sides of the political spectrum—have assured us that, even during the authoritarian era, factual details of events in the legislature were reliably reported, even if interpretation of those events may have been influenced by partisan biases.

We identified 202 days in the 1987–2019 period in which the Legislative Yuan experienced a brawl. The great majority of these were identified with the UDN database, but a handful were identified with supplemental media sources. This is the basis for the data presented in Figure 2.1 and Table A5.1.1. Of these 202 incidents, we found stories that identified at least one individual participant in 193 incidents. Again, almost all of these individual participants were identified through the UDN database. In total, 404 different legislators[6] were named, combining to identify 790 unique legislator incidents named in media reports.

Prior to a major electoral reform in 2008, more brawls took place in the first year of each three-year term. After the reform, there were more brawls in the second year of each four-year term. We suspect this might have something to do with synchronizing the presidential and legislative terms in 2008. Before that, legislators came in representing the newest expression of public opinion and were free to vigorously assert their preferences. When the terms were synchronized in 2008, the president could claim to hold a mandate just as new and arguably more national in scope, so legislators may have been hesitant to oppose the executive until they observed significant changes in public opinion. At any rate, we choose to investigate brawls and brawlers in the years with more activity and thus more data: the first year of each term before the 2008 reform and the second year of each term after the reform.[7] Eighty-nine of the 193 brawls occurred in these 10 years.

Table A5.1.1 Brawls in which individual participants were identified

Term	Unique incidents	Unique brawlers	Brawler incidents
1a*	20	24	50
1b*	46	58	214
2	36	63	133
3	13	32	41
4	7	27	32
5	19	46	58
6	13	46	73
7	8	25	36
8	8	30	44
9	23	53	109
All	193	404	790

Note: Speakers, Deputy Speakers, and "senior" legislators who were not popularly elected are excluded from this analysis.

* Starting in 1972, "supplemental" elections were held for a minority of seats for three-year terms. In this book, we only consider the last two of these supplemental terms, labeled term 1a and term 1b.

We investigated two major questions. First, did brawlers get more media attention than nonbrawlers? Second, looking only at the brawlers, did they get more media attention in the days immediately after they participated in a brawl than they did in normal (i.e., nonbrawling) times?

To answer the first question, we constructed a data set of how many stories in the UDN database mentioned each legislator in the given year.[8] Of the 1,460 legislators examined, the mean number of UDN stories in the given year was 103.3 with a standard deviation of 121.8. The minimum was 1 story, and the maximum was 1,448 stories. On average, brawlers were mentioned in 78 more stories than nonbrawlers over this entire period. To put it another way, brawlers got 87% more coverage than nonbrawlers.

It is necessary to check that this pattern still holds after controlling for different levels of media attention to the legislature over time and for legislators holding different positions of power. UDN covered the legislature more intensely in the early 1990s when there was no directly elected president and the legislature was the focus of the democratization movement. To control for this, we create dummy variables for each year investigated, with the last year (2017) as the reference category. In most legislatures, committee chairs have a certain amount of power and should be expected to receive a disproportionate amount of media coverage. Taiwan's legislative committees do not elect a single powerful chair. Rather, they elect two or three less powerful "conveners." Moreover, the conveners are almost always limited to a single six-month session in this position, so they do not accrue power over time. This is true more generally of committees. In the 1990s, it was customary to completely reshuffle committee membership every session. In recent years, most legislators have stayed on the same committee for the entire term, but there is still no seniority system that allows individual legislators to accrue power over many years in a single committee. As a result, we do not consider whether a legislator served as a committee convener during the given year. There are two institutional positions that are powerful, however. The Speaker and Deputy Speaker have a great deal of power over outcomes, especially through their informal powers to guide compromise. However, since Speakers and Deputy Speakers almost never willingly engage in brawling, we exclude them from our analysis. The other position that matters is party whips. The two big parties elect three main floor leaders, and these floor leaders guide party strategy, help to set the agenda, and negotiate compromises. As a result, they get quite a bit more media attention than ordinary backbenchers.

Table A5.1.2 shows the results of two ordinary least squares (OLS) regressions in which the cases are legislators and the dependent variable is the number of UDN stories mentioning each one in the relevant year. In Model A, the independent variable of interest is binary, indicating whether the legislator participated in any brawls. In Model B, the independent variable of interest is the number of brawls the legislator participated in. As expected, there are differences in the different years, and party whips receive more media attention than other legislators. For our purposes, the important point is that, after controlling for these other variables, brawlers receive more media attention than nonbrawlers. On average, brawlers were mentioned in 40.3 more stories than nonbrawlers over the course of the year. This is smaller than the difference in raw means, but 40.3 more stories over the course of a year should be a large enough gap to get a legislator's attention. Moreover, participating in multiple brawls brings more coverage. Legislators are mentioned in 29.2 more stories for each additional brawl.

It is possible that the people who brawl are simply more charismatic and would receive more media attention even if they did not brawl. The second question looks only at

Table A5.1.2 OLS regressions of brawling and UDN stories

	Model A			Model B		
	b	s.e.	sig	b	s.e.	sig
Constant	47.16	10.35	***	45.70	10.04	***
Y1987	20.23	15.68		21.36	15.44	
Y1990	140.98	14.29	***	123.07	14.31	***
Y1993	133.36	12.95	***	134.80	12.77	***
Y1996	33.46	12.90	**	36.05	12.71	**
Y1999	1.92	12.27		4.22	12.05	
Y2002	29.76	12.30	*	32.14	12.07	**
Y2005	28.33	12.32	*	30.73	12.11	*
Y2009	8.77	14.54		11.67	14.29	
Y2013	18.68	14.16		21.92	13.94	
Party whip	167.79	11.66	***	161.87	11.53	***
Brawler (binary)	40.27	7.53	***			
Number of brawls				29.16	3.53	***
Adj R2	.289			.308		
N	1,460			1,460		

Notes: This table includes the first year of the term through term 6, and the second year of the term starting with term 7. This excludes legislators who served as Speaker or Deputy Speaker that term or who left the legislature during the year in question. Party whip includes legislators who served as one of the three floor leaders for the KMT or DPP caucus in the relevant year. * $p < .05$, ** $p < .01$, *** $p < .001$.

brawlers, asking whether they receive more media attention when they brawl than when they do not brawl. To investigate this question, we collected the number of UDN stories for each brawler for each day of the year. The days were divided into two types: a brawling window and nonbrawling periods. The brawling window was defined as the three-day period starting on the day of the brawl.[9] Overall, we collected data on 91,279 legislator-days, during which the given legislator was mentioned in 41,556 stories; 1,159 of these legislator-days fell during a brawling window, during which the given legislator was mentioned in 1,943 stories.

There are several ways to think about these data. The first is to simply ask whether brawlers collectively were mentioned in more or fewer stories per day during the brawling window. In fact, brawlers were mentioned in roughly four times as many stories per day during their brawling window (Table A5.1.3).

Table A5.1.3 Average number of UDN stories per day mentioning brawlers

	Normal times	Brawling window	Ratio
1987	.25	1.46	5.8
1990	.77	1.95	2.5
1993	.73	2.50	3.4
1996	.32	1.75	5.5
1999	.20	1.28	6.4
2002	.30	1.58	5.3
2005	.25	1.14	4.6
2009	.32	1.17	3.7
2013	.39	1.18	3.0
2017	.31	1.08	3.5
All	.44	1.68	3.8

However, the point of this exercise is to look at individual brawlers to ensure that the difference in media coverage is not due to a selection bias in which charismatic legislators are especially prone to brawl. The next way to look at these data is to ask whether each individual legislator got more coverage during a brawling window. Table A5.1.4 shows that 238 of the 250 brawlers had a higher average number of stories per day in the brawling window, and t-tests showed that 78 of those gaps were statistically significant.

This finding perhaps should not be viewed as indicating that brawling was meaningless for the 160 legislators with higher but not statistically significant averages. The brawling window was only three days, so the variance for that group might be quite high. Consider two legislators, one who was mentioned in zero, eight, and one stories and one who was mentioned in three, three, and three stories. Both legislators got nine total stories, and they probably don't care much about the distribution over the three days. However, the standard deviation for the brawling window will be much higher for the first legislator and thus it is highly possible that the first legislator will fall in the higher but not significant category while the second will fall in the higher and significant category.

A third way of looking at these data is to look at ratios of coverage during brawling windows and normal times, which is more likely how practical politicians are prone to view things. During the brawling window, 199 of the 250 brawlers were covered in at least twice as many stories per day, and 86 received at least five times as much coverage as normal (Table A5.1.5).

Interestingly, there is not a lot of overlap between the 78 legislators who received statistically significantly higher coverage and the 86 legislators who received at least five times as much coverage during a brawling window. Just over half (131) of the brawlers fell into at least one of these categories, while only 33 fell into both.

To sum up, almost all brawlers saw their daily news coverage go up during the brawling window, and half of these increases were either statistically significant or substantively very large. Meanwhile, very few saw their coverage decrease. This is clear evidence that

Table A5.1.4 Brawlers and UDN coverage during a brawling window and normal times

	Do brawlers get more UDN stories when they brawl?				Number of brawlers
	Fewer and significant	Fewer, not significant	More, not significant	More and significant	
1987	1	0	7	3	11
1990	0	5	21	18	44
1993	0	3	23	11	37
1996	0	0	20	9	29
1999	0	0	15	7	22
2002	0	1	13	6	20
2005	0	0	18	5	23
2009	0	1	4	4	9
2013	0	0	12	2	14
2017	0	1	27	13	41
All	1	11	160	78	250

Table A5.1.5 Ratios of daily UDN stories for brawlers in brawling windows to normal times

	Ratio: (brawling window mean) / (normal times mean)						n
	< 1	1–2	2–3	3–5	5–10	> 10	
1987	1	1	2	2	1	4	11
1990	5	11	14	12	2	0	44
1993	3	6	6	10	7	5	37
1996	0	1	5	9	10	4	29
1999	0	4	2	3	7	6	22
2002	1	3	2	6	5	3	20
2005	0	3	3	8	4	5	23
2009	1	0	4	2	1	1	9
2013	0	1	3	2	7	1	14
2017	1	9	10	8	9	4	41
All	12	39	51	62	53	33	250

Note: Cells show the number of brawlers with a given ratio.

brawling does result in more media coverage for individual brawlers, indicating that they do in fact have an opportunity to transmit a signal about their type to the wider public.

Appendix 5.2 Media Coverage of Brawling in Ukraine—Data Collection and Analysis

Media coverage of Ukraine's parliament was drawn from Ukraine's top 12 most widely accessed online news sources. The data used for this analysis were collected from Ukraine's 12 most widely accessed online news sources as identified by the Institute of Mass Media and the Academy of Ukrainian Press (Matsuka et al. 2017). The political orientations of these sources effectively represent the scope of political leanings in Ukraine, ranging from pro-Russian to centrist to pro-Ukrainian. We first collected every article mentioning brawls from March 2013 to 2018 (corresponding to the 8th convocation of the Ukrainian parliament) and then selected a random sample of articles covering parliament for the same time period. Duplicate brawling articles that were picked up in the second sample were dropped so the sample of articles covering parliament effectively represents a random sample of nonbrawling articles.

To identify brawling articles, we use search terms "Rada," short for Verkhovna Rada, the official name of the Ukrainian parliament, in combination with (fights) or (fight). For nonbrawling articles only the term "Rada" was used. For both samples we supplemented searches with words like (parliament) and (legislator) if primary search terms yielded no results, though this was a rare occurrence.

To identify individual legislators in the articles, each article was preprocessed. We removed numbers, symbols, Twitter symbols, and URLs. This is particularly important as the sources we are using come from online news media sources, which often contain @ to signify who wrote the piece and # to signify important search terms. We set the package to process the text using lowercase Russian unigrams as most words in the Russian language are combined into one if two words are hyphenated to be used together. We also stemmed the documents using the Quanteda language stemmer and set the language and stop words to Russian. While Ukrainian is the official language of the country, most individuals are bilingual, and government agency resources and news sources are available in both Ukrainian and Russian. To ensure we did not use articles with limited scope, we limited the minimum word count of search terms to three per article with a minimum document frequency of 7 documents. We tested frequency with 5 and 10, but 5 allowed for far too much sparsity, ~90%, while limiting the documents to 10 removed more than half of my features, from 1,000 to 300. Using a frequency of 7 ensures that the topics covered are similar among sources and one article's discussion of a topic or use of a word is not dominating the corpus. The most frequently used words in the corpus include (deputy), Rad (stem for Rada), (stem for "which"), (stem for "this"), (parliament), (Ukraine), and (law), among several others. Finally, variables were constructed for each legislator's last name so that every article in the data set could be coded for whether a given legislator was mentioned. These mentions were summed within each sample to construct the graph seen in Figure 5.4.

Table A5.2.1 Media reporting on parliament and brawls

Media source	Number of articles mentioning parliament (nonbrawling)	Number of articles mentioning parliamentary brawling
Pro-Russian media		
Komsamolska Pravda	51	32
Fakty	57	23
Korrespondent	40	26
112UA	41	23
Pro-Ukraine media		
Obozrevatel	55	28
Cenzor	56	26
Unian	52	23
Espresso	12	5
Segodna	10	4
Ukrinform	8	4
Unclear orientation		
Liga	42	16
Ukrainska Pravda	24	12
Total	448	222

6
The Audience for Brawls

Armed with the evidence from Chapter 5 that signals are being passed to an intended audience through eager media transmission of individual brawling, we turn our attention to the audiences in question. Who is the audience to whom brawlers are attempting to signal? The answer is that it depends, though we can offer some general rules of thumb and interesting insights derived from our theory. The intended audience for a brawl depends on the strength of political parties and the institutional context, especially the electoral rules and the size of the legislature. When parties are strong, partisan actors are the intended audience for brawls. In most such systems, brawlers are trying to communicate with either party leaders or strong party supporters in the electorate. When parties are weak and legislators must rely on their own reputations and ability to garner resources, the main audiences for brawling are more likely to be nonpartisan actors: individuals who control financial resources (either licit or illicit) or narrow segments of the electorate who may support more contentious political tactics and/or may feel particularly strongly about a single issue. However, even in weak party systems, there are cases in which it makes sense to target party leaders. In either case, brawlers in both strong party systems and weak party systems are trying to signal that they are fighting the good fight.

One major challenge we have in providing empirical support for our expectations regarding the different audiences is that very few of our potentially receptive audiences are likely to identify as such. Given the general disapproval of brawling in electorates at large, party leadership is unlikely to explicitly acknowledge the utility of brawling, and citizens may have a strong enough sense of social desirability to be unwilling to openly profess an appreciation for brawling. Likewise, economic elites are unlikely to want to be seen as encouraging chaos in politics, and almost no one wants to publicly admit to a connection between violent events in the legislature and financial contributions to individual legislators.

Because we are unlikely to find meaningful evidence to evaluate our theory if we simply ask individuals whether they appreciate brawling or derive useful information from it, we must be particularly creative in our leveraging of empirical evidence regarding potential audiences. In this chapter, in addition to insights gleaned from media reports and our own interviews, we draw extensively on our previous research in which we conducted a panel survey before and after an actual brawl to see how people with different partisan orientations responded (Batto and Beaulieu 2020).

This chapter begins by arguing that brawlers are not communicating with median voters, either in their constituencies (if they are elected in single-member districts) or in the electorate as a whole. With respect to constituency communications, brawling is a crude communication tool that is not suitable for making the kinds of appeals that might appeal to a specific set of geographically concentrated voters. Further, brawls do not appeal to the general electorate. Here we present survey evidence demonstrating that most voters do not like brawling. If not the median voter either in constituencies or in the electorate as a whole, who is the target audience for brawling? In strong party systems in which many legislators do not have established reputations, the target audience will be party leaders. We use the cases of Mexico and South Korea to make this point. When legislators are already well known by party leaders, the intended audience will tend to be strong party supporters among the voting public. We demonstrate this using a panel survey before and after an actual brawl that shows how different citizens' reactions are shaped by their partisan attachments. For the target audience in weak party systems, we turn to Ukraine. Our interview evidence suggests that various brawlers were targeting party leaders, specific voting blocs, and economic elites.

Brawlers' Target Audience: NOT the General Electorate

Brawlers are not trying to communicate with the median voter either in their constituency or in the general electorate as a whole. On the one hand, brawling is a crude tool that is not well suited for the nuanced messages that might attract ordinary voters in individual districts. On the other hand, brawling is widely disliked. Public opinion data show that the general public does not approve of brawling, and many elites express the sentiment that brawling brings the disapproval of many citizens.

Brawling Is a Crude Tool for Political Communication

Brawls do not lend themselves to nuanced messages that legislators would want to craft to communicate directly with their constituency. We have argued that the most effective message is generally, "I will fight for you," where "you" can be defined in many different ways. It is not a message that the legislator supports a specific policy under specific conditions. However, appeals to the median voter in single-seat districts must be carefully crafted. For example, a legislator might want to call attention to specific issues that are relevant to that district. Given that most brawls revolve around either a partisan dispute between government and opposition or a personal dispute over character, brawls are rarely an ideal platform for individual legislators to express support for specific policies popular in their districts. At any rate, legislators have an array of superior tools for this sort of political communication, such as bringing home pork, performing constituency service, holding public forums, and publicly taking positions that align with district preferences.

Even for elections using closed list proportional representation, in which partisan positions might be critical, only a small proportion of votes for a major party will come from the narrow group of party leaders, party members, or extreme party supporters who might react enthusiastically to a purely partisan appeal. Most of the votes will come from voters who only have a mild preference for that party, and most of those voters will want to hear something that goes beyond a simple, blunt partisan appeal.

Therefore, we do not expect legislators to use brawling to broadcast a general message to their entire electorate, particularly legislators in single-member districts. At any rate, individual legislators usually need to do more than merely cultivate popularity with the electorate as a whole to be re-elected. Their future political careers depend heavily on the support of specific groups or individuals, and those critical groups or individuals are determined primarily by institutional factors such as electoral rules and the strength of parties.

Survey Evidence That Most Citizens Dislike Brawling

We have stated several times that most citizens generally dislike brawling, and this is a key assumption underlying our argument that brawling targets

Table 6.1 Reactions to brawling in Taiwan (1)

Question: "When there is a physical conflict in the legislature (such as occupying the podium, pushing and shoving, or fistfights), some people say that this shows that there is a serious problem with Taiwan's democratic system, but other people say that this is only a small problem with legislative procedures. Which of these statements do you agree with more?"

	Small problem	Serious problem
June 2016 telephone survey	41.6	58.4
June 2017 internet panel survey, wave 1	31.1	68.9
Strong KMT supporters	20.9	79.1
Moderate KMT supporters	25.8	74.2
Neutral	24.9	75.1
Moderate DPP supporters	36.6	63.4
Strong DPP supporters	48.8	51.2

specific audiences. There is plenty of anecdotal evidence for this. After most brawls, the most common reactions in mainstream media are horror, disgust, disdain, shame, condemnation, or condescension. Politicians who need to appeal to the broadest audiences, such as presidential candidates, usually try to distance themselves from brawling or even criticize it as shameful, undemocratic, or irrational. Here, we supplement this anecdotal evidence with survey data from Taiwan showing that ordinary citizens do not, in fact, like brawling.

We present results from two surveys.[1] In both surveys, we asked whether brawling was a serious problem or only a small problem. Solid majorities agreed that brawling constituted a serious problem for Taiwan's democracy (Table 6.1). Even larger majorities agreed that "forceful measures" should be used to deal with brawling (Table 6.2).

This dislike of brawling is not limited to any particular part of the political spectrum. Using the 2017 internet survey data, we classify attitudes toward the two main parties using thermometer scores, producing five groups of roughly similar size. Respondents were asked how much they liked the two main parties on a scale of 0 to 10. Those who liked the Kuomintang (KMT) at least four points more than they liked the Democratic Progressive Party (DPP) were considered strong KMT supporters, and those who liked the

Table 6.2 Reactions to brawling in Taiwan (2)

Question: "When there is a physical conflict in the legislature, some people think that the Speaker should use forceful measures (such as calling in the police) to maintain order. Do you agree with this?"

	Disagree	Agree
June 2016 telephone survey	27.0	73.0
June 2017 internet panel survey, wave 1	33.7	66.3
Strong KMT supporters	32.4	67.6
Moderate KMT supporters	22.0	78.0
Neutral	26.0	74.0
Moderate DPP supporters	40.9	59.1
Strong DPP supporters	50.0	50.0

KMT between one and three points more than the DPP were considered moderate KMT supporters. Strong and moderate DPP supporters were coded in the same way. Those who rated the two parties equally were considered neutral.[2] Three-fourths of neutral respondents thought that brawling indicated a serious problem for Taiwan's democracy, and this attitude was even more prevalent among strong KMT supporters. DPP supporters were somewhat less likely than other respondents to say that brawling was a serious problem. This difference probably reflects the DPP's frequent use of brawling during their decades in opposition. However, even among strong DPP supporters, as many people thought brawling was a serious problem as judged it only to be a small problem. KMT supporters were also more likely than DPP supporters to agree that brawls should be met with forceful measures. Interestingly, the moderates and neutrals supported this position even more than the strong partisans. At any rate, there is no part of the political spectrum that approves of brawling. Clearly, most Taiwanese citizens do not think that brawling is a good thing.

Another item illustrates the poignancy of these negative reactions. Respondents in the 2017 survey were asked how they felt when hearing of a brawl and provided with 14 statements, 7 positive and 7 negative. They were allowed to choose as many of these reactions as they felt appropriate (Table 6.3). For example, 85.9% chose the statement "The quality of our legislators is low," while only 0.9% chose "The quality of our legislators is

Table 6.3 Reactions to brawling in Taiwan (3)

Question: "What is your reaction when you hear about a physical fight in the legislature?"

	Positive sentiment	Negative sentiment
I feel (proud/ashamed) of my country.	2.8	59.0
Democracy (works well/doesn't work well) in my country.	4.5	65.5
The parties are (able/unable) to handle controversial issues.	7.0	72.8
The quality of our legislators is (high/low).	0.5	85.9
This (increases/decreases) my confidence in the Legislative Yuan.	3.1	65.9
Violent conflicts in the Legislative Yuan (resolve/create) polarization in society.	3.8	75.1
Democracy is (suitable/not suitable) for my country.	18.9	24.9

Note: Respondents were provided 14 statements, 7 positive and 7 negative. They were allowed to choose as many reactions as they agreed with.
Source: Wave 1 of internet panel survey, June 2017.

high." As this example suggests, respondents overwhelmingly ignored the positive sentiments, while large majorities agreed with 6 of the 7 negative sentiments. Brawls caused them to think that their representatives were lousy, to think that the legislature caused polarization, and to feel ashamed of their country. Notably, while brawls raised concerns that democracy was not working well, they did not bring them to conclude that democracy was unsuitable for the country. Overall, it is clear that the majority of citizens in Taiwan have a fairly strong dislike of brawling. Taiwan has experienced more legislative brawls over the past 35 years than any other country, so if citizens have become inured to brawling anywhere, it should be in Taiwan. Yet even here, we find that ordinary people still see it as a major defect in Taiwan's democratic regime and a source of national shame.

All in all, it is clear that brawls are not targeted at the entire electorate. Rather, they are targeted at narrower slices of the electorate, sometimes even specific individuals. This target audience depends on the strength of the party system and the institutional context. We should note that these two surveys were not conducted in the immediate aftermath of a brawl, so this expressed dislike of brawling should be thought of as a general or abstract dislike of brawling. As we will see, attitudes can change in concrete contexts.

The Target Audience When Parties Are Strong

Where parties are strong, we expect the intended audience of brawls to be partisan. Legislators use brawls as strategic signals to indicate their own resolve and to suggest to some audience that they are worthy of future support. Where parties hold the key to political futures, brawlers are signaling that they are literally willing to fight for the party and hoping those signals reach key members of their party. More specifically, the intended audience will be whichever group in the party wields a disproportionate influence over legislators' careers, whether this is party leaders, rank-and-file party members, or loyal party supporters in the electorate. Whatever the key audience, we should see evidence of them receiving the intended signal of brawling and responding in a way that suggests benefit to brawlers.

Party Leaders

For brawlers to want to target party leaders, two conditions must be met. Party leaders must have the power to shape legislators' career prospects, and they also must have insufficient information about the legislator to be unsure about whether they should try to promote his or her career. These considerations, in turn, depend on several institutional and contextual factors. The degree of power over career prospects depends on how much control the party leader has over the nomination process, whether the electoral rules make nomination effectively equivalent to election, or whether the partisan structure does the same thing by creating safe seats (Ferrara 2004; Jun and Hix 2010). The amount of information party leaders have about individual legislators depends on factors including the size of the legislature, whether re-election is permitted, and whether there is a robust system of local government.

Where parties are strong, and in electoral systems where party leaders control ballot access via proportional representation lists or a nomination process, we would expect that brawling legislators are trying to signal to party leadership. To evaluate this expectation, we briefly discuss the cases of Mexico and South Korea before looking more closely at Taiwan.

Mexico's experience is instructive. Mexico has had a strong three-party system for nearly 20 years (Kerevel 2015). The Institutional Revolutionary

Party (PRI) dominated the political system for several decades until 2000, while the other two major parties, the National Action Party (PAN) and Party of the Democratic Revolution (PRD) established themselves as credible opposition forces. Since 2000, each of the three main parties has won the presidency at least once.[3] Brawls are not common in the Mexican legislature—with the 2006 brawl following the disputed presidential election being the most significant recent example.

There are two reasons that the legislative experts we interviewed find the idea that participants in the 2006 brawl were trying to signal to party leadership to be plausible. On the one hand, three features of the electoral law gave party leaders an enormous amount of influence over legislators' political careers. First, until 2014 the federal constitution required political candidates to be affiliated with a party, giving leverage to party leadership. Second, 200 of the 500 seats in the chamber were elected by closed-list proportional representation, so obtaining one of these seats requires the support of the party leaders who put together these lists. Third, deputies could not stand for consecutive re-election prior to 2018. While nonconsecutive re-election was possible, only an average of 15.7% of legislators were re-elected after sitting out at least one term (Kerevel and Bárcena Juárez 2017). This meant that most deputies interested in continuing their political careers had to move into other political positions (Kerevel 2015). Many of these positions required the support of party leadership, a fact that research has shown deputies were sensitive to (Kerevel 2015). The joint effect of these rules was that Mexican party leaders had considerable influence over the careers of individual legislators.

On the other hand, Mexican party leaders did not always have ample information about each legislator. With 500 members, this was a relatively large chamber, so it was a challenge for party leaders to know all about each individual legislator. More importantly, the lack of re-election meant that each new term began with 500 individuals who had little to no prior reputation within the legislature. Thus, not only did deputies need political parties, but also party leaders' information about legislators within the chamber was compromised. As a result, information about the legislators was very useful to party leaders, giving legislators a strong incentive to use brawling to signal their type.

The story we gleaned from interviews with South Korean legislative experts is similar. As described in Chapter 2, Korea has a rich history of legislative brawling, especially during the first two decades of the democratic era.

During this period, a number of factors combined to suggest that brawlers should be primarily interested in signaling to party leaders.

While the parties frequently reorganize and rebrand themselves with new names, there have consistently been two main parties, a conservative party and a progressive party. Like Mexico, Korea has a mixed electoral system combining single-member plurality (SMP) and closed-list proportional representation, though a higher proportion of seats (currently 253 of 300) are elected in the SMP tier. As in Mexico, party leaders have quite a lot of influence over who sits in these seats. While re-election is allowed, winning re-election without the support of a major party is very difficult. Most seats outside the Seoul metro area are reliably safe seats for one party or the other. This means that securing the nomination from that party is usually both necessary and sufficient for re-election. However, party leaders have traditionally had nearly absolute freedom to nominate whomever they liked. In many cases, party leaders preferred fresh faces, since that might help their national party image. One might think that legislators with a powerful local presence might be difficult to bypass, but the extremely weak system of local governance—local governments were not elected at all prior to 1995—meant that very few politicians could rely on a powerful local base of support. The result of these factors left South Korean legislators in a similar situation as their Mexican counterparts. Their political careers were largely dependent on national party leaders. At the same time, since very few were able to establish an independent power base that might secure a lasting place in the political system, most of them were relatively unknown to those party leaders. Brawling—and the information it conveyed about them to the leaders—might help them avoid becoming a replaceable cog in the machine.

Although the idea of party leadership being the intended audience in strong party systems makes sense, it depends on leadership having sway over legislators' career prospects while also being sufficiently unfamiliar with those legislators that they might gain useful information from brawls. As these conditions are relaxed, however, we must consider another potential partisan audience: strong supporters of the party.

Strong Party Supporters

There are many reasons a party leader might not have the power to shape a legislator's career. Nominations might be decentralized. Re-election might be common, and there might be a norm that incumbents should be renominated. Legislators might do extensive constituency service or champion positions popular in their district and so develop a personal vote. A robust system of local government might allow some candidates to build up a trove of electoral resources even before entering the legislature. Whatever the reason, as the party leader's influence wanes, the sway of enthusiastic party supporters in the general electorate increases.

We can think of these strong party supporters as akin to Fenno's (1978) "inner circle," people who contribute more energy and enthusiasm as well as financial and organizational support to the party than the average voter. By virtue of these disproportionate contributions, extreme supporters also wield disproportionate clout relative to their numbers within the party. In different countries, the channels through which party loyalists exercise influence and the amount of influence they wield may vary, but die-hard party supporters are always disproportionately influential. In policy matters, if party loyalists hold different opinions than the rest of the electorate, legislators will often be tempted to cater to their most intense supporters (Cox 2009). Likewise, legislators seeking re-election will have strong incentives to curry favor with these strong party supporters.

Unlike party leaders, who may or may not have ample information about individual legislators, extreme partisans usually need information about their legislator's type. While they may be highly informed about national politics, party loyalists may not be so attuned to or concerned with local issues. When a legislator spends a great deal of time and energy maintaining a local power base, it is not unreasonable for extreme partisans to wonder if their legislator's priorities are in order. Does she care more about local development projects or the party's national agenda? Has he become so dedicated to serving the idiosyncratic needs of the district that he neglects the larger national partisan fight? In this environment, it can be very reassuring to loyal party supporters to receive a signal that the legislator is, in fact, committed to the party's ideals and is willing to fight for them.

Case Study: Strong Party Supporters' Reactions to a Brawl in Taiwan
In this section, we draw heavily from previously published research (Batto and Beaulieu 2020) to demonstrate that people with different partisan orientations reacted differently to a concrete brawl. Specifically, while most people reacted negatively, strong supporters of the opposition party—the party that instigated the brawl—reacted positively. We take

these findings as evidence of brawlers' intended audience—strong party supporters.

We conducted a three-wave internet panel survey before and after two special sessions of Taiwan's legislature in the summer of 2017. Wave 1 was collected before a special session of the legislature where there was no brawl; wave 2 was collected after that session; and wave 3 was collected after a second special session in which the legislature experienced a series of large-scale brawls that received considerable media attention. The first special session considered a reform of the pension system for public employees, a traditional KMT voting bloc. With such clear partisan interests on such a high-profile and politically difficult reform bill, we thought a brawl was quite likely. However, the KMT chose to resist through "civil" rather than "martial" means. After nearly two weeks of working until close to midnight each night, the legislature overcame the KMT's myriad dilatory tactics and passed these extremely contentious reforms. There was no physical conflict.

The second special session took up an infrastructure package. Construction projects are usually popular, but the KMT argued that this package was too expensive, the projects were too old-fashioned, and the details were inadequately documented. In private, the KMT worried that the DPP might be able to use this huge spending package to woo some of the KMT's local factions, which ran on a steady diet of patronage, over to their side. During the session, the KMT accused the DPP of several procedural violations, and brawling was a daily occurrence. Legislators threw punches, water balloons, chairs, and documents at each other. The KMT shouted slogans over megaphones and blew whistles, trying to make so much noise that it would be impossible to conduct regular business. In the end, the DPP passed the infrastructure bill in spite of the constant KMT disruptions.

We do not expect die-hard partisans supporting the majority and minority parties to respond the same way to brawls. Majority party supporters can look directly at the outcome—did their party pass the legislation or not?—to determine whether legislators have done a good job. If majority party legislators brawl, the signals they send can get noisy. They might be seen as stewards of the legislature—fighting to preserve order in the chamber so that the will of the majority might prevail. Alternatively, given that their party has the power to pass legislation, majority party brawlers might be seen as counterproductive and selfish grandstanders—interrupting a moment of critical legislative activity for their own self-aggrandizement. For minority partisans, the signal is much clearer. No one expects the minority party to pass its own legislation. The main question for minority party supporters, especially die-hard supporters, is whether the party fought hard enough. Brawls are a concrete manifestation of a minority legislator's sincerity and determination. Thus, we expect strong minority supporters to respond positively to partisan conflict, while the response of strong majority supporters will be more ambivalent.

The survey produced two types of evidence that strong partisans, especially those who support the opposition party, are different from everyone else. First, after the brawl, we asked people whether their evaluations had changed of various legislators who had and had not been active participants in the brawls. Not surprisingly, evaluations of the brawlers had declined much more than those of nonbrawlers. In fact, evaluations of nonbrawlers were only slightly lower, and, using the same five partisan categories detailed earlier in this chapter, there were only minor differences among respondents with different partisan orientations. However, there were significant differences in how people reacted to brawlers. As one might expect, neutral respondents and DPP partisans said they had a more negative view of KMT brawlers after the conflicts, and people who strongly preferred the DPP judged them even more harshly than moderate DPP supporters, who, in turn, were more critical than neutral respondents. The same pattern occurred for KMT partisans and DPP brawlers. However, we are more interested in what supporters of the brawlers' party think.

Strong KMT supporters said their evaluations of KMT brawlers had improved. This was the only combination of respondents and legislators being evaluated to record a positive impact from brawling. Moderate KMT supporters did not react negatively, but neither did they react positively. In fact, their reported net change was almost zero. On the DPP side, we expected supporters of the majority party to be less enthusiastic about brawlers, and that is what we found. Moderate DPP supporters said their opinions of DPP brawlers had gotten somewhat worse, though the magnitude of the change was smaller than that for neutral or KMT partisans. Strong DPP supporters claimed to have no change in their judgments of DPP brawlers. This was the best rating of the five groups for DPP brawlers, but it was clearly not as positive as evaluations of KMT brawlers by strong KMT partisans. Overall, strong partisans reacted more positively to brawlers from their preferred party than everyone else, and this pattern was clearer for strong supporters of the opposition party than of the majority party.

The second type of evidence came from the panel survey design and looked at changes in how well respondents thought the system was working. In each of the three waves, respondents were asked to rate the performance of the legislature and how well democracy was working in Taiwan. Please note that this was a panel survey, so the same exact set of respondents participated in all three waves. Any differences among the three waves came from individual respondents giving different answers after seeing recent events.

After the first special session, in which the legislature had successfully dealt with a thorny issue without any physical conflict, average evaluations of the legislature's performance and democracy in general both went up. After the second special session, which was marked by continual chaos and repeated brawling, average evaluations of both went down. More importantly, this pattern was observed in four of the five partisan groups. However, strong KMT supporters were different from everyone else. Their evaluations went down after the first special session and up after the second special session. That is, unlike everyone else, strong KMT partisans thought the democratic system and the legislature in particular were performing worse when KMT legislators didn't brawl and better when they did. To put it another way, this group was notably cheered by brawling. They may not have had the votes to stop the government's (lousy) policies, but at least *someone* was fighting for the "correct" positions.

Thus, this case provides clear evidence that, in a political system with strong parties, brawlers, particularly those from opposition parties, are, in fact, sending signals to the more extreme partisan supporters. In the aftermath of this concrete brawl, that target audience reacted to the brawling signal as expected: they responded positively to the brawl and judged the brawlers from their party more favorably.

The Target Audience When Parties Are Weak

Weaker parties do not dominate politics in the same way as stronger parties. They do not define political disputes, shape careers, or command the loyalties of large portions of the electorate for long periods of time. Instead, politicians are left to fend for themselves. These differences inevitably lead legislators in weak party systems to target different audiences when they brawl, something we see quite clearly in Ukraine.

For example, without large blocs of voters with solid, long-term party identities, it makes less sense to target strong party supporters the way that Taiwanese brawlers do. Indeed, the identities of the most prolific Ukrainian brawlers does not suggest that most brawls are waged for the benefit of extreme supporters of the opposition party. None of the most prominent brawlers in this era of Ukrainian politics hail from the main opposition bloc. They are either independents (Parasyuk) or from small opposition parties (Liashko and Soboliev). No one appears to be brawling in an attempt to appeal to supporters of mainstream opposition parties.

In stronger party systems, almost all brawlers in a given country target the same audience. In Mexico and South Korea, they target party leaders. In Taiwan, it is strong party supporters. In weaker party systems where legislators have to fend for themselves, different people will see different opportunities and target different audiences. We propose that Ukrainian brawlers are generally trying to appeal to one of three target audiences: party leaders, unaligned voting blocs, or economic elites.

Party Leaders

It might seem unexpected that brawlers would target the leaders of weak parties. Indeed, our interviews with political elites in Ukraine suggest that brawling is usually aimed elsewhere. Even if they are amenable to a brawling signal, Ukrainian party leaders usually do not have the combination of attractive political resources and insufficient information that we saw in Mexico and South Korea. For example, one of the prominent brawlers (Liashko) is actually the leader of a small opposition party that carries his name. As the party leader and the brawler, he presumably could not glean any new information about himself by brawling. His action must have been aimed elsewhere. Another prominent brawler, Parasyuk, who was generally reluctant to speculate about others' motivations for brawling, conceded that neither leadership from government (parties of the president and prime minister) nor large opposition parties, such as Timoshenko's Fatherland, wanted to see brawling.[4] A legislator hoping to impress party leaders would hardly be likely to try to send a signal of being a loyal party member by doing the thing that party leaders hoped to avoid. Again, the audience of brawlers must typically lie elsewhere.

If most brawls target different audiences, there may nonetheless be some cases in which the target audience is, in fact, the party leadership. As in Mexico and South Korea, if the party leaders do not know much about their members and also have control over key party resources, both legislator and leader might benefit from a brawling signal. A closer look at the experience of one party, Self-Reliance, illustrates how this might work.

Self-Reliance was a distinctive opposition party during the 8th convocation of the Verkhovna Rada. As an opposition party, it was not an ally of the main government parties, but it was also often at odds with Fatherland, the main opposition party. Self-Reliance featured leadership primarily from the Lviv area of Western Ukraine, but it had enlarged itself, as Ukrainian parties often do, by convincing other successful politicians and parties to join forces. One consequence of this hasty recruitment process was that party members did not know each other very well. Party leadership describes the party's entry into the legislature as "the faction of members that have never met before," because only two people on their party list had been members of Self-Reliance prior to this election. All the others were courted to join the party. Leaders describe the process in the following way: "we were open to making the list, because it was after the revolution. And most of the people I had never met before."[5]

In this context in which party leaders lacked even basic information about their party members, some credible information about a legislator's type would have been welcome to them. However, while party leaders might have welcomed the information, this leaves the question of why legislators would want to bear the cost of sending a signal. What did Self-Reliance leaders have that rank-and-file legislators wanted? Most obviously, they controlled spots on the party list. At the time we interviewed the leadership, the party had 26 members, 2 of whom were from districts and the rest from their party list. Less obviously, Self-Reliance was a relatively disciplined party, and its legislators, who presumably did not wish to be sanctioned, would have wanted to stay on good terms with party leaders. There was a vivid example of this discipline shortly before our interview with party leadership. The leaders identified four issue-areas where they expected members to vote a particular way, and the party had recently expelled members for violating one of these stances. The willingness of the Self-Reliance leadership to kick out members is unusual in a system where party switching is rampant and parties typically try to hold onto members. However, when circumstances arose regarding two of the core issues for Self-Reliance (war with Russia and constitutional changes), they were willing to sanction noncompliant party members. Thus, in this very specific example, legislators in Self-Reliance might have had an incentive to engage in brawls to communicate their type to party leaders. Indeed, the most prominent Self-Reliance brawler, Yehor Soboliev, observed that he was involved in physical confrontations "early on" during the legislative session when he was relatively unknown to the party leaders.

If Self-Reliance legislators brawled to communicate with party leaders early in the term, that soon ceased to be a plausible explanation. Self-Reliance leaders quickly learned enough about their members that they no longer needed new information. Self-Reliance institutionalized frequent, regular party meetings. Party members met three times per week during legislative sessions and once a week when in recess. These meetings were important, not only because they promoted party discipline by allowing members to hash out disagreements and giving the leadership an opportunity to persuade recalcitrant members, but also because over time they allowed party leadership to come to know party members very well. After three years of regular party meetings, when asked whether his party members would surprise him with their words or actions on the floor of the legislature, a party leader had this to say: "No. Usually I know everything before the floor. I know the feelings of people."[6] Increased familiarity between leaders and backbenchers had thus removed one potential incentive for brawling.

Unaligned Voting Blocs

If not party leaders, who are Ukrainian brawlers targeting? One likely target is unaligned voting blocs that care intensely about specific issues. In Ukraine, one such group is often labeled radicals. Indeed, one prominent brawler from this era who was presumably courting radicals in the electorate was Liashko, the leader of the Liashko Radical Party.

For a fuller story, we again turn to Soboliev, the prominent Self-Reliance brawler. Soboliev acknowledged that brawls produce a backlash from many citizens (including his own wife!). However, he also believed they might help you "get some support." When asked who might or might not appreciate brawling, he replied, "Radicals will allow you, but many people will ask themselves: is this about democracy, is this a good way to resolve problems?"[7] Soboliev had a very clear and specific understanding of his target audience. When asked if it was potentially less sophisticated Ukrainians who appreciated brawling, or possibly individuals from more rural parts of Ukraine, he responded, "No. I think it is radicals. Not only here. It's about people around the world that use violence with much more skills."[8] When asked to further clarify what he meant by the term "radicals," he had this to say:

> This is not about political division. Usually, such people oppose actions of the government, police, officials. . . . They are not against certain people or professions, or the state. They are strongly against some very serious actions like changing the constitution because of Russian pressure, reducing the money paid for the army, or reviving trade with occupied territories. So it's something that's very important that can raise this radicalism among some categories of the citizens.[9]

Soboliev's target audience was thus intensely concerned about specific issues though largely nonpartisan. They were not merely willing to forgive violence; they understood it as a tool to be used with skill. As a result, he thought brawling might gain him some support from these radicals. Moreover, entering the legislature as he did, having previously been a journalist with no real political experience, he would have needed some way to establish a reputation with these voters. His involvement in the Euromaidan protests may have inspired his choice to appeal to radicals with brawling, but it would not have been sufficient to make his reputation, as we repeatedly heard from experts and legislators that many of the new parliamentarians from the 2014 election had been associated with the events of the Euromaidan. Soboliev, however, seemed determined to work in a contentious vein. Beyond his brawling, Soboliev courted the radical vote by staging high-profile protests and confrontational actions. In one instance, he and a group of supporters camped outside the legislature, in the harsh Kyiv winter, for 137 days to protest the fact that the government was not bringing anticorruption legislation to the floor for a vote.[10] In another instance he worked with citizens to implement a physical blockade of railroad lines when the government decided to re-establish trade with Russia, against the wishes of many.

Here, then, we see a new legislator, with a need to build a reputation, brawling. Further, this individual's own insights, coupled with his other actions while in office, indicate that he was very clearly targeting a segment of the electorate we might characterize as radicals. And he had evidence to suggest that they were receiving his message. Recall that during our interview, he shared with us several graphics that had been created and launched as internet memes by his supporters.[11]

Economic Elites

Nonpartisan individuals in the electorate who hold extreme views are not the only potential audience in a weak party system. Given the perennial need for resources to mount effective campaigns, economic elites who control such resources are another potential audience. Influential economic actors who use their resources to influence politics can be found in every country in the world. This economic influence is particularly powerful in weak party systems where the connection between economic elites and elected representatives is arguably more direct and less likely to be filtered through strong political parties. In Ukraine, these individuals are known as oligarchs and are seen as influential to the point of perpetuating corruption in Ukrainian politics.

A Self-Reliance party leader described the influence the oligarchs had over the legislature and Ukrainian politics more generally:

> Most of the decisions for most of the people are made outside of the Rada and not by its members. I called them owners of the parliament. They are oligarchs. You know their names. More than 2/3 of these people [legislators] depend on those decisions [oligarch preferences]. Sometimes they make fantastic presentations, but we know this is not their thoughts. . . . For example, if somebody has a perfect emotional presentation, but we know it's not the presentation of their own, we are not listening to it, we are talking or doing something like that. And sometimes somebody speaks very softly, but we listen to them. It's not many such [truly independent] people in the Rada. It's used to be more 4 years (ago), like 100 people. Now it's down to 60. . . . Unfortunately, the majority is owned by oligarchs, but even those people who are dependent now, they still have that feeling that they are in there thanks to the revolution.[12]

This description mentions several widely held impressions. First, more than half of elected representatives in Ukraine's parliament are understood to be dependent on oligarchs and are essentially doing their bidding in the legislature. Second, these individuals who are working on behalf of an oligarch tend to put on fantastic displays in support of their oligarch's preferred policies, while truly independent and sincere actors in Ukrainian politics, those not catering to oligarchs, are more likely to present their arguments in a quieter, more understated manner. Finally, even many of the new legislators who were associated with the Euromaidan protests and are attempting to build a political reputation around this involvement and its associated priorities are still actually owned by oligarchs.

> It's not a matter of new faces. It's a matter of owners. A lot of the new faces have the same owners. Their owners are very smart, because they know how to get in there. They spend a lot of money for the social desire to have those new people. Sometimes those very new people, very smart ones, I'd say, they are spoiling that new novelty. People say: "Oh, they are new people." But they are not new, they are worse than new, because they are very old and performing in the sake of those very old killing instruments. . . . This is the circle of oligarchs. 7 to 10, doesn't matter how many of them. For 20 years they have been running the state without any alternative . . . the two revolutions [Orange and Euromaidan] . . . I don't call them revolutions. I call them uprisings. Because a revolution must always end with the power change. But the power [that emerged following each "revolution"] was from the same circle.[13]

The Self-Reliance leadership was not unique in its perspective that oligarchs have an effective stranglehold on Ukrainian politics and that, in fact, most legislators are behaving in ways they hope will impress these economic elites. Ukrainian legislative staff not only corroborated the idea that legislators might make showy displays in favor of policies that their oligarchs prefer but also additionally suggested that sometimes it may be the brawl itself that oligarchs want. There are certain issues that oligarchs recognize as important to people in their geographic area of influence. For example, maintenance of the Russian language is important to voters in the East, so oligarchs from this area will want the legislators they control to take a stance on this issue to placate people in the territory the oligarch controls. Thus, a legislator that seeks to curry favor with an oligarch might opt to get involved in one of the many brawls over language to occur in Ukraine to signal they are taking appropriate action. The second benefit of brawling for oligarchs highlighted by this staff member, however, is that they can cause a distraction to divert attention from other bills coming to the floor in which oligarchs might have a vested interest but not want too much voter attention. This individual went so far as to say that on days that brawls break out, she and her staff colleagues review the rest of the legislative docket and often feel they can determine the legislation that brawlers were hoping to distract from, in service to an oligarch.[14]

Whether the brawler is putting on an ostentatious display to draw attention to an issue that the oligarch wants to highlight or to divert attention away from an issue the oligarch would prefer to be obscured, the brawler is trying to convince the oligarch that he or she will work for the oligarch's interests.

The Target Audience in Brawls about Honor

Honor brawls generally follow the same broad script. One legislator makes a statement that another legislator takes offense to, and the latter responds violently. These two actors have different strategic considerations, so we must consider them separately.

Accusers are not always trying to instigate conflict. Sometimes they make what might seem like a relatively mild statement that the accused chooses to interpret as incendiary. More often, accusers know they are making a pointed statement and daring the accused to respond. Depending on the context and accusation, this will generally help the accuser appeal to some target audience, such as a bloc of nonpartisan voters who care intensely about corruption, sexism, good governance, organized crime, abuse of alcohol, or some other issue. If the attack is made in a partisan context with a partisan goal in mind, the target audience might also be partisan supporters. The stronger the response from the accused, the more the accuser looks like a champion of the cause. If the accused responds violently, so much the better. In some cases, the accuser goads the other legislator so much that it looks like the accuser is trying to instigate a brawl. As long as the accuser is confident the general public or, worse, the target audience won't think the attack is unreasonable, the main risk is physical. Getting punched, or hit with a water bottle in Oleksandra Kuzhel's case, can hurt.

The accused has different concerns. The attack is an accusation that the legislator has other priorities—sex, money, leisure, and so on—other than the interests of the voters. It says that this legislator is *not* fighting for you. A violent response to an accusation sends a message that the accused legislator is extremely offended by an unjustified accusation and wants to demonstrate in the most visceral way possible that the accusation is false and repugnant. He absolutely *is* fighting for you, and this malicious slander cannot be allowed to stand. In this sense, the accused is following the same strategies and appealing to the same target audiences as brawlers in disruption brawls, whether they be in strong or weak party systems.

However, refuting the charge is not always the purpose of an accused legislator in an honor brawl. Sometimes the legislator is influential precisely because he is corrupt or has ties with organized crime. The accusation is merely bringing an unspoken but widely understood truth out into the open. The accused legislator cannot countenance this accusation not because it is false, but because it is disrespectful and allowing it to stand unchallenged would signal weakness to all his rivals. By responding violently, the accused legislator is sending a message to rivals that he is not weak and to other legislators to think twice about disrespecting him in the future.

These various logics are illustrated quite nicely by a pair of honor brawls featuring KMT legislator Lin Ming-yi in Taiwan in the mid-1990s. The first occurred in July 1995, when DPP legislator Huang Chao-hui sarcastically commented that attendance was extremely good in the KMT caucus that day, including many faces he didn't even recognize. This was obviously because, Huang explained, the KMT was currently deciding nominations for the year-end election. When Lin charged to the front of the chamber to protest, Huang said, "You are Lin Ming-yi. I recognize you," and then added that Lin's protests were a bit insincere. Lin responded by punching Huang several times in the head before he was pulled away by other legislators. After the incident, Lin complained that the DPP was constantly smearing and slandering, and he couldn't stand this "verbal violence" any longer. He apologized to the legislature and the general public for his behavior, but he pointedly did not apologize to Huang or the DPP (Yin 1995a, 1995b).

Huang's charge, that many KMT legislators were too busy with their own matters to bother with legislative business, was a standard DPP attack, and he probably didn't expect anything to come of it. It was not directed against Lin personally, something that Huang emphasized by pointing out that he recognized Lin. However, Lin took it upon himself to defend the honor of the party. KMT members did not think they were lazy or shirking their duties. They thought they were working hard doing constituency service back in their districts and quietly arranging various matters in the capitol rather than wasting their time making superficial speeches in the legislature. Lin's violent response and subsequent explanation was an attempt to tell KMT supporters, including many of his own voters, that the DPP attack was baseless and unreasonable. KMT legislators were, in fact, working hard for them. In addition, Lin was also telling strong KMT supporters that he would fight for the party. This was useful information for many KMT sympathizers since Lin, who was not a university graduate, did not have a reputation as a sophisticated thinker with a deep ideological commitment to the KMT. While this was an honor brawl, the underlying logic is surprisingly similar to that of a disruption brawl.

The second incident took place a year later in October 1996. DPP legislator Su Huan-chih held up a sign saying, "If you don't arrest Lin Ming-yi, the campaign against organized crime is fake" and explained that 10 years prior "Little Lin" had been implicated in a murder case. After Su's speech, Lin immediately went to the microphone to defend himself. He called Su base and despicable, and Su yelled back from his desk that Lin was a murderer. The furious Lin marched through the chamber over to Lin and punched him several times in the head. Afterward Lin admitted that he had probably overreacted, but when Su had "attacked" him with "verbal violence" he couldn't stand it and lost control (Lu 1996).

In this instance, the conflict was consciously instigated by the accuser. Su chose to raise the topic of organized crime, he deliberately singled out Lin Ming-yi as a gangster, he gratuitously insulted him as "Little Lin," and then he heckled Lin from the floor. Su could hardly have done more to provoke a conflict. We can identify at least three motives for Su's actions. First, since he could be sure the KMT government wasn't about to arrest Lin, he could make a partisan argument that the current high-profile campaign against organized crime was a sham. Second, by personally facing down Lin, he could present himself as a champion of the fight against organized crime. Third, just the previous day, Su and Lin had physically clashed during a committee hearing over a proposed industrial park. By discrediting Lin as a gangster, Su might help his chances of winning a policy fight. Thus, Su was potentially simultaneously appealing to three target audiences: partisan DPP supporters, people opposed to organized crime, and environmentalists who wanted to block the industrial park.

Lin was accused of being a gangster, and he reacted passionately and violently. He could hardly have done more to convince people that the charge was warranted. This suggests that refuting the charge was not his top priority. A more reasonable explanation is that Lin wanted to project strength, or at least avoid looking weak, by punishing this brazenly disrespectful personal attack in the most visceral manner possible.

One final point to note about these two incidents is how violent they were. In most Taiwanese brawls, the violence is rather mild. Even when punches are thrown, they usually do not have much malice behind them. Brawling tends to be more ritualistic than vicious. That was not the case in these two brawls. Lin punched both Huang and Su directly in the head with all the force he could muster. Videos show both with a dazed look after the first punch, like they have just suffered a concussion, whereupon Lin punches them a few more times before he is dragged away. Participants in brawls often go to the hospital, but this is usually part of the show. Huang and Su also went to the hospital, but they genuinely seemed to need medical attention. One of the potential costs of inciting an honor brawl by questioning another legislator's character is physical harm, and Lin made sure that both Huang and Su paid a heavy price.

Conclusion

In this chapter we have addressed our theoretical expectations around intended audiences for brawling and how those audiences vary depending on particular brawling contexts. Common to both strong and weak party settings is the potential to find receptive audiences for brawls either among elites or narrow segments of the citizenry. Our evidence from Taiwan shows clearly that people with strong partisan preferences respond favorably to brawls and approve of the legislators who brawl, even as they continue to profess disapproval of brawling. Interviews from Ukraine show us the parallel audience in an electorate with weak parties, the so-called radicals. In both strong and weak party systems there are also indications of receptive elite audiences. Experts agree that party leadership was likely receptive to brawling behavior in Mexico and South Korea, for example. In Ukraine there is widespread agreement on the influence of nonpartisan oligarchs in politics and some indication that these oligarchs appreciate brawling, either around specific issues or as a more general distraction to be able to push through favored legislation with less oversight.

It is worth noting that none of the target audiences are unsophisticated simpletons who just want to see someone getting beat up. People with strong political opinions, whether partisan or not, tend to be highly engaged and informed. It goes without saying that party leaders and economic elites tend to be well educated and politically very sophisticated. Legislators brawl because they think these target audiences, the elites and opinion leaders in society, will be receptive to that behavior.

What continues to be striking around all of this discussion of various audiences for brawling is the clear evidence that most citizens do not appreciate brawling. Thus, we must confront the fact that in addition to any normative objections we might have to brawling as decreasing civility in democratic politics and delaying the policymaking process, we should recognize the damage it does to democratic representation more generally. As brawling legislators do their best to reach very narrow segments of the electorate or a small handful of influential elites, they are ignoring the representational needs of the broader citizenry and alienating them from the democratic process, causing their confidence in the legislature to decline.

7
Brawling and Re-election

Legislators instigate and participate in brawls because they make strategic calculations that doing so will yield political advantages. The most important consideration for most legislators is re-election. We have traced out the process, examining which legislators brawl, how brawls are reported in the media, and how brawls are received by the audiences that brawlers are trying to communicate with. In this chapter, we follow though the chain of logic to ask: Do brawlers actually reap political rewards? Are brawlers more likely to win re-election?

Consider, for example, Oleh Liashko, leader of the Radical Party in Ukraine. Liashko's reputation as a brawler is credited as helping win not just a seat for himself but also for 13 other people on the list of the political party he led. Profiled on the eve of 2014 legislative elections in the *New York Times*, brawling appears to have earned Liashko and his Radical Party a number of legislative seats. By contrast, we can look at Wang Shu-hui, whose story started this book. Her flamboyant actions on behalf of the Democratic Progressive Party (DPP) did not insulate her against a Kuomintang (KMT) wave in the next election, and she lost her race decisively.

In fact, we do not expect to see an unambiguous pattern in which brawlers always reap enormous benefits. There is a fundamental tension embedded inside the logic of brawling. It has the potential to convey political benefits. At the same time, most voters dislike it, so it also has the potential to produce a negative backlash. Strategic brawlers must tread very carefully, since there is always a danger that the risks will outweigh the rewards. There is a reason that legislators pick their brawls very carefully instead of constantly brawling all the time. Furthermore, when considering who is most motivated to brawl—those most in need of a reputational boost—we must acknowledge that these same individuals are likely to face more challenges in getting re-elected, and any advantages accrued from brawling may simply not be sufficient to secure career advancement.

This chapter finds that, under some circumstances, there can be a moderate electoral reward to brawling. Brawlers are re-elected at somewhat

Making Punches Count. Nathan F. Batto and Emily Beaulieu, Oxford University Press.
© Oxford University Press 2024. DOI: 10.1093/oso/9780197744420.003.0007

higher rates than nonbrawlers, and a more detailed examination of this relationship in different contexts yields results consistent with many of our theoretical expectations. However, we also find that there are many cases in which brawling does not pay off. On balance, brawlers tend to benefit more often than not, but brawling is by no means a magic bullet guaranteeing electoral success.

Theoretical Connections between Brawling and Electoral Outcomes

The central argument of this book is that strategic politicians see brawling as a tool to advance their careers. That is, brawling helps a legislator meet the challenges of democratic competition by sending costly signals to key audiences that the legislator is worth the support of the target audience because he or she is literally fighting for them. Since re-election is generally considered most legislators' goal, if we are correct about the strategic signaling nature of brawling, we should expect to see brawlers reaping concrete electoral rewards. Put simply, if brawling legislators are correct in their anticipation that signaling to specific audiences via brawling will help their careers, then we should expect to see brawling legislators improve their career prospects. For many legislators this will mean re-election, though we can also consider career advancement in legislatures where re-election was not an option, such as Mexico's Chamber of Deputies at the time of its multiday 2006 legislative brawl. Recall the prominent brawling National Action Party deputy—Francisco Dominguez Servien. He subsequently became governor of Queretaro.[1] Thus, we expect to see brawlers political careers advancing in some fashion. Before looking at the empirical record to evaluate our theoretical expectations, however, we should consider briefly some of the complications in identifying the causal relationship between brawling and re-election.

As we have indicated since the start of this book, the fundamental problem with brawling is that most voters hate it. We have shown in previous chapters that while extreme party supporters and certain narrow segments of the electorate may react positively to brawling, most ordinary citizens do not. Unfortunately for brawlers, democratic competition requires legislators to secure support from large numbers of voters, sometimes as large as pluralities or majorities. If those potential supporters react to brawls with shock, horror, disgust, distaste, or shame, brawling may lead to bad electoral outcomes. Legislators thus have to walk a very fine line when deciding whether to brawl or not. They should only brawl when they calculate that the rewards from the target audience will outweigh the backlash from the general public. These sorts of cost-benefit analyses are at the heart of legislative behavior. Representatives weigh these types of tradeoffs every time they cast a difficult vote, decide whether to endorse a presidential candidate, or show public support for a controversial social group. Legislators are experienced at judging how their target audiences and the wider public will react to a brawl and adjusting their behavior accordingly.

However, some legislators will inevitably misjudge the situation. It is not always easy to predict how the public will react to events. For example, the public disgust with a brawl may be more intense than expected. Alternatively, the brawler might make a mistake about some other part of the causal chain. For example, if a legislator instigates a brawl on behalf of a corrupt patron, that patron might not provide as much compensation as expected, or the money might not be as potent in the election as anticipated.

Moreover, some legislators do not have much time to make these difficult decisions. While the instigators of disruption may have time to carefully weigh the costs and benefits, legislators who were not privy to the initial planning may need to decide in the moment. With almost no time to think through their assumptions or confer with staff or advisors, they may overlook some important factor and plunge into the middle of a disastrous brawl. Those who overestimate the potential rewards or underestimate the potential costs may even find brawling to be a barrier, not a boon, to re-election.

Not all brawlers get involved because they see a potential electoral payoff. While we believe that the instigator almost always sees some potential political benefit, other legislators may be involved for other reasons. If, for example, a legislator decides it is a good idea to randomly punch a colleague, the latter can find themselves embroiled in a brawl against their will. More commonly, if opposition legislators start a brawl to try to stop the majority party from ramming through some agenda item, the majority legislators can find themselves needing to choose between engaging in a brawl or abandoning their political agenda. They might not think their supporters will approve of brawling, but they might also believe that their supporters will be furious if the ineffectual majority party fails to pass its agenda. Some legislators will see brawling as the least bad of several terrible options. There are other cases in which a brawl benefits a wealthy patron or helps consolidate a place in an organized crime hierarchy, and these brawlers might be more concerned with venal rewards than electoral consequences.

Another confounding factor involves the type of legislator who brawls. In Chapter 4, we found that brawlers are not simply a random selection of legislators. Instead, brawlers tend to be younger and junior legislators who need to build their reputations. To put it another way, these are likely to be electorally vulnerable politicians trying to use brawling to shore up a weakness. As such, there is a theoretical reason to believe that, absent brawling, the group of legislators coded as brawlers should be less likely to win re-election. If, in the real world, brawlers do not outperform nonbrawlers, this does not necessarily mean that brawling did not help their electoral prospects.

Finally, it is important to remember that voters rarely see elections purely as a referendum on brawling. There are many different reasons that voters choose to vote one way or another. They might want a specific tax, social welfare, or education policy. They may wish to express solidarity with a religious, linguistic, regional, or partisan identity. They may be concerned with national security or democratic reform. They may find a specific candidate to be more affable, inspirational, or energetic than others. An incumbent's behavior in a legislative showdown several months or years before the election may or may not be an important consideration, but it will almost never be the only consideration.

Brawling is a relatively rare event. Even in systems with chronic brawling, legislators usually prefer a peaceful legislative process. Most of the time, legislators understand brawling to be a bad choice. On the whole, we expect that strategic legislators will only enter these treacherous waters if they are confident they can successfully navigate them, and, more often than not, they will be correct. However, treacherous waters sometimes cause shipwrecks, and we do not expect to find that brawling is an unambiguously successful electoral strategy.

Anecdotal Evidence from Ukraine

Ukraine offers a striking example of just how murky the connection between brawling and re-election can be. Most brawlers from Ukraine's 8th convocation of parliament were not re-elected. Legislators who did not brawl in the 8th convocation of parliament were also mostly not re-elected. In fact, in the 2019 parliamentary elections in Ukraine, just after the election of former comedian Zelensky as president, approximately 80% of parliamentarians were not re-elected. It is also not the case that taking a strong stance against brawling was obviously rewarded or penalized. Parliamentarians who did not brawl and were not re-elected included both those who vocally opposed brawling (Oksana Urnets of the Klitschko fraction, for example) and those who were prominent and active in parliament in more conventional ways (Oleg Bereziuk, who was part of the leadership of Self-Reliance). In fact, a review of the electoral fortunes of many parliamentarians from the 8th convocation, including those identified in Chapter 5, shows no positive impact of brawling on re-election and no clear pattern to electoral success more generally.

None of the most prominent brawlers were-re-elected. Recall Andriy Teteruk who was reported to have attacked long-time parliamentarian Oleksandra Kuzhel in a committee session, causing her political party—Fatherland—to threaten a boycott of parliament (Farangis 2015). Teteruk ran for re-election on his party's list, but his party failed to win any seats. Kuzhel, who had been in parliament since the Kuchma era, likewise failed to be re-elected. Although her Fatherland Party won 26 seats in 2019, Kuzhel was not high enough on the list to be seated.

Noted brawler Oleh Liashko had led his Radical Party to a successful result in the 2014 election, but 2019 was not so kind to him or his party. After winning 14 seats in 2014, the Radical Party was unable to win even a single seat in 2019, so Liashko and fellow party member Serhiy Melnychuck, who had brawled several times during the 8th convocation, were both denied re-election.

Volodymyr Parasyuk, who spent the 8th convocation developing a reputation for brawling, did not even qualify for the ballot. He attempted to run for re-election, but he was barred due to questions about where the funds for his filing fees had come from.

Finally, Yehor Soboliev, who ended up not even running for re-election, is an interesting case study. Recall from Chapter 4 that Soboliev was a new member of Ukraine's parliament in 2014, and a very prominent brawler in this legislative era. Between his regular legislative activities, his brawling, and his continued protest activities outside of parliament, Soboliev was clearly ambitious. He aspired to be part of government in the future, saying:

> I'll be very unhappy to be in the next parliament in the same position as the chairman of a committee and a representative of the 4th fraction. I think

> we should make the majority or it is better not to be elected at all for the next convocation, because we should show people the difference, that we are serious.... So a better choice is to become the power, government. The second choice is not to be in the parliament at all. To be in the same position I would say is the third one, the most problematic choice now.[2]

And although he clearly desired a continued career in parliament, this was only attractive to him if he could lead a block of legislators in the governing majority. He was not interested in a career either in the opposition or as the parochial representative of a solitary single-member district.

> I think the representative of a district is a completely ineffective position without big influence ... politics is about strong teams. We should form strong teams. I should play an effective role in it. This is my ambition. But simply being in the parliament representing one district without any support from other MPs, it is very gloomy future.[3]

Soboliev himself appreciated that brawling was not guaranteed to produce career success.

> This is a risky strategy. I think it depends on political, national culture, but my experience is that I had strong physical clashes in this parliament at the beginning. And there are people who support me and people who think.... Radicals will allow you, but many people will ask themselves: is this about democracy, is this a good way to resolve problems? Even my wife criticized me for this.[4]

Ultimately, Soboliev decided not to run for re-election. His party, Self-Reliance, was roundly trounced at the polls, going from a fraction of 32 list and district members to a single district seat in the next election.

Soboliev's case illustrates the limitations of brawling as an electoral strategy. He had ambition and a clear message. He had gotten into physical conflicts early in his tenure and started to establish a reputation, successfully communicating a signal about himself to his target audience. However, his words suggest that, in retrospect, he suspects plunging into brawls may have been a mistake. He worried that too many ordinary voters had—like his wife—reacted negatively, and the costs may have outweighed the benefits. Another problem was that Soboliev did not have a solid political base to start with. In the absence of a solid personal vote or a reliable party support base, Soboliev was trying to cultivate support from a fickle bloc of voters with radical sympathies who had plenty of other options. Neither Soboliev personally nor Self-Reliance collectively was able to attract a large enough and stable enough voting bloc to satisfy Soboliev's political ambitions. The signal from a few brawls was nowhere near powerful enough to overcome these basic weaknesses. In the end, Soboliev gave up politics and went to work for an IT startup where he hoped he might be able to fight corruption through data mining (Tymoshchuk 2020).

It would be misleading, however, to present this consistent pattern of electoral defeat for brawlers as proof that brawling harmed Ukrainian legislators' electoral prospects. Many very prominent legislators who never brawled were also not re-elected. Ivan Rybak and Viktor Chumak, both part of President Poroshenko's bloc, failed to win re-election, though Chumak had left the Poroshenko bloc prior to the 2019 elections and was subsequently appointed deputy prosecutor general for the country.

Among individuals *not* known for brawling, losses accrued to members on party lists and in single-member districts alike: Ihor Moisychuck was elected as part of Liashko's Radical Party in 2014, and although he did not develop a reputation for brawling during his time in parliament, the party did not win any seats in 2019, so just like his brawling copartisans, he was not returned. Similarly, Soboliev was far from the only casualty of Self-Reliance's collapse. When the party failed to meet the threshold in 2019, even party leader Oleg Bereziuk lost. Mkihyalo Dobkin had had an extensive and successful political career. He had been elected to parliament in the early 2000s, had subsequently been mayor of Kharkiv, and then was elected to parliament again in 2014. Unfortunately, his party failed to meet the threshold in 2019, so his re-election bid failed. It was not merely a problem of being tied to an unpopular party list. Prominent nonbrawling incumbents elected from single-member districts such as Volodymir Litvin, Maksym Burbak, and Dmytro Yarosh lost as well.

Not everyone lost in 2019, and two of the winners were legislators we identified in Chapter 5 as less prominent brawlers. Viktoria Siumar had been elected in 2014 on the party list of the People's Front, a party aligned with then-president Poroshenko, and was re-elected in 2019 on the party list of European Solidarity, a newly formed but similarly oriented party. Vadim Rabinovich, who had registered as a candidate for the 2014 presidential race and then won a parliamentary seat on the pro-Russia Opposition Bloc party list, was re-elected at the top of the Opposition Platform—For Life party list. The success of these two reminds us that while association with brawling did not guarantee success in 2019, neither was it necessarily the kiss of death.

Because of the general trend of turnover following Ukraine's 8th convocation, it is difficult to assign any value to brawling in terms of legislators' political careers. Brawlers did not enjoy any clear and obvious benefit, nor did they seem to incur any unmistakable cost. In fact, it is hard to discern any common characteristics among the small fraction of legislators who won re-election in 2019. This apparent lack of correlation between brawling and electoral success is not entirely unexpected. There are many reasons brawling might not lead to re-election, and, even when it has a positive effect, we expect that effect to be relatively small. It is entirely possible that brawling did indeed have a marginal benefit in 2019, but that small benefit was swamped by much larger and more powerful forces that swept away most incumbents, brawlers and nonbrawlers alike. At any rate, 2019 did not produce anecdotal evidence similar to the triumph of Liashko's Radical Party in 2014 that might convince both political elites and ordinary voters that brawling leads to success.

Anecdotal Evidence from Taiwan

In contrast to Ukraine, Taiwanese learned very early on that brawlers do well in elections. Almost all of the highest-profile brawlers in the late 1980s and early 1990s succeeded at the ballot box, often in spectacular fashion. The few who lost tended to be less famous, and there were usually other factors that contributed to their defeats. The clear lesson from those early elections was that brawlers were rewarded.

Taiwan's most famous brawler was Chu Kao-cheng. Chu was elected to the legislature in 1986 under the DPP banner as a young lawyer who had just gotten a PhD in philosophy from the University of Bonn in West Germany. He was hardly a brutish ruffian. Chu started Taiwan's first brawl in February 1987, and he was the central actor in most brawls in 1987 and 1988. His willingness to instigate violent clashes earned him sobriquets such as "Taiwan's Rambo" and "Taiwan's Number One Battleship" in the media, but Chu and his fellow opposition leaders always had a clear political message behind their physical actions. The early brawls were almost universally about the legitimacy of the authoritarian regime and specifically about the structure of the legislature, which was still dominated by people elected four decades ago in China. The newly formed (and technically still illegal) DPP elected a handful of legislators in late 1986, and they took every opportunity to protest the undemocratic structure of the legislature. Chu's contribution was to pioneer the use of brawling inside the legislature as a way to spotlight this injustice. He and other DPP legislators would frequently insult senior legislators, insisting that they had no right to speak in the people's legislature. When the senior legislators ignored him and tried to continue speaking or voting, DPP legislators would rip out microphones, try to snatch away documents, or otherwise disrupt proceedings. A handful of KMT legislators usually intervened to restrain them, and brawls ensued. These types of conflicts were frequent until the senior legislators were forced to retire at the end of 1991 and the Second Legislative Yuan was elected at the end of 1992.

Chu was elected in 1986 in a large district covering five cities and counties with nine seats. As the main representative of the opposition movement, Chu won easily, getting 120,338 votes (11.4%). In 1989, the districts were redrawn so that Chu ran for re-election in just one of these counties, a rural area that elected three seats. Chu was a local son, but in those days the DPP usually did much better in urban areas than in the rural areas dominated by the KMT's patronage factions. The KMT nominated three candidates and divided their votes very evenly among them—a perfect example of the importance of political parties' coordination role in an single nontransferable vote (SNTV) electoral system (Cox and Niou 1994; Cox 1996).[5] To further complicate Chu's re-election, his self-identification as Chinese had started to create divisions within the DPP elite, and the DPP decided to formally nominate a different candidate. Chu could identify himself as a "self-nominated" DPP candidate, but it was widely understood that his candidacy was in defiance of party discipline. In the face of all these challenges, voters re-elected Chu with one of the most jaw-dropping mandates in Taiwan's electoral history. Chu swamped the rest of the field, winning 128,420 votes (47.6%), just shy of the combined total of the three KMT candidates and over 18 times as many votes as the official DPP nominee. Standing almost entirely on his credentials as Taiwan's foremost brawler and opponent of the authoritarian structure, Chu won re-election in stunning fashion.

Chu's breathtaking re-election was perhaps the single most important factor in creating the widespread impression that voters would reward brawling. Although he was brawling in a strong party system, Chu's relationship with the DPP was complicated. Chu was expelled from the DPP within a few months of his 1989 triumph, set up his own party, and then crossed the aisle entirely, joining the pro-unification New Party—a KMT splinter party—in 1994. He eventually won a total of five terms in the legislature, most of which were spent in strident antagonism to the DPP. It is hard to make the argument that later in his career he was trying to send the message that he was a good DPP party soldier, though he did embody (literally) the ethos of the early DPP when he first began brawling.

While Chu was the most famous brawler, the late 1980s and early 1990s produced many examples of other prominent partisan brawlers who enjoyed electoral success. You Ching, another German-educated lawyer, had come to prominence defending the leaders of the 1979 Kaohsiung Incident and had emerged as one of the prodemocracy movement's principal leaders in the mid-1980s. He was elected to the legislature in 1986 where he was not necessarily an instigator of legislative brawling, but neither did he shy away from it. His stature in the party ensured that the brawling label would be firmly attached to him. You did not run for re-election in 1989. Instead, he ran for Taipei County magistrate, which at the time was the most important office open to popular elections and one that the opposition had never come close to winning. You stunned everyone by scraping out a razor-thin victory, marking the most serious loss the KMT had ever suffered to that date.

Frank Hsieh Chang-ting and Chen Shui-bian were also Kaohsiung Incident defense lawyers. Hsieh had been educated in Japan, while Chen famously took first place in every exam at National Taiwan University. The media regularly linked the two charismatic lawyers as collaborators and rivals. Both spent the 1980s on the Taipei City council before moving up to the legislature in 1989, where they immediately became the DPP's most prominent legislators. Hsieh and Chen were serious and substantive politicians who became famous for their grasp of policy details as well as their ability to make stirring speeches. As masters of political communication, they regularly used brawling to hammer home messages about the KMT's authoritarian regime. Their message was clear: the regime was illegitimate, the DPP was standing up against it, and they were fighting for democracy and their party's ideals. They both easily won re-election in 1992, but that was hardly the high point of their political careers. Chen was elected Taipei City mayor in 1994 and then president in 2000. Hsieh served as the DPP vice presidential nominee in 1996 and then moved south to Taiwan's second city, Kaohsiung, where he was elected mayor in 1998. After winning re-election, President Chen appointed him premier in 2005. In 2008 Hsieh represented the DPP as its presidential nominee, but he was soundly defeated in that year's KMT tsunami.

The political fortunes of You, Hsieh, and Chen reinforced the popular impression established by Chu that brawling in the legislature was rewarded, not punished, at the ballot box. Far from being fatally damaged by being associated with physical violence in the legislature, these prominent politicians took advantage of brawling to move higher up in the political structure. Chen eventually went all the way to the presidency. However, it would be a mistake to think that brawling in and of itself was a path to political success. None of these legislators were mere thugs looking to bash some heads. They all had elite educations, and they were making a serious and substantive political point about their uncompromising struggle for democracy. Unfortunately, their actions probably also led Taiwan's citizens to accept brawling as a tolerable, perhaps even legitimate, part of the democratic political process. If these politicians, with all their elite education, sophistication, and dedication to democratic ideals, thought it was acceptable to engage in physical conflict on the floor of the national legislature, then maybe brawling wasn't entirely improper.

On the other side of the aisle, there was not always widespread enthusiasm within the KMT caucus to respond to these DPP-instigated brawls. Many of the supplemental KMT legislators had political bases in the local patronage factions. They and their voters were more interested in ensuring money was spent the right way than in defending the structure of the regime. Indeed, many shared the DPP's skepticism on that score. When a brawl broke out, they usually found an excuse to be somewhere else. However, there was a small faction of younger KMT legislators who were willing to stand up for the legitimacy of their senior colleagues. Most of these came out of the KMT's Huang Fu-hsing party branch for military veterans and their families, and they disproportionately represented voters who had come to Taiwan with the KMT after 1949. For them, the legitimacy of the regime was serious business. Chou Shu-fu fought with Chu Kao-cheng in the first brawl in February 1987, and he was a frequent participant in subsequent brawls. After the 1989 election, Chou was often joined by other KMT legislators from the Huang Fu-hsing branch, including Lin Shou-shan, Hsiao Chin-lan, Wang Tien-ging, Chu Feng-chih, and Chao Chen-peng. These legislators were not the charismatic media superstars found on the DPP side, but the KMT's dominance of the media before democratization ensured that they got plenty of coverage. Chou easily won re-election in 1989, and all of these KMT brawlers were comfortably re-elected in 1992. Their electoral victories were not as spectacular as those on the DPP side of the aisle, but they were victories nonetheless. The early KMT brawlers certainly did not seem to be paying a penalty at the ballot box for standing up and fighting for the KMT ideological orthodoxy.

Because almost all of the brawlers with the highest profiles did so well, it was easy for many observers to conclude that voters universally rewarded brawling. In fact, there were a few brawlers who lost. However, they tended to be less famous, and it was almost always easy to find extenuating circumstances. Wang Yi-hsiung lost his re-election bid in 1989, but he belonged to the fringe Labor Party. His election in 1986 was the thing that needed explaining, not his loss in 1989. Wang Tsung-sung and Wu Yung-hsiung were frequent DPP brawlers for six years, and both of them lost badly in 1992. However, they had both been elected in the functional constituencies as representative of laborers, and the functional constituencies were abolished in 1992. Forced to run in an ordinary geographic constituency, neither managed to get even a paltry 5,000 votes. The most famous brawler to lose was perhaps Stella Chen Wan-chen. Elected in 1992, Chen was a firebrand from the radical wing of the DPP who once went as far as bringing a baseball bat into the legislature to threaten the premier with, an action that even her DPP colleagues found a bit extreme. Chen unexpectedly lost her re-election bid in 1995, but, again, there were extenuating circumstances. The DPP egregiously overnominated in her district, running 10 candidates in a 17-seat district in which they only won 28.5% of the vote. They only won 4 seats, and 1 of those 4 winners was Lu Hsiu-yi, himself a frequent brawler.

The idea that brawlers do well in elections was established early on, and there were not many dramatic election losses to change that impression in subsequent years. Some of the more thuggish legislators of the 1990s and 2000s—archetypal honor brawlers—such as Lo Fu-chu and Lin Ming-yi (discussed in Chapters 4 and 6) as well as many of the more "colorful" partisan brawlers from this era won almost all of the races they entered.

Collectively, these anecdotes present a clear picture in which brawling was rewarded at the ballot box in Taiwan. However, there are a few reasons to be cautious with this interpretation. For one thing, brawls have also been used to undermine candidate credibility. As an example, when Han Kuo-yu suddenly rocketed into the national consciousness from two decades of obscurity to become the KMT's 2020 presidential nominee, enterprising netizens unearthed a legislative brawl from May 1993 in which the future presidential candidate punched future president Chen Shui-bian. At the time Han was a fairly standard and nondescript Huang Fu-hsing legislator, and the incident was quickly forgotten. Twenty-five years later, the rediscovered brawl was used to paint the suddenly prominent Han as a thuggish ruffian.

Another problem is that losers tend to fade into political obscurity, while winners stay on the political stage. Not many people remember Wang Tao-fu, a KMT Huang Fu-hsing legislator and frequent brawler who lost his re-election bid in 1992, or Wei Yao-chien, a frequent DPP brawler who failed to win renomination in 1995 and was forced out of the political arena. Losers tend to end up in the dustbin of history, along with memories of their brawling.

A third problem is that none of these cases represent a clear test of whether voters reward brawlers because none of these legislators were simply brawlers. All of the politicians mentioned here were complex people who represented various ideas and engaged in a variety of legislative behaviors. Even Chu Kao-cheng, who was more closely associated with brawling than any other legislator, was not merely a brawler. He was also a lawyer, an intellectual, a political dissident, a social democrat, and a charismatic and engaging speaker. Chu Kao-cheng, You Ching, Chen Shui-bian, Frank Hsieh, Chou Shu-fu, and all the others might have won elections because voters rewarded brawling, but they might have also won those elections because voters rewarded political talent more generally. Finally, the conclusion that voters unambiguously reward brawling raises an inconvenient question: if it is so clearly an electoral boon, why don't all legislators brawl all the time?

Fortunately for us, Taiwan's long and rich history of brawling allows us to look more systematically at brawlers' electoral fortunes. The anecdotal evidence is visceral and meaningful, but a look at the quantitative data tempers those initial impressions and reveals some interesting nuances.

Quantitative Evidence from Taiwan

Taiwan has held 11 general elections from 1986 to 2020, so we can compare re-election rates for the brawlers and nonbrawlers elected in the first 10 of these. We consider each legislator in each term as an individual case. For example, KMT member Huang Chao-shun won eight consecutive terms starting in 1992 before losing in 2020, so she counts as eight cases, in which she successfully won re-election in seven.

To identify brawlers, we return to the data set drawn from the *United Daily News* online database.[6] For each incident, the names of all legislators mentioned in connection with the brawl are recorded. Admittedly, it is not always clear whether a given legislator was actively involved in the physical confrontation or whether he or she was playing some other role. However, we count them as receiving media mention in an article reporting on brawling. In Chapter 5, we argued that the media plays a critical role in transmitting information about brawling to the general public, and these legislators have all been associated in some way with brawling in the media.[7] Because each legislator in each term is considered to be an independent case, the coding for brawler for a given individual is specific to a particular term. Again, using Huang Chao-shun as our example, of her eight separate cases in our data set, there are four in which she was coded as a brawler and four in which she was considered a nonbrawler, because no articles in the latter four terms mentioned her in reports of brawling.

It is relatively straightforward to determine which legislators were re-elected, but it is less clear which legislators were ultimately successful or unsuccessful. We assume that re-election to the legislature is the primary goal for the great majority of legislators, but there are other ways to characterize success that we should briefly consider. Many politicians have their eyes on even better jobs outside the legislature, and to the extent that legislators pursue and obtain such positions, we might also want to consider them as having been successful.

Careers outside the Legislature

Of the 1,513 legislators elected in the 10 general elections from 1986 to 2016, 36 resigned their seats to accept an appointment to an office in the bureaucracy. None of these ran in the next general election. Interestingly, only 1 of the 36 was a brawler. This appears to be a clear indication that brawling is not a good strategy to obtain an appointed position. Forty-four other legislators won an election to become head of a local city or county government, a position widely considered more desirable than a seat in the legislature. Nine (2.2% of all brawlers) of these winners had brawled and 35 (3.1% of all nonbrawlers) had not. Chen Shui-bian and You Ching were not the only brawlers to move up the political ladder, but neither were they representative of all upwardly mobile politicians. While these 80 legislators were politically successful, we must be careful in classifying the nonbrawlers. If someone left the legislature only a few months into the term, it is hard to say whether they were really a nonbrawler or simply didn't have the opportunity to jump into the fray. As a result, we will omit these 80 legislators and the 6 who died during their terms from the remainder of the analysis. This leaves us with 1,427 cases of individuals who actively sought to further their careers in the legislature, 394 (27.6%) of whom were coded as brawlers.

Retirement Instead of Re-election

Thinking about unsuccessful re-elections is even thornier. Sometimes it is straightforward. Some legislators want to run for re-election, obtain the party's nomination for a seat in the same district, and simply lose the election. However, there are many other stories. Sometimes legislators choose to retire and do not want to run for re-election at all. Sometimes they want to run for re-election but are convinced that it is hopeless, so they issue a public statement that they want to retire to spend more time with their families. Appearing on the ballot is not always an indicator of a more serious attempt at re-election since some legislators make half-hearted runs while others are dead serious before withdrawing at the last moment. The simplest way to deal with these problems is to assume that all legislators want to run for re-election, whether they actually appear on the ballot or not. We will generally follow that assumption and focus simply on whether or not a legislator was actually re-elected, but first we offer some observations on retirement rates.

Nonbrawlers were more likely to retire; 23.9% of nonbrawlers did not run again, while only 17.0% of brawlers surrendered their seats.[8] There are two obvious ways to interpret this result. On the one hand, it could be that brawling helped legislators secure places on the ballot. That is, higher retirement rates among nonbrawlers are evidence that brawling is beneficial to re-election. On the other hand, it could be that these legislators always planned to retire, and their brawling behavior was a consequence, not a cause, of that decision. This interpretation is also in line with our theoretical expectations. In Chapter 3, we argued that legislators don't brawl for the enjoyment of the fight. Brawling is unpleasant, distasteful, and sometimes physically traumatic. Most politicians get into politics to pursue their democratic policy ideals of a good society rather than to punch other democratic actors. Instead, they see brawling as conferring strategic advantages for their political careers. Many retiring legislators are no longer interested in developing their future political careers, so they should have less of an incentive to participate in brawls. Either way, the higher retirement rates among nonbrawlers are evidence of the link between electoral incentives and brawling.

Re-election Rates

Table 7.1 shows re-election rates among brawlers and nonbrawlers, and the most important result is that brawlers did a bit better. Overall, 62.7% of brawlers won re-election, while only 53.3% of nonbrawlers did. This is a clear advantage, but it is not as overwhelming as the anecdotal evidence might have suggested. Politicians can probably perceive a nearly 10-point advantage in re-election rates. However, they should also perceive that plenty of legislators managed to get re-elected without participating in brawls, and plenty of brawlers failed to be re-elected. Brawling might help, but it is certainly not a prerequisite or a guarantee for re-election.

This modest benefit answers the question of why all legislators don't brawl all the time. Brawlers can and do lose. Presumably the benefits do not always outweigh the costs. We have stressed that most voters do not like seeing their legislators engage in chaotic and shameful physical confrontations. Brawling is thus a card that must be played with care. It can help, but it can also backfire. Each legislator must try to sort out which brawls will pay benefits and which will impose costs. Politicians tend to be fairly good at these sorts of calculations—this is at the heart of their enterprise, after all—so we should expect them on balance to select the helpful brawls and avoid the harmful ones. However, we should also expect to see evidence of mistakes and recalibration.

Looking at the data by individual terms, there is evidence of these recalibrations. Taiwan has a fairly small legislature, so the numbers for each term are not large. Nonetheless, the same patterns show up repeatedly. Nonbrawlers are usually more likely than brawlers to retire, and brawlers usually are re-elected at higher rates than nonbrawlers. Moreover, there is evidence that legislators anticipate and respond to changes in popular support for brawling. When brawlers get re-elected at significantly higher rates than nonbrawlers, more legislators participate in brawls. When brawlers don't experience this sort of electoral advantage, fewer legislators choose to participate in brawls. Figure 7.1 shows that when the electoral payoff to brawling

Table 7.1 Brawling and re-election in Taiwan

	Nonbrawlers				Brawlers				sig
	Did not run	Ran and lost	Ran and won	n	Did not run	Ran and lost	Ran and won	n	
Elected in									
1986	35.4	12.5	52.1	48	26.1	4.4	69.6	23	
1989	24.4	29.3	46.3	41	8.5	22.0	69.5	59	*
1992	24.2	14.3	61.5	91	14.5	24.2	61.3	62	
1995	13.1	20.5	66.4	122	9.7	25.8	64.5	31	
1998	18.3	26.1	55.6	180	22.2	29.6	48.2	27	
2001	23.8	20.4	55.8	172	19.6	8.7	71.7	46	*
2004	30.9	29.8	39.3	168	15.6	33.3	51.1	45	
2008	25.0	22.5	52.5	80	13.6	18.2	68.2	22	
2012	35.4	21.5	43.0	79	10.3	27.6	62.1	29	$
2016	15.4	23.1	61.5	52	32.0	8.0	60.0	50	
Electoral system									
SNTV	17.6	23.8	58.6	648	12.6	23.1	64.4	247	
SMP	14.8	24.5	60.7	155	7.9	17.1	75.0	76	*
CLPR	47.8	18.7	33.5	230	42.3	14.1	43.7	71	

							sig
Party status							
Majority party	24.4	18.6	57.1	624	20.4	17.5	62.1	211
Opposition party	21.8	26.3	51.9	289	12.3	20.0	67.7	155	**
Small parties	26.7	35.8	37.5	120	17.9	42.9	39.3	28
SNTV and party								
Majority party	15.7	18.8	65.5	388	13.3	20.0	66.7	120
Opposition party	20.3	28.8	50.9	177	11.3	21.7	67.0	106	**
SMP and party								
Majority party	14.8	27.0	58.3	115	12.5	18.8	68.8	48
Opposition party	14.8	11.1	74.1	27	0.0	12.0	88.0	25
CLPR and party								
Majority party	61.2	9.9	28.9	121	48.8	9.3	41.9	43
Opposition party	27.1	25.9	47.1	85	29.2	20.8	50.0	24
All	23.9	22.8	53.3	1033	17.0	20.3	62.7	394	**

Notes: sig shows the results of a *t*-test comparing re-election (ran and won) rates for brawlers and nonbrawlers. ** $p < .01$; * $p < .05$; $ $p < .10$.

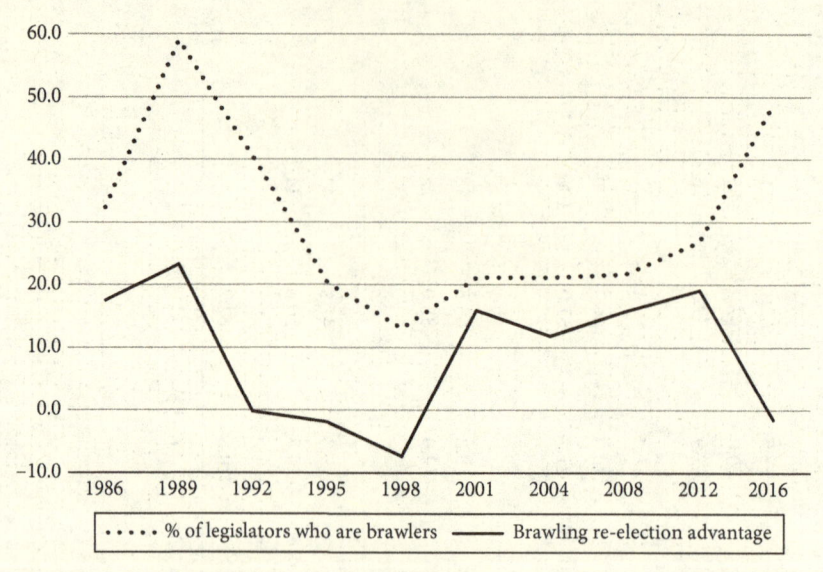

Figure 7.1 Brawling and re-election advantage.

Notes: Brawling re-election advantage is the percentage of brawlers re-elected minus the percentage of nonbrawlers re-elected. Data are taken from Table 7.1.

was higher in the late 1980s, more legislators brawled. When this payoff evaporated in the 1990s, the percentage of brawling legislators shrunk dramatically. When voters began rewarding brawlers again in the 2000s, legislators readjusted their strategies. Seeing consistently positive benefits, the share of brawlers increased noticeably from 1998 to 2012. The 2016 term may represent the point at which legislators took this trend too far, though we do not have data on whether they recalibrated by shying away from brawling in the next term. The 2016 term is arguably unique since it was the first time Taiwan had a complete rotation of power, and it was the first time the KMT had not held an outright majority or at least been able to form a majority coalition. In this new environment, the two big parties had to learn how to be effective majority and opposition parties, and they may not have figured everything out immediately. For our purposes, it is possible that the KMT overplayed the brawling card in its efforts to present itself as an energetic opposition force. However, this single term does not negate the experiences of the previous three decades in which brawling and re-election moved in predictable patterns. There have been peaks and valleys during this time period, but the overall trend is that brawling has conveyed electoral rewards.

Differences across Electoral Systems

Taiwan has used three electoral systems during this period, and all three of them show the same general trend. Brawlers have higher re-election rates in all three systems. These differences all border on conventional levels of significance, so we can be fairly confident that, at the very least, brawlers do not do worse than nonbrawlers in any of the three systems.

The main electoral system used from 1986 to 2004 was SNTV. With multimember districts, candidates often had to compete with other nominees from their party for votes. This provided a strong incentive for legislators to send a message to party supporters that they were loyal party soldiers, the purest representative of party goals from among the various party nominees.

Starting in 2008, most seats have been elected under single-member plurality (SMP) rules. SMP does not force intraparty competition in the general election, but sending a signal of party loyalty helps incumbents ward off nomination challenges and builds enthusiasm among activists, donors, and campaign workers.

From 1992 to 2004, around 20% of seats were elected by closed-list proportional representation (CLPR); in 2008 this share was increased to 30%. The connection between brawling and re-election in CLPR depends on how the lists are made up and how much information the people making the lists have about the potential nominees. The KMT and DPP have used several different methods to construct their party lists over the years, including voting by party members, voting by party elites, delegating the task to a small committee, and allowing the party chair to unilaterally decide the list. Over the years, the parties have tended to use increasingly centralized methods, with a smaller and smaller set of party elites drawing up the list. Theoretically, we argue that brawlers are trying to send a signal about their type to actors who might be able help their careers. However, with only a handful of list legislators in any given term and highly centralized decision-makers, this incentive may not translate well to Taiwanese list legislators. Indeed, in our interviews, party caucus leaders have repeatedly scoffed at the notion that they were learning anything about legislators from their brawling behavior. Party activists and supporters out in the general population may have learned something about the legislators, but the party elites inside Taiwan's small legislature insisted that they already knew their caucus members quite well. While the trend of brawlers being re-elected at higher rates seems to hold for all three systems, the theoretical linkage may not be as strong for CLPR as for SNTV or SMP. We will return to this point below.

Party Status

In Chapter 4 we established that individuals from large, opposition parties are more likely to brawl, particularly in strong party systems like Taiwan. Thus, we should consider whether the benefits of brawling also confer more regularly to individuals with this sort of partisan status. Because brawls in Taiwan have traditionally been the province of the two largest parties, we focus on the experience of the KMT and DPP.[9] The KMT was the majority party and the DPP was the main opposition party in the legislature until 2016, when the two big parties switched roles. Brawling seems to have a small electoral payoff for majority party legislators, as brawlers were re-elected roughly 5.0% more often than nonbrawlers. However, for the main opposition party, the gap between re-election rates for brawlers and nonbrawlers was three times as large (15.8%). As for smaller parties, there isn't much difference in the re-election rates between brawlers and nonbrawlers.

Electoral Systems and Party Status

Looking at the influence of electoral systems and party status in tandem is particularly interesting. Under SNTV, majority party brawlers and nonbrawlers had roughly similar re-election rates, but opposition party brawlers did much better than their nonbrawling copartisans. The re-election gap between the parties among nonbrawlers and brawlers was a substantial 14.9% (1.2% for the majority party against 16.1% for the opposition party). Under SMP, both majority party and main opposition party brawlers were re-elected at higher rates than nonbrawlers from their party, and the gap was a more modest 3.4% (10.5% for the majority party against 13.9% for the opposition party). In both electoral systems, opposition party legislators could expect to reap substantial electoral rewards by engaging in brawling.

We do not find this same pattern among CLPR legislators. Here, opposition party brawlers were re-elected at roughly the same rate as their nonbrawling colleagues. Instead, it was the majority party brawlers who saw an electoral advantage, yielding a gap in the opposite direction of 10.1% (13.0% for the majority party against 2.9% for the opposition party). The numbers of CLPR legislators are small enough that these results are not by themselves statistically significant, yet the substantive contrast in re-election rates between brawling CLPR legislators and SNTV and SMP legislators in the majority party is striking enough to demand an explanation.

Above, we argued that, due to the small number of CLPR legislators each term and the ways in which the two big parties have drawn up their lists, brawling might not confer the same benefits for legislators elected in this manner. Here, we further argue that there are important differences in what Taiwanese majority and opposition party leaders expect from list legislators. Since list legislators are elected with party votes, they are often expected to do difficult and unappealing tasks for the party. This may include sitting on less desirable committees, developing policy expertise on less salient issues, and showing up to votes that their colleagues would rather avoid (Batto 2014).

In the context of brawls, there may be different expectations for opposition and majority list legislators. Since brawls are usually instigated by the opposition, they tend to be electorally advantageous to the opposition party. There is no shortage of opposition district legislators willing to create a public spectacle, so there is no need to mobilize every opposition list legislator. Their participation is welcomed by the party, but not necessarily demanded. In contrast, the majority party often finds itself in the uncomfortable position of needing to pass an unpopular item. District legislators may be hesitant to directly engage, so it falls to the majority party list legislators, who are more insulated from public opinion, to do the party's dirty work. At re-election time, the majority party might be expected to care more about whether list legislators reliably showed up when the party needed them. Thus, in the specific context of Taiwan's small legislature and centralized list nominations, it is not altogether unreasonable to find that re-election rates are higher for majority party brawlers than nonbrawlers. And though the logic generally conforms to our expectations, we are not sure this is an observation that will generalize more broadly in the same way as some of our other findings.

Overall, the main message from Taiwan's 11 general elections is that brawlers do indeed outperform nonbrawlers. However, this advantage is modest, and there are numerous caveats. Strategic legislators might improve their odds of re-election by participating in a brawl, but they would be unwise to assume that brawling makes their re-election a foregone conclusion.

Conclusion

We have argued in this book that strategic politicians involve themselves in legislative brawls because they see a potential political advantage. Since most legislators place very high importance on winning re-election, there should be some indication that brawling helps them achieve this goal. In this chapter, we have presented evidence that this is, in fact, the case. Brawlers are more successful than nonbrawlers at winning re-election.

However, the story is not so straightforward and unambiguous. Not all brawlers win, and not all nonbrawlers lose. Brawling is neither necessary nor sufficient to win re-election. In certain conditions, however, it can provide an electoral bonus. In this sense, it is more like constituency service, a controversial vote, or a high-profile speech. None of these activities by themselves guarantee re-election, but every little bit helps.

The paradox of brawling is that legislators engage in it for electoral advantages, but most voters strongly dislike brawling. Legislators must choose their brawls very carefully, weighing the positive payoffs from the minority of people who are happy to see the brawl against the negative payoffs from the much larger group who are not. Politicians are generally very good at judging these sorts of tradeoffs, and they usually make the correct choice. However, sometimes they make mistakes, so brawling might not always convey a net-positive benefit. Sometimes, brawling might lead to electoral defeat. This potential harm is part of what makes brawls a costly—and thus credible—signal, and also the reason that legislators don't brawl all the time. The overall correlation between brawling and successful re-election relies heavily on selection bias, and it is safe to assume that strategic politicians wisely avoid most of the disadvantageous brawls.

One of the most important lessons of this chapter is that the benefits of brawling are, in the grand scheme of things, relatively modest. In Ukraine's recent legislative history, brawling did not appear to be helping legislators secure re-election, but this was an era when most politicians struggled to be re-elected. Before President Zelensky was an international sensation for his handling of Russia's invasion of Ukraine, he was a comedian who played the president of Ukraine on a television comedy show. His election to the presidency, and the legislative elections that followed shortly thereafter, clearly represented a wave of antiestablishment sentiment in Ukrainian public opinion. In the face of such a powerful trend, any effects of brawling were simply overwhelmed. Similarly, in Taiwan, Wang Shu-hui's legendary brawling behavior could not save her from the massive KMT wave that swept Taiwan's legislature in 2008. Other factors usually matter more to voting decisions than brawling.

Taiwan has experienced three decades of chronic brawling. This is driven by the widespread perception that voters usually reward brawlers and certainly do not punish them. The quantitative data show a clear electoral advantage for brawlers, but it is surprisingly small. The common wisdom that brawling pays electoral dividends was heavily influenced by a few dramatic examples early in the democratic era. Several of the highest-profile brawlers had triumphant, even smashing, electoral victories, and both elites and ordinary voters learned that brawlers could do well at the polls. In the absence of dramatic anecdotal evidence or overwhelming quantitative evidence to the contrary, there has never been a general reconsideration of this correlation. A few dramatic examples are probably disproportionately responsible for the continuation of brawling in Taiwan, and they have thus had an outsized effect on Taiwan's democratic development.

8
Conclusions

In this book we have argued that legislative brawling is a strategic choice that individual legislators make to try to further their professional goals, contra views of legislative brawling as uncontrolled, passionate outbursts or symptoms of cultural predilections for violence. Legislators try to make punches in the legislative chamber "count" as a costly signal to influential audiences about their commitments and intentions. We have argued that for the bulk of brawls—those that happen in the course of opposition disruption—these actions are, in fact, costly, and the associated costs allow brawlers to establish reputations where they may not have had them before. Further, we have argued that the specific audience will differ, depending on whether political parties are strong or weak in a given democracy, but in general there are typically some elites and some segment of the electorate more generally that brawlers are hoping will receive their signal. The signal brawlers are trying to send is that they are dedicated to fighting for what is important to the target audience—this can be a party in strong party systems or an individual or ideological position in weaker party systems. Finally, we have argued that these costly signals might help some brawlers' careers, under some circumstances, but because these are costly signals, they also carry some risk—particularly given the fact that brawling is unpopular with the public at large.

The book then investigates a number of empirical implications that follow from this general theory. In terms of who brawls, in Chapter 4, we focus on individual and contextual factors that make some legislators more prone to brawling, based on who is more likely to need the signaling opportunity presented by brawling. In terms of individual characteristics, we show that in both Ukraine and Taiwan younger and less senior legislators are more likely to brawl. We also show that, in Taiwan at least, women are at least as likely to brawl as men. In terms of our contextual factors, we show that in Taiwan's strong party system, electoral rules and party membership affect brawling behavior, with individuals who rely more on personal votes and individuals in large parties having more need to distinguish themselves and, thus, being more likely to brawl. While we do not see the same patterns in Ukraine's weak party system where everyone is trying to build a personal political brand regardless of electoral system or party, consistent across both of these countries is the fact that brawlers are more likely to be part of the political opposition. This observation makes sense both because most brawling happens in the context of opposition disruption and because members of the political opposition can send an unambiguous signal with brawling, whereas members of the party in government have to weigh the signaling potential of violence against demonstrating a commitment to upholding current institutions and passing legislation efficiently.

After showing patterns of who brawls, we move on to investigating the question of signal transmission, following the logic that if brawlers are using violence for signaling purposes, they must have some confidence that their signals will be transmitted. In Chapter 5 we review media coverage of brawling in Taiwan and Ukraine, showing that the media cover legislative brawls extensively, and identify brawling legislators by name. Furthermore, we show that brawlers receive more media coverage when they brawl than they are likely to receive in regular media coverage of parliament.

Chapter 6 then offers evidence of the audiences posited in our theory. Here we offer evidence of partisan audiences in strong party systems and largely nonpartisan audiences in weak party systems. We show that where party leaders have a great deal of control and need for information about their legislators, they are the likely audience for brawling, as in South Korea and Mexico. In systems where party leadership already knows its members, however, strong party supporters in the electorate are the likely audience. We review our previous research showing that it was only the views of strong, minority party supporters that improved in the aftermath of an actual brawl in Taiwan, even as they were openly professing a dislike of brawling. We also offer evidence of the kinds of elite audiences and segments of the electorate that are the likely audiences for brawling in weak party systems in Ukraine. Finally, in this chapter we offer concrete evidence of the general population's dislike of brawling—an important point to keep in mind as we turn to our final empirical investigation, whether brawling actually helps legislators' political careers.

In Chapter 7 we address the question of whether politicians actually realize the career benefits from brawling that we argue drives the behavior. When we examine anecdotes of legislative careers from our two main cases, Ukraine and Taiwan, the evidence cuts both ways—from any given story of a brawler one might infer that it works to further a legislator's career or that it doesn't. From our quantitative data we are able to show a systematic, over-time correlation where rates of brawling seem to respond to public sentiment on the matter, and that brawlers do enjoy modest electoral gains.

Of particular note in Chapter 7 is the fact that brawling seems to disproportionately benefit brawlers from large parties, as opposed to small parties. Schmoll and Ting (2023) have shown that brawling is more frequent in fragmented legislatures with many small parties. They reason that these small parties are likely to be more radical and less compromising, and thus their members more prone to brawling. Taiwan's smaller parties tend to occupy extreme positions, but this does not seem to lead to either more frequent brawling or clear electoral rewards for brawlers. Not only does this observation offer context for understanding when brawling will be beneficial for legislators, but also it challenges the hypothesis that extremism, in and of itself, drives brawling. While these findings are suggestive, we must remember that the number of cases is very small. This cannot constitute a definitive refutation of Scholl and Ting. It does, nonetheless, offer support for our strategic story of brawling and suggest that the role of small parties in parliamentary brawls is still insufficiently understood.

Implications for Representation and Reform

What does it mean for democratic representation if legislators are motivated to pursue violence in the hopes of boosting their career prospects? Nearly everyone agrees with the abstract notion that brawls are undesirable. We have yet to encounter an argument that parliamentary brawls are, in and of themselves, beneficial to producing good public policy, healthy party politics, citizen satisfaction, more legitimate legislative outcomes, or any other desirable aspect of democracy. In theoretical tension here are the observations that violence is never optimal in democratic processes—one of the advantages of democracy over dictatorship or anocracies is the fact that it provides mechanisms for the peaceful allocation of power and resources. At the same time, we know that most democracies tend to favor certain groups in society over others and contentious politics are often essential to achieving a higher quality of representation for groups of citizens that have been marginalized.

Brawlers almost always defend their actions as a regrettable tactic made necessary by a specific context.

Empirically, in terms of the democratic process, we know that brawls usually don't do much more than slow down the passage of legislation for a short time. At the same time, we saw in survey evidence from Taiwan that citizens generally feel worse about their legislature and democracy in the aftermath of a brawl—though the target audience for brawling in that instance actually felt better. If almost no one wants brawls and they rarely change outcomes, is there a simple institutional reform that would disincentivize brawling?

In this book, we argue that brawls are fundamentally about political communication. Legislators see brawling as a way to send signals about themselves to other actors who are critical to their careers. If we are correct, any successful reform would need to alter those payoffs. As we discuss below, this is a daunting challenge. However, there are other ways to understand brawling, and they might point to a more tractable reform strategy. One seemingly promising approach is to envision brawling as a parliamentary tactic used by minorities against overbearing majorities. Time and time again, brawlers explain their behavior in precisely these terms. The government wants to do something controversial, and it uses its numerical advantage in the legislature to ram it through with questionable parliamentary procedures. The opposition would prefer to resist the item using normal parliamentary tactics, but they simply don't have the tools to block it or even to force the majority to respect the normal procedures. All they can do to protest the majority tyranny is start a brawl. This suggests a specific reform. To prevent the opposition from ignoring the institutional rules, they need tools within those rules that will allow them to mount a substantial resistance. With those enhanced legislative powers, the opposition will no longer need to brawl.

One can see why such a reform proposal might be attractive. If the brawling is purely a problem of legislative rules, then it can be addressed with a change of the legislature's internal practices. While persuading the legislature to adopt rules empowering the minority might not be an easy package to sell, it is more focused, immediate, and feasible than a call to change broader aspects of the political system such as the political culture. Reformers should probably start with simpler plans before throwing up their hands and calling for a generation of better education. Fortunately for our purposes, South Korea has recently attempted just such a reform.

Prospects for Reform: Lessons from South Korea

After decades of chronic brawling, Korea changed its legislative rules in 2012 to empower opposition parties. Since this is theoretically so informative, we will discuss the case in detail. In fact, the results of the reform have been mixed. Brawling has been far less common, but it has not been eliminated. As we will argue, these events make more sense if brawling is understood as political communication rather than as a legislative tactic for obstruction. The reduction in brawling is probably not a result of the reform.

The 1988 Rules

South Korea experienced numerous brawls in its first few decades after democratization. Most of these were classic partisan brawls, with a large mass of legislators from the majority party trying to ram through a controversial piece of legislation facing off against a large mass of opposition party legislators trying to stop them. The legislative rules established in 1988 remained in force until a major reform in 2012, and brawlers often pointed to how these rules were used or abused to justify their actions.

The 1988 rules endowed minority parties with substantial powers. Committee chairs were distributed proportionally, so many committees were chaired by opposition legislators. These opposition chairs might kill a bill in committee by simply refusing to give it a hearing. After passing through the regular committee, all legislation went to the Legal Affairs Committee, which was supposed to inspect the wording to ensure that the content does not conflict with existing law. By tradition, the Legal Affairs Committee was chaired by an opposition legislator. Again, the minority could simply refuse to give the bill a hearing. After clearing all committees, the bill was placed on the floor docket and could be scheduled for a floor hearing. However, all legislative parties (with at least 20 members) had to agree to schedule a bill, so all parties could effectively veto it at this stage. Finally, the minority's last resort was to try to stop a bill on the floor by disrupting proceedings with a brawl. Here also, the 1988 rules empowered the minority. The 1969 brawls over presidential term limits had ended with the governing party simply moving to a new room without telling the opposition and passing the bill there. Understandably, this tactic infuriated the opposition, and it was disallowed under the 1988 rules. The Speaker or committee chair was required to be in his or her designated seat and to formally bang the gavel in order to pass a bill.

If the 1988 rules empowered the minority with several tools to resist, they also provided the majority with a trump card that could override all these consensual rules. The Speaker could unilaterally discharge a bill from committee and bring it to the floor for a vote. The threat of a discharge was a constant presence in negotiations between the majority and minority. This action was always highly controversial, and many brawls were a result of its use.

The brawls over the US-Korea Free Trade Agreement were recounted in detail in Chapter 2, and the controversial ways the rules were deployed provide a good example of why some might believe that better rules could help avoid brawls. The December 2008 brawl took place in the Foreign Affairs and Trade Committee, and the power of the committee chair was at the heart of the clash. The ruling party had a comfortable majority in the legislature (172 of 299 seats), so one might have expected them to simply vote the bill through. However, to preempt any possibility that the opposition might block proceedings, the committee chair unilaterally barred all people who might cause disruptions from entering the room. That is, the chair used his power to provide a legal rationale for keeping all opposition legislators out of the room. On the day of the hearing, ruling party legislators implemented this ruling by barricading themselves in the room before most opposition members arrived. What followed was an intense battle as opposition legislators tried to force their way in. They eventually did get in, but not before the ruling party had taken advantage of their absence to hastily declare the bill had passed.

The December 2011 brawl took place on the floor of the legislature, and rules were again an important focal point. The bill had been sent back to committee, and, in spite of the ruling party's majority, they found it difficult to get the bill to the floor for a vote. For weeks, they threatened to use the Speaker's discharge power, but the opposition parties would not budge. The Speaker ordered the chamber sealed with most of the opposition still outside. While they tried to fight their way in, the ruling party took advantage of their absence to discharge the bill and then pass it.

In both of these cases, there is a good argument that the rules made things worse. The ruling party ran roughshod over normal parliamentary procedures by locking opposition legislators out. The right to disagree and oppose is usually seen as one of the hallmarks of the democratic process. Moreover, the threat of the discharge power loomed over the entire process.

The government did not have a strong incentive to negotiate in good faith since at the end of the day they had the power to drop the discharge hammer and get exactly what they wanted. However, from the other point of view, the ruling party had nearly three-fifths of the seats, far more than the opposition. Why should the minority be able to dictate terms? Yet, the minority was able to use the rules to frustrate the majority, refuse any compromises, and prevent a floor vote. In the face of this intransigence, the ruling party felt it was justified in taking full advantage of its powers under the rules to ensure that the majority position could prevail. In the end, both sides could argue that they were defending their democratic rights while the other side was violating democratic norms. Given the unreasonable acts of the other side, they had no choice but to use physical means. If the rules had given the minority tools that would empower them to resist egregious majority tyranny while also encouraging them to ultimately accept the legitimate right of the majority to pass legislation, perhaps brawling could have been avoided.

The 2012 Reform

In 2012, in the aftermath of several spectacular and extremely violent clashes, especially those over the Free Trade Agreement and media reform, and facing uncertainty about who would win the upcoming presidential election, South Korea passed the National Assembly Advancement Reform. There were several significant changes that altered the tactical tools available to parties and the balance of power between them. First, all bills sent to committee were required to eventually be placed on the floor docket where the Speaker has discretion over whether to put them on the agenda. This meant that opposition parties could no longer try to kill a bill by refusing it a committee hearing.

Second, the new rules establish a filibuster provision. One-third of legislators can initiate a filibuster, which must involve actual talking. However, three-fifths of the body can call for an immediate vote. If the filibuster continues to the end of the legislative session, the matter must be voted on immediately at the beginning of the next session. Thus, the majority does not have to compromise if it is willing to burn time.

Third, the new rules also establish a Fast Track provision. If three-fifths of the chamber or a special committee agree, a bill can be considered under Fast Track rules. If a committee has not acted on a bill in 180 days, it is automatically reported to the Legal Affairs Committee or floor, as appropriate. After it is reported to the floor, the floor must take up the bill within 60 days.

Fourth, the new rules severely curtail the Speaker's power to unilaterally discharge a bill from committee. The Speaker now only has this power in cases of war, natural disaster, and other national emergencies.

Fifth, the new rules explicitly prohibit occupying the Speaker's or committee chair's seat and lay out enhanced penalties for brawling. In the past, violations were referred to an ethics committee, where they were watered down or simply disappeared. Now, members who improperly sit in the Speaker's chair can be referred directly to the floor, where the matter will (supposedly) receive high-profile attention. Violators can be punished in several ways, including censure, being required to issue a public apology, having their salary cut by up to one-half for some period of time, a maximum 30-day required absence from the legislature and no pay for three months, and expulsion.

The National Assembly Advancement Reform stripped both the minority and the majority of their most controversial tools. The minority lost its power to kill bills in committee and to occupy the Speaker's chair, while the majority lost its power of discharge. Both received new assurances as well. The minority was granted the right to filibuster, while the majority received more power to arrange the agenda. On balance, most observers think the reform has somewhat strengthened the minority.

The logic of this reform for the purpose of discouraging brawling is clear. The new filibuster gives the opposition a clearly sanctioned and institutionalized method to resist the majority. Rather than resorting to violence, they can act within the rules to express their opposition. The majority is also given a clear path to pursue their agenda. It can overcome the filibuster with a supermajority, and it can also expedite legislation and avoid the need to obtain consensus with the Fast Track provision. In both of these, three-fifths is defined as an important threshold. If the majority can muster a three-fifths majority, the minority should accept the majority's legitimate right to pass its agenda. Presumably if the majority cannot garner three-fifths support, it should continue to negotiate with the opposition to find a solution with a broader appeal. At any rate, the enhanced penalties for physical disruption send a clear message that legislative disputes are to be resolved within the institutional rules and not through brawling.

The 2019 Brawl over Electoral Reform

For six years after the 2012 reform, there were no major legislative brawls in South Korea. However, the reform did not definitively squelch brawling once and for all. News reports occasionally referred to minor "scuffles." If there were any doubts about the persistence of brawling, another major brouhaha occurred in April 2019.

The issue at hand was electoral reform. The ruling Democratic Party (DP) and the three minor parties agreed to change the rules from mixed-member majoritarian to mixed-member proportional while also increasing the number of party list seats from 47 to 75 (of 300 total seats). The small parties were attracted by the increased importance of the list tier, while the DP saw it as a way to weaken the main opposition Liberty Korea Party (LKP). In the previous election, the conservatives had won 90% of the seats with just over 50% of the votes in their southeastern stronghold, and they feared the more proportional new system would diminish this advantage (Y. Kim 2019). LKP floor leader Na Kyung-won minced no words: "I think the parties' move is de facto imposing the death penalty on parliamentary democracy" (Park 2019a, paragraph 14).

To ensure the reform could take effect in time for the scheduled 2020 election, the four parties agreed to use the Fast Track mechanism, which the LKP did not have enough votes to unilaterally block. Even before the special committee took up the Fast Track proposal, though, there were disputes. A committee member from the Bareunmirae Party, which was internally divided over the entire reform proposal, announced he would vote against it, which would have defeated the proposal. To avoid this, the party leader took the unusual step of asking the Speaker to replace him with a different party member who supported the package, and the Speaker quickly approved this request. This new committee member was barricaded in his office for six hours by LKP members to prevent him from reaching the committee room until he finally called police and firefighters to free him. Meanwhile, LKP legislators tried to prevent the DP from formally submitting the bills by occupying administrative offices. In the ensuing melee, legislators suffered bruises and rib fractures, and there were accusations that the other side had prepared dangerous items such as nail pullers, iron hammers, and claw hammers (B. Kim 2019; Park 2019b; Yonhap 2019a, 2019b).

After a weekend of street rallies, petition drives, and strident rhetoric about how the other side was undermining democracy, the committee met the following Monday and duly approved the Fast Track proposal. While the LKP did not instigate another full-scale brawl, it did express its continuing opposition by staging a sit-in in the committee room and shouting to try to cause disruptions (Jung 2019a; Park 2019d; Yonhap 2019c). When the full chamber took up the electoral reform bill in December 2019, proceedings were similarly bumpy. The LKP attempted to filibuster to stop the bill. However, the Speaker outright dismissed one request for a filibuster, and another filibuster attempt failed to last very long. The LKP then tried to form a circle around the Speaker's desk so that he could not reach his chair. In the end, all they could do was boycott the final vote, and the bill passed by a 156-to-10 margin as LKP members held up placards in protest (Park 2019e; Yonhap 2019e). While not utter chaos, these votes were hardly paradigms of parliamentary decorum.

Interpretations of the 2012 Reform and Its Aftereffects

Following the 2012 reform, South Korea went over six years without another major brawl. Clearly, something had changed. The reappearance of brawling in 2019 provides some clarity on which elements were more important and which were less so.

One possibility is that the enhanced penalties deterred legislative violence. This explanation is almost certainly wrong. In the aftermath of the April 2019 brawl, the DP chair vowed to seek stern punishment against the perpetrators (Park 2019c). However, the DP did not attempt to invoke the new rules to impose penalties on brawlers. There were no high-profile disciplinary hearings on the chamber floor to discuss appropriate punishments. Instead, the parties turned to the legal system. The day after the brawl, the DP filed a complaint against 18 LKP legislators, accusing them of using violence to stop the normal procedures in the National Assembly. The LKP responded by filing police charges against 17 DP legislators for assault (Lee 2019b; Park 2019c). Predictably, not much came of these gestures. When push came to shove, the National Assembly proved not to have the stomach to police itself, and the legal authorities wisely stayed out of the fray as much as possible. More broadly, there isn't much reason to expect punitive measures to deter brawling. Brawlers choose to engage in what is inherently a violation of rules because they see substantial political benefits in doing so. The penalties would need to be extremely harsh to change those calculations, perhaps even to the point that the penalties could be considered a worse violation of democratic norms than the brawling, and the penalties would need to be imposed by the other legislators, who might be hesitant to set a precedent that could be turned against them in the future.

A more plausible explanation is that the 2012 reform gave the governing party incentives to seek more consensual policies instead of turning to brute force to ram through its partisan agenda and empowered opposition parties to block the agenda within the rules so that they did not need to resort to brawling. Indeed, when we asked about the successful antibrawling reform, one scholar replied in disbelief that it could hardly be considered successful since it had prevented the legislature from passing any significant legislation.[1]

The events in 2019 provide evidence both for and against this notion. On the one hand, the reform implied that measures that could muster three-fifths support had a much higher degree of legitimacy than those that could only attract one-half. The president's party started by assembling an oversized coalition of all the parties except the LPK in favor of its bill. This was never an example of ramming something through with a narrow majority against the will of most voices in society. On the other hand, replacing the one-half threshold with a three-fifths threshold seems to have simply moved the goalposts; it does not seem to have changed how intensely the sides would contest the critical turf. To obtain the decisive last vote to fast track the bill, the coalition had to replace a recalcitrant committee member. This controversial move gave the opposition a clear rationale to claim that the bill was not legitimately passed: the government was illegally ramming its agenda through the legislature with a questionable (super)majority. The government, meanwhile, was arguably emboldened to take liberties with the rules. After all, a clear majority supported its position, both in the legislature and in society at large (Jung 2019b; Yonhap 2019d). For our purposes, the new rules did not make it much more difficult for either side to justify its brawling. The final passage vote is also informative. The LKP used the filibuster to signify its opposition to the bill. However, after the filibuster was defeated, they felt the need to further oppose the bill by surrounding the Speaker's desk. Apparently, the filibuster was not an adequate replacement for physical disruption.

While the reform might have played a role in discouraging brawling, other factors might have been more important. For one thing, the presidents in the period after the reform faced significant constraints and might not have been eager to push a maximalist legislative agenda. President Park's party only won a razor-thin majority in 2012, and her presidency was derailed by her personal controversies. No party won more than 41% of the seats in 2016, so it was unlikely that President Moon's party would be able to pass his agenda at will.

However, an antibrawling public sentiment may have been the most critical factor. Several scholars told us that there was a qualitative shift in the aftermath of several extremely violent brawls, most notably the brawls over media reform in 2009 and over the Free Trade Agreement with the US in 2008 and 2011. One legislative expert explained that before brawling became severe, most Koreans, including himself, thought that conflict was a natural part of politics, so partisan fighting could be tolerated. But after witnessing the violence of the 2008 and 2009 brawls, he continued, Koreans began to awaken to the need for some sort of reform. When the party leaders put together a reform package, they were buoyed by strong public sentiment that partisan brawling had gone too far and something needed to be done.[2]

This interpretation brings the focus back to party incentives and political communication. Korea's brawls were almost always paradigms of partisan brawls. The party had a goal that required a certain degree of physical action, and individual legislators stepped up to send a signal to a critical audience, in this case party leaders, that they were good party soldiers who would willingly fight for party interests. After the reform the parties were likely much more hesitant to ask their members to engage in physical conflict, both because the party leaders had put their prestige behind the bipartisan reform to stop brawling and because the stronger public aversion to brawling would have implied a higher cost to the instigators. In this atmosphere, the signal sent by brawling to party leaders might have been that the legislators were not good soldiers but rather loose cannons who didn't understand the party's interests.

By 2019, things had changed a bit, and the postreform disincentives to brawl had arguably faded somewhat. For one thing, the memories of the extremely violent brawls in 2008 and 2009 were no longer fresh. In the much more recent past, the LKP had suffered several years in the opposition and were frustrated with the DP agenda. A week before the April 2019 brawl, the LKP had declared "all-out protests" against a "dictatorship by leftists" after President Moon appointed several judges over their objections (Lee 2019a). For another, the LKP leadership had changed. Firebrand Na Kyung-won took over as the party's floor leader in 2018, and she consistently pushed for more aggressive action, including calling for physical resistance to the DP.

For the first time in several years, party leaders were amenable to signals that their members were good party soldiers. Arguably, Na judged that the antibrawling sentiment had faded somewhat and now was a good time to try taking this tool back out of the storage shed. This may have been a mistake. The LKP was repeatedly defeated in the fight over electoral reform, and its resistance was not rewarded with a rise in its polling numbers. The party had a disastrous showing in the 2020 legislative election, though that election was more about the government's response to the Covid pandemic than electoral reform. Na was removed as floor leader in December 2019, and she lost her re-election bid a few months later. Not all gambits work out. However, from our point of view, the critical point is that she seemed to think brawling was worth a try.

Hopes for Antibrawling Reforms

Unfortunately, the lesson of the Korean example is that there are no easy solutions to brawling. Harsher punishments will not deter brawling. Parliamentary brawling is not a criminal act. The legal system is not equipped to wade into this minefield. Legislators are also unlikely to be able to judiciously dole out appropriate punishments. Brawling is a political act, and so any punishments are also inevitably political acts. If there is a compelling political reason for the brawl, the brawlers will enjoy some degree of legitimacy. Trying to stop brawling through harsh penalties can be akin to suppressing political expression. Legislators are particularly sensitive to the importance of political expression, which makes them hesitant to judge their colleagues and set a dangerous precedent.

A better set of rules giving the minority tools to oppose and the majority tools to overcome that opposition within the legislature's institutional framework can help. Many of the Korean brawls were triggered when the majority decided to break through gridlock with a parliamentary tactic of questionable legality or legitimacy. Of course, the majority interpretation was that the opposition was using tactics of questionable legality or legitimacy to clog up the system. Rules that clearly spell out what each side is allowed to do might help to remove some of the ambiguity that can lead to conflict.

However, there are limits to the effectiveness of this strategy. For one thing, the rules cannot cover every contingency, so there will inevitably be gray zones. For example, the 2012 reform spelled out the Fast Track procedures fairly clearly, but the decision to use the Fast Track for the 2019 electoral reform nevertheless incited a brawl. In this case, the most controversial action was the replacement of a committee member who opposed the reform. Needless to say, the 2012 reform did not address the possibility of reshuffling committee memberships, so the two sides found it quite easy to disagree about whether this was a legitimate prerogative of the party leaders or an illegitimate violation of democratic procedures. More generally, parties engaged in tense legislative struggles and looking for a grievance can usually find something the other side has done that they think is unreasonable.

More fundamentally, reforms based on better rules ignore the underlying impetus for brawling. Brawlers do not want the legislature to make decisions in a quiet, dignified, and orderly manner. They want to send a message to a target audience, and political communication through the media requires a certain degree of chaos, conflict, and drama. It is much easier to ignore a speech or a vote than a physical confrontation. It is telling that when the legislature passed the electoral reform in December 2019, after the opposition's filibuster failed, they then tried to physically blockade the Speaker's desk. Apparently, the opposition did not think a few speeches were sufficient to make their point.

Ultimately, what changed in Korea were attitudes toward brawling, both in the general public and among elites. After the very violent brawls of 2008 and 2009, what had been seen as normal and acceptable became seen as uncivilized and extreme. This does not mean that the reform was useless. After all, brawls ceased after 2012, not 2009. The 2012 reform was critical because it effectively announced to the entire society that attitudes had changed and the parties were committed to acting differently in the future. However, this reform only had teeth because the underlying context had, in fact, changed.

Finally, we should make clear that we are not suggesting the way to stop brawling is to shock society with an extremely violent brawl. Extreme violence spurred reflection and reconsideration in Korea, but there is no guarantee of this outcome. Political violence is just as, and perhaps more, likely to accelerate polarization and radicalization. This brings us to our next point of consideration—in addition to thinking about legislative brawling as a part of the legislative process in democracies, we must also think about it as a form of political violence. What does our explanation of the individual logic of legislative brawling tell us about political violence more generally?

Brawling and Political Violence

This book began by defining legislative brawling as instances of actual, not merely threatened, violence in the course of legislative activity. Naturally this topic invites considerations of how brawling impacts legislative representation, accountability, and the democratic policymaking process. And while brawling often seem like a symbolic performance aimed at delaying legislation or communicating information to the electorate, it merits serious consideration as a form of political violence. In particular, there are two aspects of our strategic theory of legislative violence that stand to contribute to our understanding of political violence more broadly—the fact that in the overwhelming number of cases brawling is violence promulgated by individuals who occupy a minority power position in the political dynamics in question, as well as the relationship of violence in the legislature to the attitudes and actions of the broader polity.

Brawling as a Form of Political Violence

Like other forms of political violence, legislative violence is costly, risky, and considered suboptimal in democratic politics. There is a sense that violence is not an effective means of influencing policy either inside or outside the policymaking process itself. Chenoweth, Stephan, and Stephan (2011), for example, have argued persuasively about the superiority of nonviolent movements to influence policy and effect change. At the same time, violence occurs in democratic settings and is perceived to have some advantages.

Wilkinson (2006) argued that in the context of democratic elections, majority parties might find ethnic violence, such as riots, to be advantageous to encourage an otherwise diverse majority voting population to identify, and vote in line, with their majority status. Furthermore, democracies have been found to experience terrorist attacks under a number of different circumstances (Chenoweth 2013). How, then, does legislative brawling compare to ethnic riots and/or terrorism?

In Wilkinson's (2006) examination of communal violence in India, Hindu majority elites work to incite Hindu-Muslim violence to generate fear among Hindus that causes them to prioritize their Hindu identity when they vote. For this to work the way Wilkinson argues, it is important that the violence appear chaotic and spontaneous—and that those elites who were hoping to provoke such violence not be seen as doing so. There are both similarities and differences to brawling logic here. On one hand, brawlers too like their acts of violence to be seen as spontaneous—often part of a larger chaos of opposition disruption. Unlike the elites who foment communal violence in India, however, legislative brawlers are typically in a minority or opposition position vis-à-vis democratic power structures.

Thus, work to date on the strategic uses of seemingly spontaneous political violence for electoral gain has tended to emphasize the strategic incentives of the instigators of violence in the political majority, with the violent reactions of political actors in the minority still being seen as spontaneous. Further, when minority strategies have been investigated (such as in Scott's [1985] classic *Weapons of the Weak*, which detailed strategies of peasant resistance in Malaysia), the focus has often been on group or class dynamics. What we offer in this book suggests that even in instances of seemingly spontaneous political violence such as riots, scholars of political violence may need to give more serious consideration to the individual strategic motivations of minority actors.

This brings us to one other key distinction between the logic of political violence and brawling for career advancement: brawlers are seeking recognition for this behavior. They are hoping the violence they are engaged in will be picked up and transmitted by media—signaling their commitment and willingness to fight to a desired audience—when they lack the power to affect policy by other means. In fact, it is difficult to find other instances of political violence in domestic politics where the perpetrators of violence want to be credited. Riots are effective precisely because they are seen as spontaneous and chaotic. When the state employs repression against its own citizens in democracies, it will acknowledge doing so, but the accompanying rhetoric conveys regret. For other acts of violence where the perpetrators claim credit, we have to look to acts of terrorism. In the case of terrorism, typically some nonstate actor takes credit for having committed the violence. With this credit-claiming for terrorism, there is more a sense of a desire to send a costly signal, akin to the logic we have presented here vis-à-vis brawling.

While both legislative brawlers and terrorists have incentives to publicly claim credit for their actions, they have very different relationships with the public. For one thing, legislative brawling, unlike terrorism (or ethnic rioting), is a contained, controlled form of violence that occurs in a venue set apart from, rather than in the midst of, a democratic society. It does not inspire the same sort of reflexive and visceral sympathy for the victims of such violence; unlike the innocent bystander, legislators are not necessarily viewed favorably by society (whether they are brawling or not). Legislative brawling is there for citizens to observe from a distance with a certain detachment. It may reflect a general mood in society—there are times when brawls in both Ukraine and Taiwan have coincided with popular protest—or it may be wholly divorced from contentious politics in society more broadly. Brawlers simply do not impose themselves and their demands on the public in the same way that terrorists and rioters do. Furthermore, brawlers are never really trying to communicate with citizens as a whole, or even with large swaths of the electorate. Contrast this with the fact that the majority party that foments a riot hopes to scare majority voters into voting a particular way. The signaling purpose of brawling for the individual legislator is always to connect with a very specific, targeted audience—elites, extreme partisans, or a very specific voting bloc. For the brawler, then, public sentiment is something to be navigated rather than activated.

Finally, then, what we can say about brawling based on both the logic of political violence and our earlier discussion of reforms is that the role of political elites and public opinion are critical in shaping brawlers' incentives. Legislators are willing to commit violence despite general public disapproval because some small group of actors—very often elites—may just reward them for this behavior. If elites did not respond positively, however, or if public disapproval presented a truly formidable risk, then strategic legislators might well reconsider the signaling value of brawling.

Brawling in the Shadow of Conflict

There is one other aspect of political violence with respect to brawls that we would be remiss not to remark upon before concluding our book. The two countries we have featured here are noteworthy not only because of the serial brawling activity in their legislatures but also because they are democracies that exist in the shadow of interstate conflict. For Taiwan the question of relations with China and the threat of military action from China hang over all politics. For Ukraine questions of conflict with Russia have been ever-present, first with fighting in the East and more recently with an open invasion by Russia. Our featured case in this chapter, South Korea, offers another instance of repeated legislative brawling in a democracy facing an existential security threat. And while three cases do not present a pattern sufficient for us to investigate systematically, they do raise the question of some possible relationship between these phenomena. One possibility is that politics in democracies operating in the shadow of major interstate conflict simply run hotter, that there is a heightened pressure in these places that makes violence more appealing to legislators and citizens. Given our argument that brawls are actually strategic, however, we are skeptical that this is the case. Instead, we think that very often this potential for conflict at a broader scale is reflected in societal divisions, which fuel political polarization and incivility in politics. In both Taiwan and Ukraine, the dominant political cleavage is defined by differing attitudes about how the country should relate to and interact with the neighboring giant. Perhaps such circumstances foster the breakdown of civility in democratic deliberation as basic democratic norms and values take a backseat to strong attachments to political identity.

We can think of what has happened and is currently happening in the US through this lens. Perhaps the division between North and South that ultimately produced the Civil War first drove a breakdown in democratic norms of civility and increased legislative violence. The contemporary American case reminds us that major societal divisions that produce polarization don't necessarily have to be fueled by a threat of civil or interstate war. The US has seen violence in the US Congress—if not directly perpetrated by legislators—and a more general decline in civility as the country becomes increasingly polarized along a divide between white Christian nationalists (McDaniel, Nooruddin, and Shortle 2022) and the rest of the country. It would not shock us to see a legislative brawl occur in this highly charged context.

We are not in a position, based on the research in this book, to say definitively whether strong cleavages and identity politics fuel legislative violence. But what is instructive from our research, and offers some cautious optimism, is that this is a phenomenon driven by individuals who are out of power attempting to communicate effectively with a relatively small audience. While the violence itself may somehow be related to broader societal divisions, this kind of violence has a very narrow appeal. Curbing such violence is not an impossible task.

It is not clear that legislative brawling in polarized democracies signals a death knell for democracy. Examples of polarized democracies that do not experience perpetual brawls in the legislatures abound—countries such as Nigeria, Indonesia, and several South American democracies in the 1960s and 1970s come to mind. In such cases, one might argue that rather than producing legislative violence, societal divisions in these cases led to a complete breakdown in democracy—typically in the form of civil conflicts and/or military coups. An optimistic interpretation of this observation is that where we see legislative brawls, we may actually see democracy enduring in the face of political polarization. Because of its contained nature and remove from society, legislative brawling may represent a kind of safety valve to release some tensions that might otherwise boil over into society.

Lest we risk being overly sanguine, however, we conclude by suggesting that those who would like to curb brawling in legislatures may need to consider the context of political polarization, particularly as we look to elites and the public to shift legislators' incentives for violence. So long as legislators perceive that those audiences will reward them and there may be career gains to be made by signaling that they are a fighter, we are likely to continue to see brawling as a regular feature of democratic legislatures.

Notes

Chapter 1

1. Taiwan's president has only a very weak veto that can be overridden by a simple legislative majority.
2. Answer: only one of the authors has been.
3. Interview, June 13, 2018, Kyiv, Ukraine.
4. Freeman describes some of the individuals involved in congressional violence in such terms. For example, Lawrence Keitt, a Democrat from South Carolina, is described as "an almost comically hot-tempered fire-eater" (Freeman 2018, 238).
5. For example, one can hardly argue that Ukraine and Taiwan are both culturally predisposed to violence. In 2014, Ukraine had 6.34 homicides per 100,000 people, close to the global average, while Taiwan in 2015 had only 0.82, one of the lowest homicide rates in the world.
6. With this description, we are essentially applying Mainwaring and Scully's (1995) description of an entire political party system to describe individual parties.

Chapter 2

1. m has ranged from 1 to 17.
2. Since re-election was not possible for senior legislators, the First Legislature officially lasted from May 1948 to January 1993. September 1992 to January 1993 was thus the 90th Session of the First Legislature.
3. Interview, June 12, 2018, Lviv, Ukraine.
4. Interview, December 3, 2017, Kuala Lumpur, Malaysia.

Chapter 3

1. For more on the value of signaling in the mafia as described here see Gambetta (2011).
2. Interview, June 18, 2018, Kyiv, Ukraine.
3. There are some exceptions to this general observation. Vicente Fox, for example, made a reputation for himself with his individual outbursts in the Mexican Chamber of Deputies.

4. Here *m* refers to the total number of seats in the district. For example, in a district with three seats, the top three vote getters would win those seats.

Chapter 4

1. Mexico did not allow consecutive re-election until 2018, so most, but not all, deputies were, like Dominguez, in their first term.
2. See Eibach (2016) for a review of this connection.
3. Interview, June 13, 2018, Lviv, Ukraine.
4. Interview, June 13, 2018, Lviv, Ukraine.
5. Interview, June 18, 2018, Kyiv, Ukraine.
6. Interview, June 14, 2018, Kyiv, Ukraine.
7. The number fluctuates between a half-dozen to more than a dozen.
8. Taiwan had divided government from 2000 to 2008, with the DPP holding the presidency and the blue camp maintaining a majority in the legislature. It is thus a bit awkward to refer to the green camp as an opposition party during the 2005–2007 period. In this book, however, we will ignore the executive branch and consider the blue camp's legislative majority to define it as a party in power.

Chapter 5

1. Interview, June 17, 2017, Taipei, Taiwan.
2. A more detailed description of the data, methods, and results is provided in Appendix 5.1.
3. For more information about this data set, see Appendix 5.2.
4. The fact that the nonbrawling articles were randomly sampled prevents us from specifying the proportion of total legislative coverage devoted to brawls.
5. Interview, June 4, 2018, Kiyv Ukraine.
6. We consider each term separately. That is, Chu Kao-cheng in the 2nd Term and Chu Kao-cheng in the 3rd Term are considered to be two different individuals.
7. The legislative year runs from February 1 through January 31. For simplicity, we refer to the entire period by the calendar year from February to December.
8. More specifically, we searched for the legislator's name in the three major UDN newspapers, the *United Daily News*, the *United Evening News*, and the *Economic Daily News*, during the relevant year. Since many people might share the same name if the person's name has common characters, we also required that the story include either "legislator" or "Legislative Yuan" (*liwei, lifaweiyuan, lifayuan*). Because the Speaker and Deputy Speaker receive so much coverage due to their institutional positions, they were excluded from this analysis.
9. The United Evening News publishes in the afternoon, so events taking place before noon are often published in that afternoon's paper. We extended the window for

Chapter 6

1. The first survey was a telephone survey with a representative national sample conducted in June 2016. The second was the first wave of the internet panel survey described in this chapter, conducted in June 2017. While the internet survey has a nonrepresentative sample, the results are nonetheless quite striking.
2. All analyses presented in this chapter are robust to alternative codings of partisanship.
3. In more recent years, traditional party divisions have broken down and re-formed, leaving the 2018 legislature with a number of new coalitions. Nonetheless, there are still three major voting blocs (Castro Cornejo 2023).
4. Interview, June 13, 2018, Kyiv, Ukraine.
5. Interview, June 5, 2018, Kiyv, Ukraine.
6. Interview, June 5, 2018, Kiyv, Ukraine.
7. Interview, June 8, 2018, Kiyv, Ukraine.
8. Interview, June 8, 2018, Kiyv Ukraine.
9. Interview, June 8, 2018, Kiyv Ukraine.
10. Note: average temperatures are below freezing in Kyiv, Ukraine, in the winter. Sobolev reported to us that the coldest it got during that protest encampment was 25 degrees (Celsius) below zero.
11. Interview, June 6, 2018, Kyiv, Ukraine.
12. Interview, June 5, 2018, Kiyv, Ukraine.
13. Interview, June 5, 2018, Kiyv, Ukraine.
14. Interview, June 5, 2018, Kyiv, Ukraine.

Chapter 7

1. Interview, July 27, 2017, Mexico City, Mexico.
2. Interview, June 8, 2018, Kiyv, Ukraine.
3. Interview, June 8, 2018, Kiyv, Ukraine.
4. Interview, June 8, 2018, Kiyv, Ukraine.
5. Chapter 4 describes the SNTV electoral system in more detail.
6. For a description of this data source, see Appendix 5.1.
7. An alternative operational definition is to look at the video evidence we presented in Chapter 4 and define brawlers as people we have seen engaging in physical conflicts. Theoretically, this approach strips out the media's intermediary role in identifying brawlers for the general public, which may or may not be desirable. However, since we only have video data from 2004, this approach would cut the period of study by more than half. This definition yielded a much higher proportion of brawling legislators,

but the patterns between brawling and re-election were substantively very similar to the results presented here. For the sake of simplicity, we do not present data from this alternative definition.
8. A standard t-test shows this difference to be statistically significant. $t = 2.82, p = 0.005$.
9. We make an exception for the People First Party (PFP) in the 2002–2007 period. During this period, the DPP was the largest party in the legislature, but the KMT and PFP formed a majority coalition that set the legislative agenda. Since PFP votes were necessary for this majority, we code the PFP in these two terms as a majority party. Other small parties have cooperated with majority parties at various times, but their votes were never necessary to form a majority.

Chapter 8

1. Interview, October 28, 2017, Seoul, South Korea.
2. Interview, October 31, 2017, Seoul, South Korea.

References

"100 Most Influential Ukrainians." 2019. *Focus*, December 23, 2019.

Achen, Christopher H., and T. Y. Wang, eds. 2017. *The Taiwan Voter*. Ann Arbor: University of Michigan Press.

Auel, Katrin, Olga Eisele, and Lucy Kinski. 2018. "What Happens in Parliament Stays in Parliament? Newspaper Coverage of National Parliaments in EU Affairs." *JCMS: Journal of Common Market Studies* 56 (3): 628–645.

Bacchus, Emily Beaulieu, and Carew Boulding. 2021. "Corruption Perceptions: Confidence in Elections and Evaluations of Clientelism." *Governance* 35 (2): 609–632.

Barnes, Tiffany D. 2016. *Gendering Legislative Behavior*. New York: Cambridge University Press.

Barnes, Tiffany D., and Emily Beaulieu. 2019. "Women Politicians, Institutions, and Perceptions of Corruption." *Comparative Political Studies* 52 (1): 134–167.

Barnes, Tiffany D., Emily Beaulieu, and Gregory W. Saxton. 2020. "Sex and Corruption: How Sexism Shapes Voters' Responses to Scandal." *Politics, Groups, and Identities* 8 (1): 103–121.

Batto, Nathan F. 2012. "Differing Mandates and Party Loyalty in Mixed-Member Systems: Taiwan as a Baseline Case." *Electoral Studies* 31 (2): 384–392.

Batto, Nathan F. 2014. "Was Taiwan's Electoral Reform Good for Women? SNTV, MMM, Gender Quotas, and Female Representation." *Issues & Studies* 50 (2): 39–76.

Batto, Nathan F., and Emily Beaulieu. 2020. "Partisan Conflict and Citizens' Democratic Attitudes: How Partisanship Shapes Reactions to Legislative Brawls." *Journal of Politics* 82 (1): 315–328.

Batto, Nathan F., Chi Huang, Alexander C. Tan, and Gary W. Cox, eds. 2016. *Mixed-Member Electoral Systems in Constitutional Context: Taiwan, Japan, and Beyond*. Ann Arbor: University of Michigan Press.

BBC. 2010. "Ukraine MPs Hurt in Parliament Brawl." December 17, 2010. https://www.bbc.com/news/world-europe-12019273.

BBC. 2017. "Turkey's President Erdogan Wins Power-Boosting Vote." January 21, 2017. https://www.bbc.com/news/world-europe-38703704.

Binder, Sarah A. 1997. *Minority Rights, Majority Rule: Partisanship and the Development of Congress*. New York: Cambridge University Press.

Biryabarema, Elias. 2017. "Uganda Bans Live Coverage after House Fistfights, Protests against Museveni." Reuters, September 27, 2017. https://www.reuters.com/article/ozatp-uk-uganda-politics-idAFKCN1C21JV-OZATP.

Brass, Paul R. 2003. *The Production of Hindu-Muslim Violence in Contemporary India*. Seattle: University of Washington Press.

Brescoll, Victoria L., Tyler G. Okimoto, and Andrea C. Vial. 2018. "You've Come a Long Way . . . Maybe: How Moral Emotions Trigger Backlash against Women Leaders." *Journal of Social Issues* 74 (1): 144–164.

Brooks, Deborah Jordan. 2011. "Testing the Double Standard for Candidate Emotionality: Voter Reactions to the Tears and Anger of Male and Female Politicians." *Journal of Politics* 73 (2): 597–615.

Campbell, Angus, Philip E. Converse, Warren E. Miller, and Donald E. Stokes. 1960. *The American Voter*. Chicago: University of Chicago Press.

Carey, John M. 2007. "Competing Principals, Political Institutions, and Party Unity in Legislative Voting." *American Journal of Political Science* 51 (1): 92–107.

Carey, John M., and Matthew Soberg Shugart. 1995. "Incentives to Cultivate a Personal Vote: A Rank Ordering of Electoral Formulas." *Electoral Studies* 14 (4): 417–439.

Castro Cornejo, Rodrigo. 2023. "The AMLO Voter: Affective Polarization and the Rise of the Left in Mexico." *Journal of Politics in Latin America* 15 (1): 96–112.

Chang, Chien-ping. 2001. "Jingwen an: jiaozhang cheng you mindai guanqie; buzhi youwu heidao jieru" [Chingwen case: Education Minister shares representatives' concerns; unsure if organized crime involved]. *United Daily News*, March 27, 2001.

Chang, Jae-soon, and Eun-jung Kim. 2011. "(2nd LD) Lee Offers to Seek Renegotiation on Key Clause after U.S. FTA Takes Effect." Yonhap, November 15, 2011. https://en.yna.co.kr/view/AEN20111115010051315.

Chen, Chih-ping. 2006. "zhihang tiaokuan biaojue: ta cangsai kouzhong" [Vote on direct flights clause: She stuffs it in her mouth]. *United Daily News*, May 31, 2006.

Chen, Yen-po. 2001. "LiYuan bao chongtu Li Qing'an zao Luo Fuzhu dashang" [Conflict erupts in Legislative Yuan; Lee Ching-an injured by Lo Fu-chu]. *United Evening News*, March 28, 2001.

Cheng, Feng-hsing. 2006. "Wei Taiwan dapin Wang Shuhui huanxing Minjindang" [Fighting for Taiwan Wang Shu-hui wakes up DPP]. *Taiwan Daily*, May 31, 2006.

Cheng, Tun-jen, and Yung-ming Hsu. 1996. "Issue Structure, the DPP's Factionalism, and Party Realignment." In *Taiwan's Electoral Politics and Democratic Transition: Riding the Third Wave*, edited by Hung-mao Tien, 137–173. Armonk, NY: M. E. Sharpe.

Chenoweth, Erica. 2013. "Terrorism and Democracy." *Annual Review of Political Science* 16: 355–378.

Chenoweth, Erica, Maria J. Stephan, and Maria Stephan. 2011. *Why Civil Resistance Works: The Strategic Logic of Nonviolent Conflict*. New York: Columbia University Press.

Chu, Yun-han, and Tse-min Lin. 1996. "The Process of Democratic Consolidation in Taiwan: Social Cleavage, Electoral Competition, and the Emerging Party System." In *Taiwan's Electoral Politics and Democratic Transition: Riding the Third Wave*, edited by Hung-mao Tien, 79–104. Armonk, NY: M. E. Sharpe.

Chung, Min-uck. 2011. "Survey Shows Mixed Responses to FTA." *Korea Times*, November 25, 2011. https://www.koreatimes.co.kr/www/nation/2011/11/113_99468.html.

Clark, Justin. 2017. "The 'Black Day' of the General Assembly." *Hoosier State Chronicles*, February 24, 2017. https://blog.newspapers.library.in.gov/black-day-general-assembly.

Cook, Timothy E. 1986. "House Members as Newsmakers: The Effects of Televising Congress." *Legislative Studies Quarterly* 11 (2): 203–226.

Courtemanche, Marie, and Joanne Connor Green. 2020. "A Fall from Grace: Women, Scandals, and Perceptions of Politicians." *Journal of Women, Politics & Policy* 41 (2): 219–240.

Cox, Gary W. 1987. *The Efficient Secret: The Cabinet and the Development of Political Parties in Victorian England*. New York: Cambridge University Press.

Cox, Gary W. 1990. "Centripetal and Centrifugal Incentives in Electoral Systems." *American Journal of Political Science* 34 (4): 903–935.

Cox, Gary W. 1996. "Is the Single Nontransferable Vote Superproportional? Evidence from Japan and Taiwan." *American Journal of Political Science* 40 (3): 740–755.

Cox, Gary W. 2009. "Swing Voters, Core Voters, and Distributive Politics." In *Political Representation*, edited by Ian Shapiro, Susan C. Stokes, Elisabeth Jean Wood, and Alexander S. Kirshner, 342–357. New York: Cambridge University Press.

Cox, Gary W., and Mathew D. McCubbins. 1993. *Legislative Leviathan: Party Government in the House*. Berkeley: University of California Press.

Cox, Gary W., and Mathew D. McCubbins. 2005. *Setting the Agenda: Responsible Party Government in the US House of Representatives*. New York: Cambridge University Press.

Cox, Gary W., and Emerson Niou. 1994. "Seat Bonuses under the Single Nontransferable Vote System: Evidence from Japan and Taiwan." *Comparative Politics* 26 (2): 221–236.

Dawley, Evan N. 2019. *Becoming Taiwanese: Ethnogenesis in a Colonial City, 1880s to 1950s*. Cambridge: Harvard University Asia Center.

Deutsche Welle. 2017. "Brawl Erupts in Turkey's Parliament over Constitutional Reform." January 20, 2017. https://www.dw.com/en/brawl-erupts-in-turkeys-parliament-over-constitutional-reform/a-37202195.

Dion, Douglas. 2001. *Turning the Legislative Thumbscrew: Minority Rights and Procedural Change in Legislative Politics*. Ann Arbor: University of Michigan Press.

Eagly, Alice H., and Steven J. Karau. 2002. "Role Congruity Theory of Prejudice toward Female Leaders." *Psychological Review* 109 (3): 573–598.

Eibach, Joachim. 2016. "Violence and Masculinity." In *The Oxford Handbook of the History of Crime and Criminal Justice*, edited by Paul Knepper and Anja Johansen, 229–249. New York: Oxford University Press.

Esarey, Justin, and Leslie A. Schwindt-Bayer. 2018. "Women's Representation, Accountability and Corruption in Democracies." *British Journal of Political Science* 48 (3): 659–690.

Fallows, James. 1996. *Breaking the News: How the Media Undermine American Democracy*. New York: Vintage.

Farangis, Najibullah. 2015. "Ukrainian Parliamentarian Accused of Striking Female Lawmaker with Bottle." Radio Free Europe/Radio Liberty, November 6, 2015.

Fenno, Richard F. 1978. *Home Style: House Members in Their Districts*. Little, Brown.

Ferrara, Federico. 2004. "Frogs, Mice and Mixed Electoral Institutions: Party Discipline in Italy's XIV Chamber of Deputies." *The Journal of Legislative Studies* 10 (4): 10–31.

Flores, Thomas Edward, and Irfan Nooruddin. 2016. *Elections in Hard Times: Building Stronger Democracies in the 21st Century*. Cambridge University Press.

Fox, Kara. 2017. "Female Lawmakers Brawl in Turkish Parliament." *CNN*, January 20, 2017. https://edition.cnn.com/2017/01/20/europe/turkey-parliament-brawl/index.html.

France24. 2017. "Turkey's Parliament Approve Bill to Expand President Erdogan's Powers." January 21, 2017. https://www.france24.com/en/20170121-turkey-parliament-approves-constitutional-reform-bill-erdogan.

Fraser, Suzan. 2017. "Protest, Fight in Turkish Parliament Sends 2 Female Legislators to Hospital." *Global News*, January 19, 2017. https://globalnews.ca/news/3192509/protest-fight-in-turkish-parliament-sends-2-female-legislators-to-hospital/.

Freeman, Joanne B. 2001. *Affairs of Honor: National Politics in the New Republic*. New Haven, CT: Yale University Press.

Freeman, Joanne B. 2018. *The Field of Blood: Violence in Congress and the Road to Civil War*. New York: Farrar, Straus and Giroux.

Gambetta, Diego. 2011. *Codes of the Underworld: How Criminals Communicate*. Princeton: Princeton University Press.

Gandhi, Mahatma. 1938. *Indian Home Rule: Or, Hind Swaraj*. Pothi.com.

Gandrud, Christopher. 2016. "Two Sword Lengths Apart: Credible Commitment Problems and Physical Violence in Democratic National Legislatures." *Journal of Peace Research* 53 (1): 130–145.

Glionna, John H. 2009. "South Korea Lawmakers: Reaching across the Aisle with a Sledgehammer." *Los Angeles Times*, January 28, 2009. https://www.latimes.com/world/la-fg-korea-fight28-2009jan28-story.html.

Grofman, Bernard, Sung-Chull Lee, Edwin Winckler, and Brian Woodall, eds. 1999. *Elections in Japan, Korea, and Taiwan under the Single Non-transferable Vote: The Comparative Study of an Embedded Institution*. Ann Arbor: University of Michigan Press.

The Guardian. 2017. "Bill to Cement Erdoğan's Power Passes First Vote in Turkey." January 16, 2017. https://www.theguardian.com/world/2017/jan/16/bill-to-cement-erdogans-power-passes-first-vote-in-turkey.

Gurr, Ted Robert. 1970. *Why Men Rebel*. Princeton: Princeton University Press.

Guyana Chronicle. 2021. "Mace Protector: 'I Would Do It Again If I Have To.'" December 21, 2021. https://guyanachronicle.com/2021/12/31/mace-protector-i-would-do-it-again-if-i-have-to/.

Hankyoreh. 2008a. "Lawmakers Make and Break Alliances over FTA Ratification." November 11, 2008. https://www.hani.co.kr/arti/PRINT/321117.html.

Hankyoreh. 2008b. "GNP Goes Solo Again to Submit FTA Bill for Ratification." December 19, 2008. http://english.hani.co.kr/arti/english_edition/e_national/328625.html.

Hankyoreh. 2008c. "Assembly Speaker Apologizes for GNP's Unilateral Actions." December 20, 2008. https://english.hani.co.kr/arti/english_edition/e_national/328785.html.

Harbridge, Laurel, and Neil Malhotra. 2011. "Electoral Incentives and Partisan Conflict in Congress: Evidence from Survey Experiments." *American Journal of Political Science* 55 (3): 494–510.

Helfer, Luzia, and Peter Van Aelst. 2016. "What Makes Party Messages Fit for Reporting? An Experimental Study of Journalistic News Selection." *Political Communication* 33 (1): 59–77.

Hemphill, Libby, and Matthew A. Shapiro. 2019. "Appealing to the Base or to the Moveable Middle? Incumbents' Partisan Messaging before the 2016 US Congressional Elections." *Journal of Information Technology & Politics* 16 (4): 325–341.

Herron, Erik S. 2002a. "Causes and Consequences of Fluid Faction Membership in Ukraine." *Europe-Asia Studies* 54 (4): 625–639.

Herron, Erik S. 2002b. "Electoral Influences on Legislative Behavior in Mixed-Member Systems: Evidence from Ukraine's Verkhovna Rada." *Legislative Studies Quarterly* 27 (3): 361–382.

Herron, Erik S., Brian Fitzpatrick, and Maksym Palamarenko. 2019. "The Practice and Implications of Legislative Proxy Voting in Ukraine." *Post-Soviet Affairs* 35 (1): 41–62.

Herszenhorn, David M. 2014. "With Stunts and Vigilante Escapades, a Populist Gains Ground in Ukraine." *New York Times*, October 24, 2014. https://www.nytimes.com/2014/10/25/world/europe/with-stunts-and-vigilante-escapades-a-populist-gains-ground-in-ukraine.html.

Hess, David, and Brian Martin. 2006. "Repression, Backfire, and the Theory of Transformative Events." *Mobilization: An International Quarterly* 11 (2): 249–267.

Hicken, Allen. 2009. *Building Party Systems in Developing Democracies*. New York: Cambridge University Press.

Ho, Samuel P. S. 1978. *Economic Development of Taiwan, 1860–1970*. New Haven, CT: Yale University Press.

Holman, Mirya R., Jennifer L. Merolla, and Elizabeth J. Zechmeister. 2016. "Terrorist Threat, Male Stereotypes, and Candidate Evaluations." *Political Research Quarterly* 69 (1): 134–147.

Huang, Jewel. 2006. "Links Bill Nixed Amid Legislative Chaos." *Taipei Times*, May 31, 2006.

Huang, Ming-hsi. 2006. "zhihang tiaokuan chongtu. Wang Jin-ping: dongyong jingchaquan zhisi yifen" [Conflict over direct flights clause. Wang Jin-pyng: Using police powers would bring chaos]. Central News Agency, May 30, 2006.

Huddy, Leonie, and Nayda Terkildsen. 1993. "Gender Stereotypes and the Perception of Male and Female Candidates." *American Journal of Political Science*: 37 (1): 119–147.

Hürriyet Daily News. 2017. "Three MPs Sent to Hospital after Violent Altercation Following Handcuff Protest." January 20, 2017. https://www.hurriyetdailynews.com/three-mps-sent-to-hospital-after-violent-altercation-following-handcuff-protest-108754.

Hyde, Susan D. 2011. *The Pseudo-Democrat's Dilemma: Why Election Observation Became an International Norm*. Ithaca, NY: Cornell University Press.

Ilie, Cornelia. 2013. "Gendering Confrontational Rhetoric: Discursive Disorder in the British and Swedish Parliaments." *Democratization* 20 (3): 501–521.

Interfax-Ukraine. 2015. "Member of Parliament Parasyuk Faces 5 Years in Jail for Attacking SBU Officer." *Kyiv Post*, November 20, 2015. https://www.kyivpost.com/article/content/ukraine-politics/member-of-parliament-parasyuk-faces-5-years-in-jail-for-attacking-on-duty-officer-pgo-402519.html.

Irish Times. 2001. "Turkish MP Dies as Debate Descends to a Brawl." January 31, 2001. https://www.irishtimes.com/news/turkish-mp-dies-as-debate-descends-to-a-brawl-1.373225.

Jennings, George Henry. 1881. *An Anecdotal History of the British Parliament from the Earliest Periods to the Present Time*. New York: D. Appleton & Company.

Jun, Hae-Won, and Simon Hix. 2010. "Electoral Systems, Political Career Paths and Legislative Behavior: Evidence from South Korea's Mixed-Member System." *Japanese Journal of Political Science* 11 (2): 153–171.

Jung, Da-min. 2019a. "Over 1 Million Sign Petition Demanding LKP Disbandment." *Korea Times*, April 30, 2019. https://www.koreatimes.co.kr/www/nation/2023/02/356_268066.html.

Jung, Da-min. 2019b. "52% of Voters Support Fast-Tracking of Reform Bills: Poll." *Korea Times*, May 2, 2019. http://www.koreatimes.co.kr/www/nation/2019/08/356_268209.html.

Kahn, Kim Fridkin. 1994. "Does Gender Make a Difference? An Experimental Examination of Sex Stereotypes and Press Patterns in Statewide Campaigns." *American Journal of Political Science*: 38 (1): 162–195.

Kang, Hyun-kyung. 2008. "Assembly in FTA Conflict." *Korea Times*, December 18, 2008. https://www.koreatimes.co.kr/www/news/nation/2008/12/116_36329.html.

Kerevel, Yann P. 2015. "(Sub) National Principals, Legislative Agents: Patronage and Political Careers in Mexico." *Comparative Political Studies* 48 (8): 1020–1050.

Kerevel, Yann P., and Sergio A. Bárcena Juárez. 2017. "Democratización y representación legislativa en México." *Revista Uruguaya de Ciencia Política* 26 (1): 59–83.

Kim, Bo-gyung. 2019. "Standoff between Ruling and Main Opposition Results in Violent Clash." *Korea Herald*, April 26, 2019. https://www.koreaherald.com/view.php?ud=20190426000630.

Kim, Eun-jung. 2011a. "(2nd LD) Main Opposition Party Refuses Lee's Renegotiation Offer on U.S. FTA." Yonhap, November 16, 2011. https://en.yna.co.kr/view/AEN20111116002552315.

Kim, Eun-jung. 2011b. "(2nd LD) U.S. FTA Clash Looms in S. Korean Parliament." Yonhap, November 17, 2011. https://en.yna.co.kr/view/AEN20111117004052315.

Kim, Eun-jung. 2011c. "(5th LD) S. Korean Parliament Approves Free Trade Pact with U.S." Yonhap, November 22, 2011. https://en.yna.co.kr/view/AEN20111122009055315.

Kim, Eun-jung. 2011d. "(LEAD) Opposition Parties Boycott Assembly Sessions in Protest of FTA Passage." Yonhap, November 23, 2011. https://en.yna.co.kr/view/AEN20111123003051315.

Kim, Eun-jung. 2011e. "Parliamentary Trade Committee Chairman Offers to Resign over U.S. FTA." Yonhap, November 24, 2011. https://en.yna.co.kr/view/AEN20111124002600315.

Kim, Yoo-chul. 2019. "LKP Fears Losing Influence." *Korea Times*, April 26, 2019. https://www.koreatimes.co.kr/www/nation/2023/01/356_267846.html.

Kizil, Nurbanu. 2017. "Everything You Need to Know about Turkey's Constitutional Reform." *Daily Sabah*, January 18, 2017. https://www.dailysabah.com/legislation/2017/01/18/everything-you-need-to-know-about-turkeys-constitutional-reform.

Lai, Tse-han, Ramon H. Myers, and Wei Wou. 1991. *A Tragic Beginning: The Taiwan Uprising of February 28, 1947*. Stanford: Stanford University Press.

Lamley, Harry J. 1999. "Taiwan Under Japanese Rule, 1895–1945: The Vicissitudes of Colonialism." In *Taiwan: A New History*, edited by Murray Rubinstein, 201–260. Armonck, NY: M.E. Sharpe.

Lee, Min-hyung. 2019a. "LKP Declares All-Out Struggle against Moon." *Korea Times*, April 19, 2019. https://www.koreatimes.co.kr/www/nation/2019/12/356_267469.html.

Lee, Min-hyung. 2019b. "Party Standoff Deepens over Fast-Track Reform Bills." *Korea Times*, April 28, 2019. https://www.koreatimes.co.kr/www/nation/2019/06/356_267917.html.

Liao, Da-chi. 1997. *Lifa Yuan Chongtu Xianxiang Lunheng* [Conflict in the Legislative Yuan]. Kaohsiung: Kaohsiung Fuwen Press.

Lin, Ho-ming, Hsueh-mei Wang, and Hsu-tsen Hsiao. 2002. "Jianpiaoren kan liangbian renma; zheng zhiti chongtu yibazhua dai toupiao" [Voting supervisors watch both sides; physical conflict grabbing proxy voters]. *United Daily News*, June 21, 2002.

Lu, Chien-yao. 1996. "LiYuan Guoshiluntan kaida; Lin Mingyi da Su Huanzhi shu quan" [Fighting starts in Legislative Yuan during the National Affairs Forum; Lin Ming-yi punches Su Huan-chih several times]. *United Daily News*, October 9, 1996.

Mainwaring, Scott, and Timothy Scully, eds. 1995. *Building Democratic Institutions: Party Systems in Latin America*. Stanford: Stanford University Press.

Mainwaring, Scott, and Matthew Soberg Shugart, eds. 1997. *Presidentialism and Democracy in Latin America*. New York: Cambridge University Press.

Matsuka, Oleksii, Serhi Tomilenko, Oleksii Pohorelov, Oles Hoian, Andrii Yurychko, Tetiana Lebediva, and Vitalii Moroz. 2017. *Ukrainian Media Landscape-2017*. Konrad Adenauer Foundation. Academy of Ukrainian Press.

McDaniel, Eric L., Irfan Nooruddin, and Allyson F. Shortle. 2022. *The Everyday Crusade: Christian Nationalism in American Politics*. New York: Cambridge University Press.

Modern Japan in Archives. "Parliament in Brawl and Lament by Secretary General of House of Representatives." National Diet Library. https://www.ndl.go.jp/modern/e/column/09.html.

Morris, Jonathan S., and Rosalee Clawson. 2005. "Media Coverage of Congress in the 1990s: Scandals, Personalities, and the Prevalence of Policy and Process." *Political Communication* 22: 297–313.

Morrow, James D. 1999. "The Strategic Setting of Choices: Signaling, Commitment, and Negotiation in International Politics." In *Strategic Choice and International Relations*, edited by David A. Lake and Robert Powell, 77–114. Princeton: Princeton University Press.

Mutz, Diana C., and Byron Reeves. 2005. "The New Videomalaise: Effects of Televised Incivility on Political Trust." *American Political Science Review* 99 (1): 1–15.

Nepstad, Sharon Erickson. 2013. "Mutiny and Nonviolence in the Arab Spring: Exploring Military Defections and Loyalty in Egypt, Bahrain, and Syria." *Journal of Peace Research* 50 (3): 337–349.

News Room. 2021. "APNU's Annette Ferguson Attempts to Steal Speaker's Mace." December 29, 2021. https://newsroom.gy/2021/12/29/apnus-annette-ferguson-attempts-to-steal-speakers-mace/.

Nordland, Rob. 2017. "Amid Fistfights, Turkey's Parliament Backs a New Constitution." *New York Times*, January 20, 2017. https://www.nytimes.com/2017/01/20/world/middleeast/turkey-new-constitution-fight.html.

Okello, Dickens, H. 2017. "Kadaga: Minister Kibuule Had a Gun at Parliament." *ChimpReports*. https://chimpreports.com/kadaga-minister-kibuule-had-a-gun-at-parliament/.

Park, Ji-won. 2019a. "LKP Goes All Out to Block Reform Bills." *Korea Times*, April 23, 2019. https://www.koreatimes.co.kr/www/nation/2019/04/113_267650.html.

Park, Ji-won. 2019b. "National Assembly Set to Put Reform Bills on Fast Track despite Protest." *Korea Times*, April 25, 2019. https://www.koreatimes.co.kr/www/nation/2019/07/356_267790.html.

Park, Ji-won. 2019c. "Ruling Party Head Vows Stern Handling of 'Law-Breaking' LKP Members." *Korea Times*, April 29, 2019. https://www.koreatimes.co.kr/www/nation/2019/04/113_267979.html.

Park, Ji-won. 2019d. "Four Parties Put Reform Bills on Fast Track." *Korea Times*, April 30, 2019. https://www.koreatimes.co.kr/www/nation/2019/05/356_268024.html.

Park, Ji-won. 2019e. "New Election Bill Passed amid Clashes." *Korea Times*, December 27, 2019. https://www.koreatimes.co.kr/www/nation/2019/12/356_280985.html.

Plokhy, Serhii. 2015. *The Gates of Europe: A History of Ukraine*. New York: Basic Books.

Rahat, Gideon, and Reuven Y. Hazan. 2001. "Candidate Selection Methods: An Analytical Framework." *Party Politics* 7 (3): 297–322.

Ramani, Samuel. 2017. "Interview with Former Aidar Battalion Commander and Ukrainian Rada Member Serhiy Melnychuck on 'Myths' about Aidar Battalion and Ukraine's Future." HuffPost, September 5, 2017. https://www.huffpost.com/entry/interview-with-former-aidar-battalion-commander-and_b_59aee24ee4b0c50640cd625d.

Ramseyer, J. Mark, and Frances McCall Rosenbluth. 1993. *Japan's Political Marketplace*. Cambridge, MA: Harvard University Press.

Ranney, Austin. 1983. *Channels of Power: The Impact of Television on American Politics*. New York: Perseus Books.

Reuters. 2014. "Meet the Man Who Forced Ukraine's President to Run for His Life." *New York Post*, February 25, 2014. https://nypost.com/2014/02/25/meet-the-man-who-forced-ukraines-president-to-run-for-his-life/.

RFE/RL. 2013. "Ukrainian Deputies Throw Punches in Parliament." Radio Free Europe/Radio Liberty, March 19, 2013. https://www.rferl.org/a/24933141.html.

Rigger, Shelley. 1999. *Politics in Taiwan: Voting for Democracy*. New York: Routledge.

Romanenko, Maria. 2017. "Over 500 Police Officers Call for Lawmaker Parasiuk to Be Stripped of Immunity." *Kyiv Post*, March 17, 2017. https://www.kyivpost.com/ukraine-politics/500-police-officers-call-lawmaker-parasiuk-stripped-immunity.html.

Rosenthal, Cindy Simon. 2000. "Gender Styles in State Legislative Committees: Raising Their Voices in Resolving Conflict." *Women & Politics* 21 (2): 21–45.

Roy, Denny. 2003. *Taiwan: A Political History*. Ithaca, NY: Cornell University Press.

Rozelle, Mark J. 1994. "Press Coverage of Congress, 1946–92." In *Congress, the Press, and the Public*, edited by Thomas E. Mann and Norman J. Ornstein, 59–130. Washington, DC: American Enterprise Institute and Brookings Institution.

Rudman, Laurie A., and Peter Glick. 1999. "Feminized Management and Backlash toward Agentic Women: The Hidden Costs to Women of a Kinder, Gentler Image of Middle Managers." *Journal of Personality and Social Psychology* 77 (5): 1004.

Russell, Jan Jaboe. 1992. "The Eternal Challenger." *Texas Monthly*, October 1992. https://www.texasmonthly.com/news-politics/the-eternal-challenger.

Sabato, Larry J. 1991. *Feeding Frenzy: How Attack Journalism Has Transformed American Politics*. New York: Free Press.

Schmoll, Moritz, and Wang Leung Ting. 2023. "Explaining Physical Violence in Parliaments." *Journal of Conflict Resolution* 67 (2–3): 375–401.

Schneider, Monica C., Mirya R. Holman, Amanda B. Diekman, and Thomas McAndrew. 2016. "Power, Conflict, and Community: How Gendered Views of Political Power Influence Women's Political Ambition." *Political Psychology* 37 (4): 515–531.

Scott, James C. 1985. *Weapons of the Weak: Everyday Forms of Peasant Resistance*. Yale University Press.

Sharp, Gene. 1973. *The Politics of Nonviolent Action*. 3 vols. Boston: Porter Sargent.

Shepherd, John R. 1999. "The Island Frontier of the Ch'ing, 1684–1780." In *Taiwan: A New History*, edited by Murray A. Rubinstein, 107–132. Armonk, NY: M. E. Sharpe.

Shukan, Ioulia. 2013. "Intentional Disruptions and Violence in Ukraine's Supreme Rada: Political Competition, Order, and Disorder in a Post-Soviet Chamber, 2006–2012." *Post-Soviet Affairs* 29 (5): 439–456.

Slomczynski, Kazimierz M., Goldie Shabad, and Jakub Zielinski. 2008. "Fluid Party Systems, Electoral Rules and Accountability of Legislators in Emerging Democracies: The Case of Ukraine." *Party Politics* 14 (1): 91–112.

Spary, Carole. 2010. "Disrupting Rituals of Debate in the Indian Parliament." *Journal of Legislative Studies* 16 (3): 338–351.

Spary, Carole. 2013. "Legislative Protest as Disruptive Democratic Practice." *Democratization* 20 (3): 392–416.

Sputnik. 2017. "Lawmaker Reveals Why Ukrainian Parliament Keeps Breaking Out in Fisticuffs." February 13, 2017. https://sputniknews.com/20170213/krainian-parliament-brawls-reasons-revealed-1050629855.html.

Sullivan, Jonathan, and James Smyth. 2018. "The KMT's China Policy: Gains and Failures." In *Assessing the Presidency of Ma Ying-jiu in Taiwan: Hopeful Beginning, Hopeless End?*, edited by André Beckershoff and Gunter Schubert, 17–36. London: Routledge.

Tarrow, Sidney. 1998. *Power in Movement: Collective Action, Social Movements and Politics*. New York: Cambridge University Press.

Tasker, John Paul. 2016. "Justin Trudeau's Elbowing Incident Leaves House in an Uproar." *CBC News*, May 18, 2016.

Thames, Frank C. 2005. "Searching for Party Effects in Post-Communist Ukraine." *Communist and Post-Communist Studies* 38 (1): 89–108.

Thames, Frank C. 2007. "Searching for the Electoral Connection: Parliamentary Party Switching in the Ukrainian Rada, 1998–2002." *Legislative Studies Quarterly* 32 (2): 223–256.

Thames, Frank. 2016. "Electoral Rules and Legislative Parties in the Ukrainian Rada." *Legislative Studies Quarterly* 41 (1): 35–59.

Thames, Frank, and Melanie Castleberg. 2006. "Electoral Incentives and Party Switching in Mixed-System Legislatures." Paper presented at the annual meeting of the American Political Science Association, Philadelphia.

Tien, Hung-mao. 1989. *The Great Transition: Political and Social Change in the Republic of China*. Stanford: Hoover Institution Press.

Tien, Hung-mao. 1996. "Elections and Taiwan's Democratic Development." In *Taiwan's Electoral Politics and Democratic Transition: Riding the Third Wave*, edited by Hung-mao Tien, 3–26. Armonk, NY: M. E. Sharpe.

The Times. 1923. "Parliament." April 12, 1923, p 7.

The Times. 1931. "Disorder in the Commons." July 3, 1931, p 9.

Tsfati, Y., D. M. Elfassi, and I. Waismel-Manor. 2010. "Exploring the Association between Israeli Legislators' Physical Attractiveness and Their Television News Coverage." *International Journal of Press/Politics* 15 (2): 175–192.

Tymoshchuk, Yaroslava. 2020. "Former Deputy Yehor Soboliev—About the Path to Programming." *Dou*, June 16, 2020.

UDN. 1987. "Li Yuan chaofantian. Yichang tuole xian" [Legislative Yuan argues all day. Chamber goes off the rails]. *United Daily News*, October 24, 1987.

Vakulyuk, Dmitriy. 2015. "Fight Cuts Short March 3 Session of Parliament." *Kyiv Post*, March 3, 2015.

Van Santen, Rosa, Luzia Helfer, and Peter Van Aelst. 2015. "When Politics Becomes News: An Analysis of Parliamentary Questions and Press Coverage in Three West European Countries." *Acta Politica* 50: 45–63.

Vos, Debby. 2014. "Which Politicians Pass the News Gates and Why? Explaining Inconsistencies in Research on News Coverage of Individual Politicians." *International Journal of Communication* 8: 2438–2461.

Vos, Debby. 2016. "How Ordinary MPs Can Make It into the News: A Factorial Survey Experiment with Political Journalists to Explain the Newsworthiness of MPs." *Mass Communication and Society* 19 (6): 738–757.

Wikipedia. n.d. "Black Day of the Indiana General Assembly." https://en.wikipedia.org/wiki/Black_Day_of_the_Indiana_General_Assembly.

Wilkinson, Steven. 2006. *Votes and Violence: Electoral Competition and Ethnic Riots in India*. Cambridge University Press.

Williams, Melissa J., and Larissa Z. Tiedens. 2016. "The Subtle Suspension of Backlash: A Meta-Analysis of Penalties for Women's Implicit and Explicit Dominance Behavior." *Psychological Bulletin* 142 (2): 165.

Wills Jr., John E. 1999. "The Seventeenth-Century Transformation: Taiwan under the Dutch and the Cheng Regime." In *Taiwan: A New History*, edited by Murray A. Rubinstein, 84–106. Armonk, NY: M. E. Sharpe.

Yang, Sheng-ju. 2006. "zhihang tiaokuan you bao chongtu nülüwei tun an yan chu" [Direct flights bill erupts in conflict again; green female legislator swallows bill]. *United Evening News*, May 30, 2006.

Yin, Nai-hsin. 1995a. "Lin Mingyi lian hui jiu quan; Huang Zhaohui zao ji wei huanshou" [Lin Ming-yi throws nine punches; Huang Chao-hui is attacked but doesn't hit back]. *United Daily News*, July 19, 1995.

Yin, Nai-hsin. 1995b. "Lin Mingyi: bu neng renshou yuyan baoli" [Lin Ming-yi: I can't stand the verbal violence]. *United Daily News*, July 19, 1995.

Yomiuri Shinbun. 1954. "Senseless Violence—Four Hours of Chaos" [in Japanese]. June 4, 1954.

Yonhap. 2011a. "Ruling Party Lawmaker Begins Hunger Strike for Vote on U.S. FTA." November 13, 2011. https://en.yna.co.kr/view/AEN20111113003000315.

Yonhap. 2011b. "Ruling Party Set to Ram through U.S. FTA." November 22, 2011. https://en.yna.co.kr/view/AEN20111122007500315.

Yonhap. 2011c. "Opposition Lawmaker Detonates Tear Gas Bomb inside Assembly Chamber to Protest FTA." November 22, 2011. https://en.yna.co.kr/view/AEN20111122008300315.

Yonhap. 2019a. "(3rd LD) Speaker OKs Change of Judiciary Reform Panel Members amid Political Turmoil." Yonhap News Agency, April 25, 2019. https://en.yna.co.kr/view/AEN20190425003453315.

Yonhap. 2019b. "(LEAD) Rival Parties Clash over Whether to Fast-Track Key Reform Bills." Yonhap News Agency, April 26, 2019. https://en.yna.co.kr/view/AEN20190426007852315.

Yonhap. 2019c. "(LEAD) Opposition Party Stages Massive Street Protest against Move to Fast-Track Key Bills." Yonhap News Agency, April 27, 2019. https://en.yna.co.kr/view/AEN20190427001251325.

Yonhap. 2019d. "Moon's Approval Rating Goes Up despite Parliament Limbo." Yonhap News Agency, May 6, 2019. https://en.yna.co.kr/view/AEN20190506001200325.

Yonhap. 2019e. "Assembly Convenes to Deal with Election, Prosecution Bills." *Korea Herald*, December 23, 2019. https://www.koreaherald.com/view.php?ud=20191223000844.

Yu, Eric Chen-hua, Kaori Shoji, and Nathan F. Batto. 2016. "Innovations in Candidate Selection Methods." In *Mixed-Member Electoral Systems in Constitutional Context: Taiwan, Japan, and Beyond*, edited by Nathan F. Batto, Chi Huang, Alexander C. Tan, and Gary W. Cox, 135–164. Ann Arbor: University of Michigan Press.

Index

For the benefit of digital users, indexed terms that span two pages (e.g., 52–53) may, on occasion, appear on only one of those pages.

Note: Tables and figures are indicated by *t* and *f* following the page number

accusations
  improper actions during brawls, 33, 38, 143
  improper actions leading to brawls, 26, 33–34, 39, 88–89, 91, 132, 143
  motives for, 14–15, 70–71, 71*f*, 72–74, 92, 93–94, 141–42
ad hominem attacks, 36
age, 75, 82, 89, 90–91, 95, 100, 149, 156–57, 170–71
AKP. *See* Justice and Development Party
antebellum culture, 3–4, 11–12
anthropological explanations of brawling, 9, 11–12, 15
archetypes of honor brawlers, 92–93

ballot access, 17
blue camp, 27, 99, 190n.8
Boyko, Yuriy, 91
brawling. *See specific topics*
Burbak, Maksym, 152

Calderon, Felipe, 46–47, 81
Canada, 6–7
careers, *See also* re-election
  as a motive to brawl, 7–8, 9, 11–12, 15, 17–18, 19, 52–53, 55, 78–79, 100, 114, 124, 146, 147, 151, 153, 160–61, 165–66, 170, 171–73, 185, 188
  outside the legislature, 10, 88, 89, 147, 159–60
  strong parties and, 14, 61, 63–64, 128–31
  weak parties and, 14, 68–70, 76–77, 134

Chang Hung-hsueh, 26
Chao Chen-peng, 156–57
character attacks, 72
Cheng family, 20
Chen Shui-bian, 27, 109–10, 155–56, 157–58, 159–60
Chen Wan-chen, Stella, 157
Chiang Ching-kuo, 22
Chiang Kai-shek, 21
China
  immigration to Taiwan from, 20
  KMT and, 22
  during ROC era, 21
  Taiwan and, 1, 8, 24, 153–54, 186–87
Chou Shu-fu, 156–57, 158
CHP. *See* Republican People's Party
Chu Feng-chih, 156–57
Chu Kao-cheng, 10, 26, 153–55, 156–57, 158, 190n.6
Chumak, Viktor, 152
Civil War, US, 3–4, 11, 39–40, 51, 80
closed-list proportional representation (CLPR) electoral rules
  brawling and, 63–64, 65–66, 69, 76–77, 79, 85–86, 98–99, 124, 136, 165–66
  brawling and re-election in, 146, 150, 151, 152–53, 166–67
  in Korea, 130, 178
  in Mexico, 128–29
  in Taiwan, 16–17, 24–25, 65–66, 98–99, 165–67
  in Ukraine, 16–17, 30–31, 32, 89, 90–91, 92, 136, 146, 150, 151, 152–53
CLPR. *See* closed-list proportional representation

corruption
  accusations of, in brawls, 7, 92
  and electoral rules, 76–77
  as a motive for brawls, 72–73, 74, 139, 141, 142, 148
  in South Africa, 48
  in Taiwan, 2, 21
  in Ukraine, 29, 30, 33, 34, 88–90, 138, 151–52
costly signals
  brawls as, 33–34, 52–55, 170
  credibility of, 13, 56, 59–60, 62, 168
  and political violence, 184, 185
  transmission of, 77–78
  who sends, 60, 62–63, 72–73, 75, 82, 84, 85–86
Crimean War, 28–29

Daisuke Yoshie, 41
data collection, 16, 94, 101–2, 107–8, 114–20, 115t–21t
delegation, 76–77
democracy
  breakdown, 80, 187–88
  democratic process, 3–4, 28, 56–57, 137–38, 145, 147–48, 151, 160–61, 175–76, 182–83, 184
  frequency of brawls in, 8, 16–17, 34–36, 42, 56, 129–30
  norms, 3–4, 175–76, 179–80
  quality of, 3–4, 8–9, 32, 43, 45, 49–50, 60, 80, 124–27, 125t–27t, 134, 169, 178–79, 184–86
  representation, 8, 19, 69, 80, 100, 145, 172–73
  suppression of, 20–22
Democratic Alliance (South Africa), 48
Democratic Labor Party (South Korea), 43, 44
Democratic Party (South Korea), 42–45, 178–80, 181–82
Democratic Party (US), 40
Democratic Progressive Party (DPP) (Taiwan)
  and democratization, 22–23, 24, 25–27, 56
  in disruption brawls, 1–2, 26–27, 28, 34, 132, 156–57

  election results, 27, 28, 146, 153–56, 157, 158
  in honor brawls, 142–41
  as a large party, 99, 166
  nominations, 158, 165–66
  party image, 5
  party supporters, 125–26, 125t, 126t, 133
  as a strong party, 65
  United Daily News position toward, 114–15
democratization
  brawls and, 16–17, 25–26, 27, 42, 45, 56, 153–56
  election observation and, 13, 62–63
  in Taiwan, 22–23
destruction, of property, 4–5, 6–7, 27, 95t, 102, 153–54
disruption
  characteristics of disruption brawls, 50–51, 74
  definition of, 5–7
  examples of, 1–2, 32–34, 37–49, 81, 94, 132, 178–79, 180
  gender and, 79–80, 85
  honor and, 7
  legislative, 3–4, 57–61
  legislators and, 52, 87
  nonviolent, 6, 46–47, 59, 75–76
  opposition disruption, 5, 7, 36, 52, 55–70, 55f, 73, 75–76, 87, 105–6, 170–71
  in politics, 10, 57–59, 184–85
  and representation, 11
  strong parties and, 14, 60, 61–63, 76–77
  violence and, 6–7, 61–62, 75–76, 94–95, 95t, 153–54
  weak parties and, 68–70
Dominguez Servien, Francisco, 81, 147, 190n.1
DPP. *See* Democratic Progressive Party

economic elites, 14, 30, 55f, 68, 70, 122, 123, 135, 139–41, 144–45. *See also* oligarchs
election observation, 13, 62–63
electoral rules, *See also* CLPR; mixed-member; SMP; SNTV
  impact of, 8, 11–12, 14, 52–53, 60, 63–64, 79, 85–86, 100, 122, 124, 128, 129

Korean reform, 42, 170–71, 178–79, 181–82, 183
English Civil War, 37
Erdoğan, Recep Tayyip, 45
Euromaidan protests
  consequences of, 16–17, 30, 33–34, 69
  legislators in, 10–11, 30, 69, 88, 89, 113, 138
  to oligarchs, 139–40
Europe (in Ukrainian politics), 28–29, 30, 35–36, 152–53
extremism, 87, 134

Fast Track provision (in Korea), 170, 176–77, 178–79, 182–83
Fatherland Party (Ukraine), 33, 92–93, 135, 136, 150
Ferguson, Annette, 47–48
filibuster (in Korea), 5–6, 176, 177, 178–79, 180, 183
Foreman, Ed, 40
Fox, Vicente, 47, 56, 189n.3
France, 28–29, 35–36
Freeman, Joanne, 3–4, 9–10, 11, 39–40, 71–72, 80, 104, 189n.4

Gandrud, Christopher, 34–36, 55–56
gender. *See also* women
  in honor brawls, 73–74
  incentives to brawl, 79–80, 83–85, 98, 100–1
  signaling, 79–80, 83, 84, 98
  stereotypes, 73–74, 79–80, 83–85
  in Taiwan, 98
  in Ukraine, 83
general electorate, 13–14, 18–19, 52–53, 54–55, 64–65, 78–79, 80, 122, 123–27, 185–86
Gonzalez, Henry, 40
Grand National Party (GNP) (Korea), 42–45
green camp, 27, 99, 190n.8
Griswold, Roger, 39
Guinness, Walter, 38
Guyana, 46, 47–48

Han Kuo-yu, 157–58
HDP. *See* People's Democratic Party

honor brawls
  compared to opposition disruption brawls, 74–75, 94
  gender in, 73–74
  honor as a motive to brawl, 7, 14–15, 51
  re-election and, 157
  signaling in, 70–71, 72–73, 141–44
  in Taiwan, 93–94, 142–44
  in Ukraine, 34, 92–94, 100
  in US, 11, 39–40, 71–72
  worldwide, 7, 36
Hsiao Chin-lan, 156–57
Hsieh Chang-ting, Frank, 155–56, 158
Huang Chao-hui, 142–44
Huang Chao-shun, 158–59
Huang Chih-hsiung, 10–11
Hung Hsiu-chu, 2
Hwang Woo-yea, 43–44

identity politics, 187
Institutional Revolutionary Party (PRI) (Mexico), 46–47, 56, 65, 81, 128–29
intensity index, 94, 95, 95t, 96t, 97t
Italy, 35–36

Japan
  strong parties and brawling in, 98
  Taiwan colony, 20–21, 22, 40–41
  US-Japan Security Treaty, 40–42
Japan Socialist Party (Japan), 41
Jeong Tae-Keun, 43–44
Justice and Development Party (AKP) (Turkey), 45–46

Kadaga, Rebecca, 49
Kaohsuing Incident, 22, 155–56
Keitt, Lawrence, 189n.4
Kibuule, Ronald, 49
Kilicdaroglu, Kemal, 46
Kim Hyong-o, 43, 44
Kim Sun-dong, 44, 50
Klitschko, Vitali, 10–11, 149–50
KMT. *See* Kuomintang
Kolomoysky, Ihor, 70
Kuchma, Leonid, 29, 32–33, 150

Kuomintang (KMT) (Taiwan)
  authoritarian era, 21–22, 24
  blue camp, 27, 99
  democratization and, 22–23, 24, 25–27, 56
  in disruption brawls, 1–2, 26–27, 28, 34, 132, 156–57
  election results, 27, 28, 146, 154, 156–57, 158, 168–69
  in honor brawls, 93–94, 142–44
  Huang Fu-hsing legislators, 156–58
  Issue positions, 1–2, 23, 132
  as a large party, 99, 166
  local factions, 26, 132
  as a majority party, 1–2, 5, 99
  nominations, 165–66
  as an opposition party, 99, 132–34, 161–64
  party supporters, 125–26, 125t, 126t, 132, 133, 134
  ROC era in China, 21
  as a strong party, 34, 65
Kuzhel, Oleksandra, 92–94, 141, 150

Labour Party (UK), 38
large parties and brawling
  large opposition parties, 100–1, 172
  media coverage, 78, 105–6
  need to send signals, 87, 135, 170–71
  nonviolent disruption, 75–76
  in Ukraine, 89, 90, 91, 100
  in Taiwan, 99, 100, 166
Lee Ching-an, 93–94
Lee Teng-hui, 22–23
Legal Affairs Committee (Korea), 174–75, 176–77
Leschenko, Serhiy, 34
Levchenko, Nikolai, 33–34
Liashko, Oleh, 88, 90–91, 94, 114, 115, 135, 137, 146, 150
Liashko Radical Party (Ukraine), 34, 90–91, 135, 137, 146, 150, 152, 153
Liberty Korea Party (LKP) (Korea), 178–80, 181–82
Lin Ming-yi, 142–44, 157
Lin Nan-sheng, 109–10
Litvin, Volodymir, 152
Lo Fu-chu, 93–94, 157
Lopez Obrador, Andres Manuel, 46–47

Lu Hsiu-yi, 157
Lyon, Matthew, 39

majoritarian systems and brawling, 8, 28, 55–56
majority parties and brawling
  incentives to brawl, 3–5, 59, 75–76, 78, 87, 132–33, 148–49, 173, 177
  re-election, 166–67
Ma Ying-jeou, 2, 5
McGovern, John, 38
media
  as a data source, 3, 16, 34–35, 36, 94, 107, 110, 115, 120, 159
  social media, 34, 90
  in Taiwan, 94, 114–15
  in Ukraine, 70, 88–89, 121t
media coverage
  brawling, as a topic, 2–3, 50, 67–68, 77–78, 103, 104, 124–25
  brawls and brawlers, 1–2, 41, 49, 92, 93, 103, 107–13, 132, 153–54, 155–57
  in contentious politics, 58–59
  legislators trying to obtain, 18, 67–68, 77–78, 88–89, 103, 104, 106–7, 108–9, 114
  parties and, 56–57
  public consumption of, 80
  sensationalism, 67–68, 104–5
  in signaling theory, 14, 78, 103, 104, 113–14, 171, 183, 185
  types of legislators covered, 78, 82–83, 96–97, 104–6
median voters, 64–65, 106–7, 123–24
Medvedchuk, Viktor, 33–34, 50
Melnychuck, Serhiy Ivan, 34, 91, 150
Mexico
  Brawls in, 34–35, 46–47, 81
  disruptions in, 56
  executive-legislative relations, 50–51
  re-election, 147
  strong parties, 65
  target audience of brawls, 18–19, 66–67, 123, 128–29, 130, 135–36, 144, 171
MHP. See Nationalist Movement Party
mixed-member electoral system, 16–17, 24–25, 31, 130, 178
Moisychuck, Ihor, 152
Moon Jae-in, 180–81

Morton, Wendy, 38
Murray, Robert, 38
Museveni, Yoweri, 48–49

Na Kyung-won, 178, 181–82
Nam Kyung-pil, 44–45
National Action Party (PAN) (Mexico), 46–47, 56, 65, 81, 128–29, 147
National Assembly Advancement Reform, 176–77, 179–83
Nationalist Movement Party (MHP) (Turkey), 45
National Resource Fund bill, 47–48
national security, 8, 19, 41, 186–87
Nazliaka, Aylin, 45–46
New Party (Taiwan), 154–55
New Zealand, 35–36
Nganda, Ibrahim Ssemujju, 49
nominations
   decision to seek, 160
   in SMP systems, 165
   in SNTV systems, 24, 86, 142, 154, 157, 158
   who influences, 17, 63, 64, 65–67, 79, 93, 128, 130–31, 167
nonviolent disruption, 6, 7, 10, 55–56, 59, 75–76

Opposition Bloc party (Ukraine), 97*t*, 152–53
opposition disruption, 7, 55–70, 55*f*, 73, 75–76
   as a context of brawls, 5, 7, 17–18, 36, 50–51, 52, 55–70, 55*f*, 170–71
   and escalation of violence, 60, 61–62, 95, 184–85
   overcoming, 32–33
   and party incentives, 59–60, 75–76, 87
   and signaling, 33–34, 73
   and strong parties, 14, 46–47, 61, 63–67
   and weak parties, 14, 61, 68–70
opposition parties and brawling
   and democratic regime, 16–17, 32–33, 43, 45–46, 49–51
   incentives to brawl, 3–5, 55–70, 75–76, 78, 87, 100–1, 131–34, 148–49, 173, 177
   and large parties, 100–1, 131–34, 135
   re-election, 166–67

Orange Revolution, 29, 30, 140

Palamarenko, Maksym, 31–32
PAN. *See* National Action Party
Parasyuk, Volodymyr
   career of, 69, 88, 150
   characteristics of, 89, 90, 91, 92, 94, 135
   media coverage of, 112–13
   motives for brawling, 88–89, 135
   reputation of, 88–89
Park Geun-hye, 180–81
Park Hee-tae, 44
parties. *See also specific parties*
   and brawls, 75–76, 167
   and disruptions, 7, 55–61, 76–77 (*see also* opposition disruption)
   leaders, 60, 61–64, 67, 122, 128–30, 135–37
   legislative violence, 59–60, 62–63
   and legislators' gender, 84–85, 98
   nominations (*see* nominations)
   size (*see* large parties and brawling; small parties and brawling)
   status (*see* majority parties; opposition parties)
   strength of parties (*see* strong parties; weak parties)
   supporters, 63–64, 122, 130–34
Party of the Democratic Revolution (PRD) (Mexico), 46–47, 56, 65, 81, 128–29
party supporters
   electoral rules and, 86, 165
   in honor brawls, 72, 142–43
   party status and, 75–76
   in Taiwan, 17, 65–66, 124–27, 131–34, 142–43
   as a target audience, 5, 14–15, 61, 63, 67, 122, 123, 130–34, 135, 141, 147–49, 171
   value to legislators, 64, 124, 131
   violence and, 80, 124–27
Pavey, Şafak, 45–46, 50
People First Party (PFP) Taiwan, 27, 192n.9
People's Democratic Party (HDP) (Turkey), 45
PFP. *See* People First Party
political communication, 4, 49–50, 124, 155–56, 173, 174, 181, 183

political violence, 9–10, 15, 19, 183, 184–88
Poroshenko, Petro, 34, 70, 89, 90, 92, 152–53
PRD. *See* Party of the Democratic Revolution
PRI. *See* Institutional Revolutionary Party
psychological explanations of brawling, 9–12, 15
public opinion, 15, 18–19, 26, 44–45, 58–59, 75–76, 115, 123, 167, 168–69, 186
Putin, Vladimir, 33–34

Quanteda language stemmer, 120

Rabinovich, Vadiim, 152–53
Radical Party. *See* Liashko Radical Party
re-election
  brawling and, 100, 146–49, 168–69
  careers outside the legislature and, 147, 155–56, 159–60
  in electoral systems, 165–66
  the electorate and, 14, 63
  in Mexico, 66–67
  as a motivation, 12, 53, 79, 81, 146
  party status and, 166
  party switching and, 30–31, 32
  permitted or not, 12, 65, 66–67, 100, 128, 129, 130
  of presidents, 29, 42, 47–49, 103
  rates, 161–64
  retirement compared to, 160–61
  for "senior" legislators in Taiwan, 24, 189n.2
  in South Korea, 66–67, 172
  in strong parties, 130–31
  in Taiwan, 65, 153–67
  in Ukraine, 149–53
  in weak parties, 32
representation, 8, 11, 19, 80, 100, 145, 172–73, 184
Republican People's Party (CHP) (Turkey), 45–46
Republic of China (ROC), 21, 24, 26
retirement, 160–61
ROC. *See* Republic of China
Russia
  Europe and, 28–29

  Orange Revolution and, 30
  Russian language, 33–34, 120, 140–41
  as Soviet Union, 30
  Ukraine and, 8, 28–29, 33, 61, 89–90, 91, 110, 121*t*, 136, 138, 152–53, 168–69, 186–87
Rybak, Ivan, 152

Schmoll, Moritz, 7, 35–36, 49–50, 87, 172
Self-Reliance Party, 89, 90, 136–41, 149–50, 151–52
seniority, 18, 59, 81, 82–83, 88, 89, 91, 92, 96–97, 100, 113, 116, 149, 190n.1
Shufrych, Nestor, 33–34
signaling. *See also* costly signals
  content of, 67–68, 70, 87, 181
  in election monitoring, 13
  gender and, 79–80, 83–85
  in honor brawls, 14–15, 70–75, 141–44
  in international relations, 13
  in opposition disruption brawls, 17–18, 55–70
  in organized crime, 13
  target audience, 11–12, 14, 63–67, 68–70, 78–79, 80, 122–45
  theory, 13–14, 52–55, 82, 185–86
  transmission, 77–78, 103–20
Sihanlioglu, Mehmet Fevzi, 45
single member plurality (SMP) electoral rules
  brawling and, 76–77, 98–99
  brawling and re-election in, 151, 152, 165, 166
  in Korea, 130, 178
  in Mexico, 129
  in Taiwan, 16–17, 24–25, 98–99, 165, 166
  in Ukraine, 16–17, 31, 151, 152
single nontransferable vote (SNTV) rules
  brawling and, 76–77, 98–99
  brawling and re-election in, 153–58, 165, 166
  coordination, 154
  mechanics of, 24, 65–66, 86
  personal vote, 86
  in Taiwan, 24, 25, 98–99, 153–58, 165, 166
Sino-Japanese War, 20

Siumar, Viktoria, 152–53
slander, 72
small parties and brawling, 87, 89, 90, 91, 99, 100, 166, 172
SMP. *See* single member plurality districts
SNTV. *See* single nontransferable vote rules
Soboliev, Yehor
   career of, 54–55, 69, 137–39, 150–52
   career of, 89–90, 150–52
   characteristics of, 90, 94, 135
   on costs and benefits of brawling, 54–55, 136, 137–39, 151–52
   Euromaidan protests and, 69, 89, 138
   reputation of, 88, 89–90, 91, 92, 94, 138–39
social media, 34, 90, 120
Sohn Hak-kyu, 44–45
South Africa, 48, 50–51
South Korea. *See also specific topics*
   1988 legislative rules, 174–76
   2012 legislative reform (*see* National Assembly Advancement Reform)
   electoral reform brawl, 178–79
   history of brawling, 8, 19, 34–35, 42, 50–51, 174
   Japan and, 40–41
   language, 3, 36
   lessons for anti-brawling reforms, 182–83
   media coverage of brawls, 50
   media reform brawl, 42, 181
   national security, 186–87
   party status, 87
   strong parties, 65, 128, 135, 171
   target audience, 66–67, 123, 129–30, 135, 144, 171, 181–82
   US-Korea Free Trade Agreement brawls, 42–45, 175, 181
   violence in brawls, 42, 54–55, 181, 183
strong parties
   age and, 100
   brawls and, 60, 80, 87
   characteristics of, 14, 30–31, 61, 189n.6
   disruption and, 46–47, 60, 61–63
   electoral rules and, 76–77, 79, 100
   gender and, 98, 100
   honor brawls and, 71–72, 74, 141–42
   in Japan, 98
   media coverage, 114
   in Mexico, 46–47, 66–67, 128–29, 171
   party size and, 100
   seniority and, 100
   signal content, 5, 61, 62–63, 67–68
   in South Korea, 66–67, 129–30, 171
   in Taiwan, 17, 18–19, 23, 65–66, 94, 98, 131–34, 154–55, 170–71
   target audience, 14, 17, 18–19, 61, 62–67, 78–79, 103, 122, 123, 128–34, 144, 170, 171
   violence and, 60, 62–63
Su Huan-chih, 143–44
Sumner, Charles, 39–40
symbols and brawls, 6–7, 11, 27, 36, 45–46, 47, 48, 49–51, 153–54, 184

Taekwondo, 10–11
Taiwan. *See also specific topics*
   brawling in, 3, 25–28, 34–35, 36, 93–99, 107–10, 142–44, 153–67
   democratization and brawling, 25–27, 56
   history of, 20–23
   Kaohsiung Incident, 22, 155–56
   media in, 114
   national security, 8, 186–87
   political institutions, 23–25
   "senior" legislators in, 22, 24, 25–27, 153–54, 156–57, 189n.2
   United Daily News, 107–10, 114–20, 159, 190n.8
   video evidence of brawling, 94–99, 101–2
Taiwan Solidarity Union (TSU) (Taiwan), 27
target audiences
   economic elites, 14, 69–70, 139–41
   electorate at large, 13–14, 64–65, 123–27, 147–48
   general public (*see* electorate at large)
   honor brawls and, 14–15, 70–71, 72–73, 141–44
   median voter (*see* electorate at large)
   in Mexico, 65, 66–67, 128–29
   party leaders, 14, 63–64, 65–66, 69, 128–30, 135–37

target audiences (*cont.*)
  in South Korea, 65, 66–67, 129–30
    strong parties and, 14, 61, 63–67, 122, 123, 128–34
    strong party supporters, 14, 63–64, 130–34
  in Taiwan, 65–66, 124–27, 131–34, 142–44
  in Ukraine, 69–70, 135–41
  unaligned voting blocs, 14, 69, 137–39
  weak parties and, 14, 68–70, 122, 123, 134–41
Tarrow, Sidney, 57–59
terrorism, 185–86
Teteruk, Andriy, 88, 92–93, 100, 150
Ting, Wang Leung, 7, 35–36, 49–50, 87, 172
Trudeau, Justin, 6
TSU. *See* Taiwan Solidarity Union
Tsutsumi, Yasujiro, 41
Turkey, 3, 8, 34–35, 36, 45–46, 50–51
2012 legislative reform. *See* National Assembly Advancement Reform
Tymoshenko, Yulia, 29, 33, 90–91

Uganda, 18–19, 48–49, 50–51, 82–83, 103
Ukraine. *See also specific topics*
  brawling in, 32–34, 69, 88–91, 92–93, 135–41, 149–53
  history of, 28–30
  media in, 16, 70, 78, 88–89, 92, 103, 110–14, 120, 168–69, 171
  national security, 8, 186–87
  oligarchs, 29, 30, 70, 88–89, 139–41, 144
  political institutions, 30–32
  radicals, 68, 137–39, 144, 151
  Russia and, 8, 28–30, 33–34, 61, 89–90, 91, 110, 121*t*, 136, 138, 140–41, 152–53, 168–69, 186–87
United Kingdom, 3, 37–38, 47–48, 49, 103–4
United States (US)
  Black Day of the Indiana General Assembly, 40
  brawls in, 3–4, 39–40
  Civil War, 3–4, 39–40, 51, 80
  honor in early US, 39–40, 51, 71–72

US-Japan Security Treaty, 41
US-Korea Free Trade Agreement, 42–45, 50, 175, 181
violence and culture in, 11–12, 72
white Christian nationalism, 187

violence in brawls
  anthropological explanations, 9, 11–12, 15
  definition of brawling, 5–7
  escalation of, 7, 39–40, 49–50, 59–60, 87
  gender and, 83–85
  in honor brawls, 71*f*, 72–73
  intensity index (in Taiwan), 94, 95*t*
  legislators' motives, 12–15, 60, 61–62
  majority and minority parties and, 75–76
  parties and, 59–60, 62–63
  party strength and, 14, 60, 76–77
  psychological explanations, 9–12, 15
  risks of, 13, 59, 75–76, 137–38
  signaling and, 12–15, 32–33, 53–55

Wang Jin-pyng, 2
Wang Shu-hui, 1, 2, 28, 168–69
Wang Tao-fu, 158
Wang Tien-ging, 156–57
Wang Tsung-sung, 157
Wang Yi-hsiung, 157
weak parties
  age and, 100
  brawls and, 100–1
  characteristics of, 14, 30–31, 32, 68–69, 134, 189n.6
  disruption and, 60, 61, 68–70
  electoral rules and, 76–77, 100
  gender and, 98
  honor brawls and, 71–72, 74, 141–42
  media coverage, 114
  party size and, 100
  seniority and, 100
  signal content, 68, 70
  target audience, 14, 17, 18–19, 68, 69–70, 78–79, 103, 122, 123, 134–41, 144, 170, 171
  in Ukraine, 17, 18–19, 30–31, 32, 34, 61, 94, 135–41
Wei Yao-chien, 158

Whittaker, Craig, 38
Women. *See also* gender
  in Guyana, 48
  in Japan, 41
  in South Korea, 181–82
  in Taiwan, 1–2, 93–94, 98, 100, 146, 157, 158–59, 170–71
  in Turkey, 45–46
  in Uganda, 49
  in Ukraine, 83, 92–94

Wu Yung-hsiung, 157

Yanukovych, Viktor, 10, 29, 30, 32–33
Yarosh, Dymetro, 152
Yildirim, Binali, 46
You Ching, 155, 156, 158, 159–60
Yurnyets, Oksana, 78

Zelensky, Volodymyr, 149–50, 168–69
Zuma, Jacob, 48